D0375964

THE FIRST ADMINISTRATION

OF

THOMAS JEFFERSON

1801—1805

HISTORY OF THE UNITED STATES.

BY

HENRY ADAMS.

HISTORY

OF THE

UNITED STATES OF AMERICA

DURING THE FIRST ADMINISTRATION OF

THOMAS JEFFERSON

By HENRY ADAMS

Vol. I.

ANTIQUARIAN PRESS LTD.
New York
1962

First Published
1891-1896
by
Charles Scribner's Sons

———

Reprinted 1962
by
Antiquarian Press, Ltd.
New York, N.Y.

LIBRARY

FEB 1 3 1963

UNIVERSITY OF THE PACIFIC

Edition Limited to 750 Sets

115469

Library of Congress Catalog Card Number: 61-8054

Printed in the U.S.A.
———
NOBLE OFFSET PRINTERS, INC.
NEW YORK 3, N.Y.

CONTENTS OF VOL. I.

HISTORY OF THE UNITED STATES.

CHAPTER I.

ACCORDING to the census of 1800, the United States of America contained 5,308,483 persons. In the same year the British Islands contained upwards of fifteen millions; the French Republic, more than twenty-seven millions. Nearly one fifth of the American people were negro slaves; the true political population consisted of four and a half million free whites, or less than one million able-bodied males, on whose shoulders fell the burden of a continent. Even after two centuries of struggle the land was still untamed; forest covered every portion, except here and there a strip of cultivated soil; the minerals lay undisturbed in their rocky beds, and more than two thirds of the people clung to the seaboard within fifty miles of tide-water, where alone the wants of civilized life could be supplied. The centre of population rested within eighteen miles of Baltimore, north and east of Washington. Except in political arrangement, the interior was little more civilized than in 1750,

and was not much easier to penetrate than when La
Salle and Hennepin found their way to the Mississippi more than a century before.

A great exception broke this rule. Two wagon-
roads crossed the Alleghany Mountains in Pennsylvania, — one leading from Philadelphia to Pittsburg;
one from the Potomac to the Monongahela; while a
third passed through Virginia southwestward to the
Holston River and Knoxville in Tennessee, with a
branch through the Cumberland Gap into Kentucky.
By these roads and by trails less passable from
North and South Carolina, or by water-ways from
the lakes, between four and five hundred thousand
persons had invaded the country beyond the Alleghanies. At Pittsburg and on the Monongahela
existed a society, already old, numbering seventy or
eighty thousand persons, while on the Ohio River
the settlements had grown to an importance which
threatened to force a difficult problem on the union
of the older States. One hundred and eighty thousand whites, with forty thousand negro slaves, made
Kentucky the largest community west of the mountains; and about ninety thousand whites and fourteen thousand slaves were scattered over Tennessee.
In the territory north of the Ohio less progress had
been made. A New England colony existed at Mari-
etta; some fifteen thousand people were gathered at
Cincinnati; half-way between the two, a small town
had grown up at Chillicothe, and other villages or
straggling cabins were to be found elsewhere; but

the whole Ohio territory contained only forty-five thousand inhabitants. The entire population, both free and slave, west of the mountains, reached not yet half a million; but already they were partly disposed to think themselves, and the old thirteen States were not altogether unwilling to consider them, the germ of an independent empire, which was to find its outlet, not through the Alleghanies to the seaboard, but by the Mississippi River to the Gulf.

Nowhere did eastern settlements touch the western. At least one hundred miles of mountainous country held the two regions everywhere apart. The shore of Lake Erie, where alone contact seemed easy, was still unsettled. The Indians had been pushed back to the Cuyahoga River, and a few cabins were built on the site of Cleveland; but in 1800, as in 1700, this intermediate region was only a portage where emigrants and merchandise were transferred from Lake Erie to the Muskingum and Ohio valleys. Even western New York remained a wilderness: Buffalo was not laid out; Indian titles were not extinguished; Rochester did not exist; and the county of Onondaga numbered a population of less than eight thousand. In 1799 Utica contained fifty houses, mostly small and temporary. Albany was still a Dutch city, with some five thousand inhabitants; and the tide of immigration flowed slowly through it into the valley of the Mohawk, while another stream from Pennsylvania, following the Susquehanna, spread toward the Genesee country.

The people of the old thirteen States, along the
Atlantic seaboard, thus sent westward a wedge-shaped
mass of nearly half a million persons, penetrating by
the Tennessee, Cumberland, and Ohio rivers toward
the western limit of the Union. The Indians offered
sharp resistance to this invasion, exacting life for life,
and yielding only as their warriors perished. By the
close of the century the wedge of white settlements,
with its apex at Nashville and its flanks covered by
the Ohio and Tennessee rivers, nearly split the Indian
country in halves. The northern half — consisting
of the later States of Wisconsin, Michigan, Illinois,
Indiana, and one third of Ohio — contained Wyan-
dottes and Shawanese, Miamis, Kickapoos, and other
tribes, able to send some five thousand warriors to
hunt or fight. In the southern half, powerful confederacies of Creeks, Cherokees, Chickasaws, and
Choctaws lived and hunted where the States of Mississippi, Alabama, and the western parts of Georgia,
Tennessee, and Kentucky were to extend ; and so
weak was the State of Georgia, which claimed the
southwestern territory for its own, that a well-con-
certed movement of Indians might without much
difficulty have swept back its white population of one
hundred thousand toward the ocean or across the
Savannah River. The Indian power had been broken
in halves, but each half was still terrible to the colonists on the edges of their vast domain, and was used
as a political weapon by the Governments whose territory bounded the Union on the north and south.

The governors-general of Canada intrigued with the northwestern Indians, that they might hold in check any aggression from Washington; while the Spanish governors of West Florida and Louisiana maintained equally close relations with the Indian confederacies of the Georgia territory.

With the exception that half a million people had crossed the Alleghanies and were struggling with difficulties all their own, in an isolation like that of Jutes or Angles in the fifth century, America, so far as concerned physical problems, had changed little in fifty years. The old landmarks remained nearly where they stood before. The same bad roads and difficult rivers, connecting the same small towns, stretched into the same forests in 1800 as when the armies of Braddock and Amherst pierced the western and northern wilderness, except that these roads extended a few miles farther from the seacoast. Nature was rather man's master than his servant, and the five million Americans struggling with the untamed continent seemed hardly more competent to their task than the beavers and buffalo which had for countless generations made bridges and roads of their own.

Even by water, along the seaboard, communication was as slow and almost as irregular as in colonial times. The wars in Europe caused a sudden and great increase in American shipping employed in foreign commerce, without yet leading to general improvement in navigation. The ordinary sea-going

vessel carried a freight of about two hundred and
fifty tons; the largest merchant ships hardly reached
four hundred tons; the largest frigate in the United
States navy, the " line-of-battle ship in disguise," had
a capacity of fifteen hundred and seventy-six tons.
Elaborately rigged as ships or brigs, the small merchant craft required large crews and were slow sail-
ers; but the voyage to Europe was comparatively
more comfortable and more regular than the voyage
from New York to Albany, or through Long Island
Sound to Providence. No regular packet plied between New York and Albany. Passengers waited till
a sloop was advertised to sail; they provided their
own bedding and supplies; and within the nineteenth
century Captain Elias Bunker won much fame by
building the sloop "Experiment," of one hundred
and ten tons, to start regularly on a fixed day for
Albany, for the convenience of passengers only, supplying beds, wine, and provisions for the voyage of
one hundred and fifty miles. A week on the North
River or on the Sound was an experience not at all
unknown to travellers.

While little improvement had been made in water-
travel, every increase of distance added to the difficulties of the westward journey. The settler who
after buying wagon and horses hauled his family
and goods across the mountains, might buy or build
a broad flat-bottomed ark, to float with him and his
fortunes down the Ohio, in constant peril of upsetting
or of being sunk; but only light boats with strong

oars could mount the stream, or boats forced against the current by laboriously poling in shallow water. If he carried his tobacco and wheat down the Mississippi to the Spanish port of New Orleans, and sold it, he might return to his home in Kentucky or Ohio by a long and dangerous journey on horseback through the Indian country from Natchez to Nashville, or he might take ship to Philadelphia, if a ship were about to sail, and again cross the Alleghanies. Compared with river travel, the sea was commonly an easy and safe highway. Nearly all the rivers which penetrated the interior were unsure, liable to be made dangerous by freshets, and both dangerous and impassable by drought; yet such as they were, these streams made the main paths of traffic. Through the mountainous gorges of the Susquehanna the produce of western New York first found an outlet; the Cuyahoga and Muskingum were the first highway from the Lakes to the Ohio; the Ohio itself, with its great tributaries the Cumberland and the Tennessee, marked the lines of western migration; and every stream which could at high water float a boat was thought likely to become a path for commerce. As General Washington, not twenty years earlier, hoped that the brawling waters of the Cheat and Youghiogheny might become the channel of trade between Chesapeake Bay and Pittsburg, so the Americans of 1800 were prepared to risk life and property on any streamlet that fell foaming down either flank of the Alleghanies. The experience of mankind proved trade to be dependent on water communications, and as yet Americans did not dream that the experience of mankind was useless to them.

If America was to be developed along the lines of water communication alone, by such means as were known to Europe, Nature had decided that the experiment of a single republican government must meet extreme difficulties. The valley of the Ohio had no more to do with that of the Hudson, the Susquehanna, the Potomac, the Roanoke, and the Santee, than the valley of the Danube with that of the Rhone, the Po, or the Elbe. Close communication by land could alone hold the great geographical divisions together either in interest or in fear. The union of New England with New York and Pennsylvania was not an easy task even as a problem of geography, and with an ocean highway; but the union of New England with the Carolinas, and of the seacoast with the interior, promised to be a hopeless undertaking. Physical contact alone could make one country of these isolated empires, but to the patriotic American of 1800, struggling for the continued existence of an embryo nation, with machinery so inadequate, the idea of ever bringing the Mississippi River, either by land or water, into close contact with New England, must have seemed wild. By water, an Erie Canal was already foreseen; by land, centuries of labor could alone conquer those obstacles which Nature permitted to be overcome.

In the minds of practical men, the experience of

Europe left few doubts on this point. After two thousand years of public labor and private savings, even despotic monarchs, who employed the resources of their subjects as they pleased, could in 1800 pass from one part of their European dominions to another little more quickly than they might have done in the age of the Antonines. A few short canals had been made, a few bridges had been built, an excellent post-road extended from Madrid to St. Petersburg; but the heavy diligence that rumbled from Calais to Paris required three days for its journey of one hundred and fifty miles, and if travellers ventured on a trip to Marseilles they met with rough roads and hardships like those of the Middle Ages. Italy was in 1800 almost as remote from the north of Europe as when carriage-roads were first built. Neither in time nor in thought was Florence or Rome much nearer to London in Wordsworth's youth than in the youth of Milton or Gray. Indeed, such changes as had occurred were partly for the worse, owing to the violence of revolutionary wars during the last ten years of the eighteenth century. Horace Walpole at his life's close saw about him a world which in many respects was less civilized than when as a boy he made the grand tour of Europe.

While so little had been done on the great highways of European travel, these highways were themselves luxuries which furnished no sure measure of progress. The post-horses toiled as painfully as ever through the sand from Hamburg to Berlin, while the

coach between York and London rolled along an excellent road at the rate of ten miles an hour; yet
neither in England nor on the Continent was the
post-road a great channel of commerce. No matter
how good the road, it could not compete with water,
nor could heavy freights in great quantities be hauled
long distances without extravagant cost. Water communication was as necessary for European commerce
in 1800 as it had been for the Phœnicians and Egyp-
tians; the Rhine, the Rhone, the Danube, the Elbe,
were still the true commercial highways, and except
for government post-roads, Europe was as dependent on these rivers in the eighteenth century as in
the thirteenth. No certainty could be offered of more
rapid progress in the coming century than in the
past; the chief hope seemed to lie in the construction of canals.

While Europe had thus consumed centuries in im-
proving paths of trade, until merchandise could be
brought by canal a few score miles from the Rhone
to the Loire and Seine, to the Garonne and the
Rhine, and while all her wealth and energy had not
yet united the Danube with other river systems,
America was required to construct, without delay,
at least three great roads and canals, each several
hundred miles long, across mountain ranges, through
a country not yet inhabited, to points where no great
markets existed, — and this under constant peril of
losing her political union, which could not even by
such connections be with certainty secured. After

this should be accomplished, the Alleghanies must still remain between the eastern and western States, and at any known rate of travel Nashville could not be reached in less than a fortnight or three weeks from Philadelphia. Meanwhile the simpler problem of bringing New England nearer to Virginia and Georgia had not advanced even with the aid of a direct ocean highway. In becoming politically independent of England, the old thirteen provinces developed little more commercial intercourse with each other in proportion to their wealth and population than they had maintained in colonial days. The material ties that united them grew in strength no more rapidly than the ties which bound them to Europe. Each group of States lived a life apart.

Even the lightly equipped traveller found a short journey no slight effort. Between Boston and New York was a tolerable highway, along which, thrice a week, light stage-coaches carried passengers and the mail, in three days. From New York a stage-coach started every week-day for Philadelphia, consuming the greater part of two days in the journey; and the road between Paulus Hook, the modern Jersey City, and Hackensack, was declared by the newspapers in 1802 to be as bad as any other part of the route between Maine and Georgia. South of Philadelphia the road was tolerable as far as Baltimore, but between Baltimore and the new city of Washington it meandered through forests; the driver chose the track which seemed least dangerous, and rejoiced

if in wet seasons he reached Washington without
miring or upsetting his wagon. In the Northern
States, four miles an hour was the average speed for
any coach between Bangor and Baltimore. Beyond
the Potomac the roads became steadily worse, until
south of Petersburg even the mails were carried on
horseback. Except for a stage-coach which plied
between Charleston and Savannah, no public conveyance of any kind was mentioned in the three south-
ernmost States.

The stage-coach was itself a rude conveyance, of a
kind still familiar to experienced travellers. Twelve
persons, crowded into one wagon, were jolted over
rough roads, their bags and parcels, thrust inside,
cramping their legs, while they were protected from
the heat and dust of mid-summer and the intense
cold and driving snow of winter only by leather flaps
buttoned to the roof and sides. In fine, dry weather
this mode of travel was not unpleasant, when compared with the heavy vehicles of Europe and the hard
English turnpikes; but when spring rains drew the
frost from the ground the roads became nearly impassable, and in winter, when the rivers froze, a serious peril was added, for the Susquehanna or the North
River at Paulus Hook must be crossed in an open
boat, — an affair of hours at best, sometimes leading to fatal accidents. Smaller annoyances of many
kinds were habitual. The public, as a rule, grumbled
less than might have been expected, but occasionally
newspapers contained bitter complaints. An angry

Philadelphian, probably a foreigner, wrote in 1796 that, " with a few exceptions, brutality, negligence, and filching are as naturally expected by people accustomed to travelling in America, as a mouth, a nose, and two eyes are looked for in a man's face." This sweeping charge, probably unjust, and certainly supported by little public evidence, was chiefly founded on the experience of an alleged journey from New York : —

" At Bordentown we went into a second boat where we met with very sorry accommodation. This was about four o'clock in the afternoon. We had about twenty miles down the Delaware to reach Philadelphia. The captain, who had a most provoking tongue, was a boy about eighteen years of age. He and a few companions despatched a dozen or eighteen bottles of porter. We ran three different times against other vessels that were coming up the stream. The women and children lay all night on the bare boards of the cabin floor. . . . We reached Arch Street wharf about eight o'clock on the Wednesday morning, having been about sixteen hours on a voyage of twenty miles."

In the Southern States the difficulties and perils of travel were so great as to form a barrier almost insuperable. Even Virginia was no exception to this rule. At each interval of a few miles the horseman found himself stopped by a river, liable to sudden freshets, and rarely bridged. Jefferson in his frequent journeys between Monticello and Washington was happy to reach the end of the hundred miles

without some vexatious delay. " Of eight rivers between here and Washington," he wrote to his Attorney-General in 1801, " five have neither bridges
nor boats."

Expense caused an equally serious obstacle to
travel. The usual charge in the Northern States
was six cents a mile by stage. In the year 1796,
according to Francis Baily, President of the Royal
Astronomical Society, three or four stages ran daily
from Baltimore to Philadelphia, the fare six dollars,
with charges amounting to two dollars and a quarter a day at the inns on the road. Baily was three
days in making the journey. From Philadelphia
to New York he paid the same fare and charges,
arriving in one day and a half. The entire journey
of two hundred miles cost him twenty-one dollars.
He remarked that travelling on the main lines of road
in the settled country was about as expensive as in
England, and when the roads were good, about as
rapid. Congress allowed its members six dollars
for every twenty miles travelled. The actual cost,
including hotel expenses, could hardly have fallen
below ten cents a mile.

Heavy traffic never used stage routes if it could
find cheaper. Commerce between one State and another, or even between the seaboard and the interior
of the same State, was scarcely possible on any large
scale unless navigable water connected them. Except
the great highway to Pittsburg, no road served as a
channel of commerce between different regions of the

country. In this respect New England east of the Connecticut was as independent of New York as both were independent of Virginia, and as Virginia in her turn was independent of Georgia and South Carolina. The chief value of inter-State communication by land rested in the postal system; but the post furnished another illustration of the difficulties which barred progress. In the year 1800 one general mail-route extended from Portland in Maine to Louisville in Georgia, the time required for the trip being twenty days. Between New York and Petersburg in Virginia was a daily service; between New York and Boston, and also between Petersburg and Augusta, the mail was carried thrice a week. Branching from the main line at New York, a mail went to Canandaigua in ten days; from Philadelphia another branch line went to Lexington in sixteen days, to Nashville in twenty-two days. Thus more than twenty thousand miles of post-road, with nine hundred post-offices, proved the vastness of the country and the smallness of the result; for the gross receipts for postage in the year ending Oct. 1, 1801, were only $320,000.

Throughout the land the eighteenth century ruled supreme. Only within a few years had the New Englander begun to abandon his struggle with a barren soil, among granite hills, to learn the comforts of easier existence in the valleys of the Mohawk and Ohio; yet the New England man was thought the shrewdest and most enterprising of Americans. If

the Puritans and the Dutch needed a century or
more to reach the Mohawk, when would they reach
the Mississippi ? The distance from New York to
the Mississippi was about one thousand miles ; from
Washington to the extreme southwestern military
post, below Natchez, was about twelve hundred.
Scarcely a portion of western Europe was three
hundred miles distant from some sea, but a width
of three hundred miles was hardly more than an
outskirt of the United States. No civilized country
had yet been required to deal with physical difficulties so serious, nor did experience warrant conviction
that such difficulties could be overcome.

If the physical task which lay before the American
people had advanced but a short way toward comple-
tion, little more change could be seen in the economical conditions of American life. The man who in
the year 1800 ventured to hope for a new era in the
coming century, could lay his hand on no statistics
that silenced doubt. The machinery of production
showed no radical difference from that familiar to
ages long past. The Saxon farmer of the eighth century enjoyed most of the comforts known to Saxon
farmers of the eighteenth. The eorls and ceorls of
Offa and Ecgbert could not read or write, and did not
receive a weekly newspaper with such information
as newspapers in that age could supply ; yet neither
their houses, their clothing, their food and drink, their
agricultural tools and methods, their stock, nor their

habits were so greatly altered or improved by time
that they would have found much difficulty in accom-
modating their lives to that of their descendants in
the eighteenth century. In this respect America was
backward. Fifty or a hundred miles inland more
than half the houses were log-cabins, which might
or might not enjoy the luxury of a glass window.
Throughout the South and West houses showed little attempt at luxury; but even in New England
the ordinary farmhouse was hardly so well built,
so spacious, or so warm as that of a well-to-do contemporary of Charlemagne. The cloth which the
farmer's family wore was still homespun. The hats
were manufactured by the village hatter; the clothes
were cut and made at home; the shirts, socks, and
nearly every other article of dress were also home-
made. Hence came a marked air of rusticity which
distinguished country from town, — awkward shapes
of hat, coat, and trousers, which gave to the Yankee
caricature those typical traits that soon disappeared
almost as completely as coats of mail and steel head-
pieces. The plough was rude and clumsy; the sickle
as old as Tubal Cain, and even the cradle not in
general use; the flail was unchanged since the Aryan
exodus; in Virginia, grain was still commonly trod-
den out by horses. Enterprising gentlemen-farmers
introduced threshing-machines and invented scientific
ploughs; but these were novelties. Stock was as a
rule not only unimproved, but ill cared for. The
swine ran loose; the cattle were left to feed on what

pasture they could find, and even in New England
were not housed until the severest frosts, on the
excuse that exposure hardened them. Near half a
century afterward a competent judge asserted that
the general treatment of cows in New England was
fair matter of presentment by a grand jury. Except
among the best farmers, drainage, manures, and rota-
tion of crops were uncommon. The ordinary culti-
vator planted his corn as his father had planted it,
sowing as much rye to the acre, using the same number of oxen to plough, and getting in his crops on
the same day. He was even known to remove his
barn on account of the manure accumulated round
it, although the New England soil was never so rich
as to warrant neglect to enrich it. The money for
which he sold his wheat and chickens was of the Old
World ; he reckoned in shillings or pistareens, and
rarely handled an American coin more valuable than
a large copper cent.

At a time when the wealth and science of London
and Paris could not supply an article so necessary
as a common sulphur-match, the backwardness of
remote country districts could hardly be exaggerated. Yet remote districts were not the only suf-
ferers. Of the whole United States New England
claimed to be the most civilized province, yet New
England was a region in which life had yet gained
few charms of sense and few advantages over its
rivals.   Wilson, the ornithologist, a Pennsylvania
Scotchman, a confirmed grumbler, but a shrewd judge,

and the most thorough of American travellers, said
in 1808: "My journey through almost the whole of
New England has rather lowered the Yankees in my
esteem. Except a few neat academies, I found their
schoolhouses equally ruinous and deserted with ours;
fields covered with stones; stone fences; scrubby
oaks and pine-trees; wretched orchards; scarcely
one grain-field in twenty miles; the taverns along
the road dirty, and filled with loungers brawling
about lawsuits and politics; the people snappish and
extortioners, lazy, and two hundred years behind the
Pennsylvanians in agricultural improvements." The
description was exaggerated, for Wilson forgot to
speak of the districts where fields were not covered
with stones, and where wheat could be grown to advantage. Twenty years earlier, Albert Gallatin, who
knew Pennsylvania well, having reached Hartford
on his way to Boston, wrote: "I have seen nothing
in America equal to the establishments on the Connecticut River." Yet Wilson's account described the
first general effect of districts in the New England
States, where agriculture was backward and the
country poor. The houses were thin wooden buildings, not well suited to the climate; the churches
were unwarmed; the clothing was poor; sanitary
laws were few, and a bathroom or a soil-pipe was
unknown. Consumption, typhoid, scarlet fever, diph-
theria, and rheumatic fevers were common; habits
of drinking were still a scourge in every family, and
dyspepsia destroyed more victims than were con-

sumed by drink. Population increased slowly, as
though the conditions of life were more than usually
hard. A century earlier, Massachusetts was supposed to contain sixty thousand inhabitants. Governor Hutchinson complained that while the other
colonies quadrupled their numbers, Massachusetts
failed to double its population in fifty years. In
1790 the State contained 378,000 people, not including the province of Maine; in 1800 the number rose
to 423,000, which showed that a period of more rapid
growth had begun, for the emigration into other
States was also large.

A better measure of the difficulties with which
New England struggled was given by the progress of
Boston, which was supposed to have contained about
eighteen thousand inhabitants as early as 1730, and
twenty thousand in 1770. For several years after the
Revolution it numbered less than twenty thousand,
but in 1800 the census showed twenty-five thousand
inhabitants. In appearance, Boston resembled an
English market-town, of a kind even then old-fashioned. The footways or sidewalks were paved, like
the crooked and narrow streets, with round cobble-
stones, and were divided from the carriage way only
by posts and a gutter. The streets were almost un-
lighted at night, a few oil-lamps rendering the dark-
ness more visible and the rough pavement rougher.
Police hardly existed. The system of taxation was
defective. The town was managed by selectmen, the
elected instruments of town-meetings whose jealousy

of granting power was even greater than their objection to spending money, and whose hostility to city government was not to be overcome.

Although on all sides increase of ease and comfort was evident, and roads, canals, and new buildings, public and private, were already in course of construction on a scale before unknown, yet in spite of more than a century and a half of incessant industry, intelligent labor, and pinching economy Boston and New England were still poor. A few merchants enjoyed incomes derived from foreign trade, which allowed them to imitate in a quiet way the style of the English mercantile class; but the clergy and the lawyers, who stood at the head of society, lived with much economy. Many a country clergyman, eminent for piety and even for hospitality, brought up a family and laid aside some savings on a salary of five hundred dollars a year. President Dwight, who knew well the class to which he belonged, eulogizing the life of Abijah Weld, pastor of Attleborough, declared that on a salary of two hundred and twenty dollars a year Mr. Weld brought up eleven children, besides keeping a hospitable house and maintaining charity to the poor.

On the Exchange a few merchants had done most of the business of Boston since the peace of 1783, but a mail thrice a week to New York, and an occasional arrival from Europe or the departure of a ship to China, left ample leisure for correspondence and even for gossip. The habits of the commercial class

had not been greatly affected by recent prosperity.
Within ten or fifteen years before 1800 three Banks
had been created to supply the commercial needs of
Boston. One of these was a branch Bank of the
United States, which employed there whatever part
of its capital it could profitably use; the two others
were local Banks, with capital of $1,600,000, toward
which the State subscribed $400,000. Altogether the
banking capital of Boston might amount to two millions and a half. A number of small Banks, representing in all about two and a half millions more,
were scattered through the smaller New England
towns. The extraordinary prosperity caused by the
French wars opened to Boston a new career. Wealth
and population were doubling; the exports and imports of New England were surprisingly large, and
the shipping was greater than that of New York
and Pennsylvania combined; but Boston had already
learned, and was to learn again, how fleeting were
the riches that depended on foreign commerce, and
conservative habits were not easily changed by a few
years of accidental gain.

Of manufactures New England had many, but none
on a large scale. The people could feed or clothe
themselves only by household industry; their whale-
oil, salt fish, lumber, and rum were mostly sent
abroad; but they freighted coasters with turners'
articles, home-made linens and cloths, cheese, butter,
shoes, nails, and what were called Yankee Notions
of all sorts, which were sent to Norfolk and the

Southern ports, and often peddled from the deck, as goods of every sort were peddled on the flat-boats of the Ohio. Two or three small mills spun cotton with doubtful success; but England supplied ordinary manufactures more cheaply and better than Massachusetts could hope to do. A tri-weekly mail and a few coasting sloops provided for the business of New England with domestic ports. One packet sloop plied regularly to New York.

The State of New York was little in advance of Massachusetts and Maine. In 1800 for the first time New York gained the lead in population by the difference between 589,000 and 573,000. The valuation of New York for the direct tax in 1799 was $100,000,000; that of Massachusetts was $84,000,000. New York was still a frontier State, and although the city was European in its age and habits, travellers needed to go few miles from the Hudson in order to find a wilderness like that of Ohio and Tennessee. In most material respects the State was behind New England; outside the city was to be seen less wealth and less appearance of comfort. The first impression commonly received of any new country was from its inns, and on the whole few better tests of material condition then existed. President Dwight, though maintaining that the best old-fashioned inns of New England were in their way perfect, being in fact excellent private houses, could not wholly approve what he called the modern inns, even in Connecticut; but when he passed into New

York he asserted that everything suffered an instant change for the worse. He explained that in Massachusetts the authorities were strict in refusing licenses to any but respectable and responsible persons, whereas in New York licenses were granted to any one who would pay for them, — which caused a multiplication of dram-shops, bad accommodations, and a gathering of loafers and tipplers about every tavern porch, whose rude appearance, clownish manners, drunkenness, swearing, and obscenity confirmed the chief of Federalist clergymen in his belief that democracy had an evil influence on morals.

Far more movement was to be seen, and accumulation was more rapid than in colonial days; but little had yet been done for improvement, either by Government or by individuals, beyond some provision for extending roads and clearing watercourses behind the advancing settlers. If Washington Irving was right, Rip Van Winkle, who woke from his long slumber about the year 1800, saw little that was new to him, except the head of President Washington where that of King George had once hung, and strange faces instead of familiar ones. Except in numbers, the city was relatively no farther advanced than the country. Between 1790 and 1800 its population rose from 33,000 to 60,000; and if Boston resembled an old-fashioned English market-town, New York was like a foreign seaport, badly paved, undrained, and as foul as a town surrounded by the tides could be. Although the Manhattan Company was laying wooden pipes for a water supply, no sanitary regulations were enforced, and every few years — as in 1798 and 1803 — yellow fever swept away crowds of victims, and drove the rest of the population, panic stricken, into the highlands. No day-police existed; constables were still officers of the courts; the night-police consisted of two captains, two deputies, and seventy-two men. The estimate for the city's expenses in 1800 amounted to $130,000. One marked advantage New York enjoyed over Boston, in the possession of a city government able to introduce reforms. Thus, although still mediæval in regard to drainage and cleanliness, the town had taken advantage of recurring fires to rebuild some of the streets with brick sidewalks and curbstones. Travellers dwelt much on this improvement, which only New York and Philadelphia had yet adopted, and Europeans agreed that both had the air of true cities: that while Boston was the Bristol of America, New York was the Liverpool, and Philadelphia the London.

In respect to trade and capital, New York possessed growing advantages, supplying half New Jersey and Connecticut, a part of Massachusetts, and all the rapidly increasing settlements on the branches of the Hudson; but no great amount of wealth, no considerable industry or new creation of power was yet to be seen. Two Banks, besides the branch Bank of the United States, supplied the business wants of the city, and employed about the same amount of

capital in loans and discounts as was required for
Boston.   Besides these city institutions but two other
Banks existed in the State, — at Hudson and at
Albany.

The proportion of capital in private hands seemed
to be no larger.   The value of exports from New
York in 1800 was but $14,000,000; the net revenue
on imports for 1799 was $2,373,000, against $1,607,000
collected in Massachusetts.   Such a foreign trade required little capital, yet these values represented a
great proportion of all the exchanges.   Domestic
manufactures could not compete with foreign, and
employed little bank credit.   Speculation was slow,
mostly confined to lands which required patience to
exchange or sell.   The most important undertakings
were turnpikes, bridges such as Boston built across
the Charles, or new blocks of houses; and a canal,
such as Boston designed to. the Merrimac, over-
strained the resources of capital.   The entire banking
means of the United States in 1800 would not have
answered the stock-jobbing purposes of one great op-
erator of Wall Street in 1875.   The nominal capital
of all the Banks, including the Bank of the United
States, fell short of $29,000,000.   The limit of credit
was quickly reached, for only the richest could borrow more than fifteen or twenty thousand dollars at
a time, and the United States Government itself
was gravely embarrassed whenever obliged to raise
money.   In 1798 the Secretary of the Treasury could
obtain five million dollars only by paying eight per

cent interest for a term of years; and in 1814 the
Government was forced to stop payments for the
want of twenty millions.

The precise value of American trade was uncertain,
but in 1800 the gross exports and imports of the
United States may have balanced at about seventy-five
million dollars. The actual consumption of foreign
merchandise amounted perhaps to the value of forty
or fifty million dollars, paid in wheat, cotton, and
other staples, and by the profits on the shipping
employed in carrying West India produce to Europe.
The amount of American capital involved in a trade
of fifty millions, with credits of three, six, and nine
months, must have been small, and the rates of profit
large.

As a rule American capital was absorbed in shipping or agriculture, whence it could not be suddenly
withdrawn. No stock-exchange existed, and no broker
exclusively engaged in stock-jobbing, for there were
few stocks. The national debt, of about eighty millions, was held abroad, or as a permanent investment
at home. States and municipalities had not learned
to borrow. Except for a few banks and insurance
offices, turnpikes, bridges, canals, and land-companies,
neither bonds nor stocks were known. The city of
New York was so small as to make extravagance
difficult; the Battery was a fashionable walk, Broad-
way a country drive, and Wall Street an uptown residence. Great accumulations of wealth had hardly
begun. The Patroon was still the richest man in the

State. John Jacob Astor was a fur-merchant living
where the Astor House afterward stood, and had
not yet begun those purchases of real estate which
secured his fortune. Cornelius Vanderbilt was a
boy six years old, playing about his father's ferry-
boat at Staten Island. New York city itself was
what it had been for a hundred years past, — a local
market.

As a national capital New York made no claim to
consideration. If Bostonians for a moment forgot
their town-meetings, or if Virginians overcame their
dislike for cities and pavements, they visited and admired, not New York, but Philadelphia. " Philadelphia," wrote the Duc de Liancourt, " is not only the
finest city in the United States, but may be deemed
one of the most beautiful cities in the world." In
truth, it surpassed any of its size on either side of the
Atlantic for most of the comforts and some of the ele-
gancies of life. While Boston contained twenty-five
thousand inhabitants and New York sixty thousand,
the census of 1800 showed that Philadelphia was
about the size of Liverpool, — a city of seventy thousand people. The repeated ravages of yellow fever
roused there a regard for sanitary precautions and
cleanliness; the city, well paved and partly drained,
was supplied with water in wooden pipes, and was
the best-lighted town in America; its market was a
model, and its jail was intended also for a model, —
although the first experiment proved unsuccessful,
because the prisoners went mad or idiotic in solitary

confinement. In and about the city flourished in-
dustries considerable for the time. The iron-works
were already important; paper and gunpowder, pleasure carriages and many other manufactures, were
produced on a larger scale than elsewhere in the
Union. Philadelphia held the seat of government
until July, 1800, and continued to hold the Bank of
the United States, with its capital of ten millions,
besides private banking capital to the amount of
five millions more. Public spirit was more active in
Pennsylvania than in New York. More roads and
canals were building; a new turnpike ran from
Philadelphia to Lancaster, and the great highway
to Pittsburg was a more important artery of national life than was controlled by any other State.
The exports of Pennsylvania amounted to $12,000,-
000, and the custom-house produced $1,350,000.
The State contained six hundred thousand inhabitants, — a population somewhat larger than that of
New York.

Of all parts of the Union, Pennsylvania seemed to
have made most use of her national advantages; but
her progress was not more rapid than the natural increase of population and wealth demanded, while to
deal with the needs of America, man's resources and
his power over Nature must be increased in a ratio
far more rapid than that which governed his numbers. Nevertheless, Pennsylvania was the most encouraging spectacle in the field of vision. Baltimore,
which had suddenly sprung to a population and

commerce greater than those of Boston, also offered
strong hope of future improvement; but farther South
the people showed fewer signs of change.

The city of Washington, rising in a solitude on the
banks of the Potomac, was a symbol of American
nationality in the Southern States. The contrast between the immensity of the task and the paucity of
means seemed to challenge suspicion that the nation
itself was a magnificent scheme like the federal city,
which could show only a few log-cabins and negro
quarters where the plan provided for the traffic of
London and the elegance of Versailles. When in
the summer of 1800 the government was transferred
to what was regarded by most persons as a fever-
stricken morass, the half-finished White House stood
in a naked field overlooking the Potomac, with two
awkward Department buildings near it, a single row
of brick houses and a few isolated dwellings within
sight, and nothing more; until across a swamp, a
mile and a half away, the shapeless, unfinished Capitol was seen, two wings without a body, ambitious
enough in design to make more grotesque the nature
of its surroundings. The conception proved that the
United States understood the vastness of their task,
and were willing to stake something on their faith
in it. Never did hermit or saint condemn himself
to solitude more consciously than Congress and the
Executive in removing the government from Philadelphia to Washington: the discontented men clus-
tered together in eight or ten boarding-houses as

near as possible to the Capitol, and there lived, like a convent of monks, with no other amusement or occupation than that of going from their lodgings to the Chambers and back again. Even private wealth could do little to improve their situation, for there was nothing which wealth could buy; there were in Washington no shops or markets, skilled labor, commerce, or people. Public efforts and lavish use of public money could alone make the place tolerable; but Congress doled out funds for this national and personal object with so sparing a hand, that their Capitol threatened to crumble in pieces and crush Senate and House under the ruins, long before the building was complete.

A government capable of sketching a magnificent plan, and willing to give only a half-hearted pledge for its fulfilment; a people eager to advertise a vast undertaking beyond their present powers, which when completed would become an object of jealousy and fear, — this was the impression made upon the traveller who visited Washington in 1800, and mused among the unraised columns of the Capitol upon the destiny of the United States. As he travelled farther south his doubts were strengthened, for across the Potomac he could detect no sign of a new spirit. Manufactures had no existence. Alexandria owned a bank with half a million of capital, but no other was to be found between Washington and Charleston, except the branch Bank of the United States at Norfolk, nor any industry to which loans and discounts

could safely be made. Virginia, the most populous
and powerful of all the States, had a white population
of 514,000, nearly equal to that of Pennsylvania and
New York, besides about 350,000 slaves. Her energies had pierced the mountains and settled the western territory before the slow-moving Northern people
had torn themselves from the safer and more comfortable life by the seaboard ; but the Virginia ideal
was patriarchal, and an American continent on the
Virginia type might reproduce the virtues of Cato,
and perhaps the eloquence of Cicero, but was little
likely to produce anything more practical in the way
of modern progress. The Shenandoah Valley rivalled
Pennsylvania and Connecticut in richness and skill of
husbandry ; but even agriculture, the favorite industry in Virginia, had suffered from the competition
of Kentucky and Tennessee, and from the emigration
which had drawn away fully one hundred thousand
people. The land was no longer very productive.
Even Jefferson, the most active-minded and sanguine
of all Virginians, — the inventor of the first scientific
plough, the importer of the first threshing-machine
known in Virginia, the experimenter with a new
drilling-machine, the owner of one hundred and fifty
slaves and ten thousand acres of land, whose negroes
were trained to carpentry, cabinet-making, house-
building, weaving, tailoring, shoe-making, — claimed
to get from his land no more than six or eight bushels of wheat to an acre, and had been forced to
abandon the more profitable cultivation of tobacco.

Except in a few favored districts like the Shenandoah Valley, land in Virginia did not average eight bushels of wheat to an acre. The cultivation of tobacco had been almost the sole object of land-owners, and even where the lands were not exhausted, a bad system of agriculture and the force of habit prevented improvement.

The great planters lavished money in vain on experiments to improve their crops and their stock. They devoted themselves to the task with energy and knowledge; but they needed a diversity of interests and local markets, and except at Baltimore these were far from making their appearance. Neither the products, the markets, the relative amount of capital, nor the machinery of production had perceptibly changed. "The Virginians are not generally rich," said the Duc de Liancourt, "especially in net revenue. Thus one often finds a well-served table, covered with silver, in a room where for ten years half the window panes have been missing, and where they will be missed for ten years more. There are few houses in a passable state of repair, and of all parts of the establishment those best cared for are the stables." Wealth reckoned in slaves or land was plenty; but the best Virginians, from President Washington downward, were most outspoken in their warnings against the Virginia system both of slavery and agriculture.

The contrast between Virginia and Pennsylvania was the subject of incessant comment.

" In Pennsylvania," said Robert Sutcliffe, an English Friend who published travels made in 1804–1806, " we meet great numbers of wagons drawn by four or more fine fat horses, the carriages firm and well made, and covered with stout good linen, bleached almost white; and it is not uncommon to see ten or fifteen together travelling cheerfully along the road, the driver riding on one of his horses. Many of these come more than three hundred miles to Philadelphia from the Ohio, Pittsburg, and other places, and I have been told by a respectable Friend, a native of Philadelphia, that more than one thousand covered carriages frequently come to Philadelphia market. . . . The appearance of things in the Slave States is quite the reverse of this. We sometimes meet a ragged black boy or girl driving a team consisting of a lean cow and a mule; sometimes a lean bull or an ox and a mule; and I have seen a mule, a bull, and a cow each miserable in its appearance, composing one team, with a half-naked black slave or two riding or driving as occasion suited. The carriage or wagon, if it may be called such, appeared in as wretched a condition as the team and its driver. Sometimes a couple of horses, mules, or cows would be dragging a hogshead of tobacco, with a pivot or axle driven into each end of the hogshead, and something like a shaft attached, by which it was drawn or rolled along the road. I have seen two oxen and two slaves pretty fully employed in getting along a single hogshead; and some of these come from a great distance inland."

In the middle of these primitive sights, Sutcliffe was startled by a contrast such as Virginia could always show. Between Richmond and Fredericksburg, —

" In the afternoon, as our road lay through the woods, I was surprised to meet a family party travelling along in as elegant a coach as is usually met with in the neighborhood of London, and attended by several gayly dressed footmen."

The country south of Virginia seemed unpromising even to Virginians. In the year 1796 President Washington gave to Sir John Sinclair his opinion upon the relative value of American lands. He then thought the valley of Virginia the garden of America ; but he would say nothing to induce others to settle in more southern regions.

" The uplands of North and South Carolina and Georgia are not dissimilar in soil," he wrote, " but as they approach the lower latitudes are less congenial to wheat, and are supposed to be proportionably more unhealthy. Towards the seaboard of all the Southern States, and farther south more so, the lands are low, sandy, and unhealthy ; for which reason I shall say little concerning them, for as I should not choose to be an inhabitant of them myself, I ought not to say anything that would induce others to be so. . . . I understand that from thirty to forty dollars per acre may be denominated the medium price in the vicinity of the Susquehanna in the State of Pennsylvania, from twenty to thirty on the Potomac in what is called the Valley, . . . and less, as I have noticed before, as you proceed southerly."

Whatever was the cause, the State of North Carolina seemed to offer few·temptations to immigrants or capital. Even in white population ranking fifth among the sixteen States, her 478,000 inhabitants were unknown to the world. The beautiful upper country attracted travellers neither for pleasure nor for gain, while the country along the sea-coast was avoided except by hardy wanderers. The grumbling Wilson, who knew every nook and corner of the United States, and who found New England so dreary, painted this part of North Carolina in colors compared with which his sketch of New England was gay. " The taverns are the most desolate and beggarly imaginable; bare, bleak, and dirty walls, one or two old broken chairs and a bench form all the furniture. The white females seldom make their appearance. At supper you sit down to a meal the very sight of which is sufficient to deaden the most eager appetite, and you are surrounded by half-a-dozen dirty, half-naked blacks, male and female, whom any man of common scent might smell a quarter of a mile off. The house itself is raised upon props four or five feet, and the space below is left open for the hogs, with whose charming vocal performance the wearied traveller is serenaded the whole night long." The landscape pleased him no better, — " immense solitary pine savannahs through which the road winds among stagnant ponds; dark, sluggish creeks of the color of brandy, over which are thrown high wooden bridges without railings," crazy and rotten.

North Carolina was relatively among the poorest States. The exports and imports were of trifling value, less than one tenth of those returned for Mas-

sachusetts, which were more than twice as great as
those of North Carolina and Virginia together. That
under these conditions America should receive any
strong impulse from such a quarter seemed unlikely;
yet perhaps for the moment more was to be expected
from the Carolinas than from Virginia. Backward as
these States in some respects were, they possessed
one new element of wealth which promised more for
them than anything Virginia could hope. The steam-
engines of Watt had been applied in England to
spinning, weaving, and printing cotton; an immense
demand had risen for that staple, and the cotton-gin
had been simultaneously invented. A sudden impetus
was given to industry; land which had been worthless and estates which had become bankrupt acquired
new value, and in 1800 every planter was growing cotton, buying negroes, and breaking fresh soil. North
Carolina felt the strong flood of prosperity, but South
Carolina, and particularly the town of Charleston,
had most to hope. The exports of South Carolina
were nearly equal in value to those of Massachusetts
or Pennsylvania; the imports were equally large.
Charleston might reasonably expect to rival Boston,
New York, Philadelphia, and Baltimore. In 1800
these cities still stood, as far as concerned their foreign trade, within some range of comparison; and
between Boston, Baltimore, and Charleston, many
plausible reasons could be given for thinking that the
last might have the most brilliant future. The three
towns stood abreast. If Charleston had but about

eighteen thousand inhabitants, this was the number
reported by Boston only ten years before, and was
five thousand more than Baltimore then boasted.
Neither Boston nor Baltimore saw about them a
vaster region to supply, or so profitable a staple to
export. A cotton crop of two hundred thousand
pounds sent abroad in 1791 grew to twenty millions
in 1801, and was to double again by 1803. An export of fifty thousand bales was enormous, yet was
only the beginning. What use might not Charleston,
the only considerable town in the entire South, make
of this golden flood?

The town promised hopefully to prove equal to its
task. Nowhere in the Union was intelligence, wealth,
and education greater in proportion to numbers than
in the little society of cotton and rice planters who
ruled South Carolina; and they were in 1800 not behind — they hoped soon to outstrip — their rivals.
If Boston was building a canal to the Merrimac, and
Philadelphia one along the Schuylkill to the Susquehanna, Charleston had nearly completed another
which brought the Santee River to its harbor, and
was planning a road to Tennessee which should draw
the whole interior within reach. Nashville was nearer
to Charleston than to any other seaport of the Union,
and Charleston lay nearest to the rich trade of the
West Indies. Not even New York seemed more
clearly marked for prosperity than this solitary Southern city, which already possessed banking capital in
abundance, intelligence, enterprise, the traditions of

high culture and aristocratic ambition, all supported by slave-labor, which could be indefinitely increased by the African slave-trade.

If any portion of the United States might hope for a sudden and magnificent bloom, South Carolina seemed entitled to expect it. Rarely had such a situation, combined with such resources, failed to produce some wonderful result. Yet as Washington warned Sinclair, these advantages were counterbalanced by serious evils. The climate in summer was too relaxing. The sun was too hot. The sea-coast was unhealthy, and at certain seasons even deadly to the whites. Finally, if history was a guide, no permanent success could be prophesied for a society like that of the low country in South Carolina, where some thirty thousand whites were surrounded by a dense mass of nearly one hundred thousand negro slaves. Even Georgia, then only partially settled, contained sixty thousand slaves and but one hundred thousand whites. The cotton States might still argue that if slavery, malaria, or summer heat barred civilization, all the civilization that was ever known must have been blighted in its infancy; but although the future of South Carolina might be brilliant, like that of other oligarchies in which only a few thousand freemen took part, such a development seemed to diverge far from the path likely to be followed by Northern society, and bade fair to increase and complicate the social and economical difficulties with which Americans had to deal.

A probable valuation of the whole United States in 1800 was eighteen hundred million dollars, equal to $328 for each human being, including slaves; or $418 to each free white. This property was distributed with an approach to equality, except in a few of the Southern States. In New York and Philadelphia a private fortune of one hundred thousand dollars was considered handsome, and three hundred thousand was great wealth. Inequalities were frequent; but they were chiefly those of a landed aristocracy. Equality was so far the rule that every white family of five persons might be supposed to own land, stock, or utensils, a house and furniture, worth about two thousand dollars; and as the only considerable industry was agriculture, their scale of life was easy to calculate, — taxes amounting to little or nothing, and wages averaging about a dollar a day.

Not only were these slender resources, but they were also of a kind not easily converted to the ready uses required for rapid development. Among the numerous difficulties with which the Union was to struggle, and which were to form the interest of American history, the disproportion between the physical obstacles and the material means for overcoming them was one of the most striking.

CHAPTER II.

THE growth of character, social and national, — the formation of men's minds, — more interesting than any territorial or industrial growth, defied the tests of censuses and surveys. No people could be expected, least of all when in infancy, to understand the intricacies of its own character, and rarely has a foreigner been gifted with insight to explain what natives did not comprehend. Only with diffidence could the best-informed Americans venture, in 1800, to generalize on the subject of their own national habits of life and thought. Of all American travellers President Dwight was the most experienced; yet his four volumes of travels were remarkable for no trait more uniform than their reticence in regard to the United States. Clear and emphatic wherever New England was in discussion, Dwight claimed no knowledge of other regions. Where so good a judge professed ignorance, other observers were likely to mislead; and Frenchmen like Liancourt, Englishmen like Weld, or Germans like Bülow, were almost equally worthless authorities on a subject which none understood. The newspapers of the time were little more trustworthy than the books of travel, and hardly so well written. The literature of a higher kind was

chiefly limited to New England, New York, and Pennsylvania. From materials so poor no precision of
result could be expected. A few customs, more or
less local; a few prejudices, more or less popular;
a few traits of thought, suggesting habits of mind,
— must form the entire material for a study more
important than that of politics or economics.

The standard of comfort had much to do with the
standard of character; and in the United States, except among the slaves, the laboring class enjoyed an
ample supply of the necessaries of life. In this respect, as in some others, they claimed superiority over
the laboring class in Europe, and the claim would
have been still stronger had they shown more skill in
using the abundance that surrounded them. The
Duc de Liancourt, among foreigners the best and
kindest observer, made this remark on the mode of
life he saw in Pennsylvania : —

" There is a contrast of cleanliness with its opposite
which to a stranger is very remarkable. The people of
the country are as astonished that one should object to
sleeping two or three in the same bed and in dirty sheets,
or to drink from the same dirty glass after half a score
of others, as to see one neglect to wash one's hands and
face of a morning. Whiskey diluted with water is the
ordinary country drink. There is no settler, however
poor, whose family does not take coffee or chocolate for
breakfast, and always a little salt meat; at dinner, salt
meat, or salt fish, and eggs; at supper again salt meat
and coffee. This is also the common regime of the
taverns."

An amusing, though quite untrustworthy English-man named Ashe, who invented an American journey in 1806, described the fare of a Kentucky cabin : —

" The dinner consisted of a large piece of salt bacon, a dish of hominy, and a tureen of squirrel broth. I dined entirely on the last dish, which I found incomparably good, and the meat equal to the most delicate chicken. The Kentuckian eat nothing but bacon, which indeed is the favorite diet of all the inhabitants of the State, and drank nothing but whiskey, which soon made him more than two-thirds drunk. In this last practice he is also supported by the public habit. In a country, then, where bacon and spirits form the favorite summer repast, it cannot be just to attribute entirely the causes of infirmity to the climate. No people on earth live with less regard to regimen. They eat salt meat three times a day, seldom or never have any vegetables, and drink ardent spirits from morning till night. They have not only an aversion to fresh meat, but a vulgar prejudice that it is unwholesome. The truth is, their stomachs are depraved by burning liquors, and they have no appetite for anything but what is high-flavored and strongly impregnated by salt."

Salt pork three times a day was regarded as an essential part of American diet. In the " Chain-bearer," Cooper described what he called American poverty as it existed in 1784. " As for bread," said the mother, " I count that for nothing. We always have bread and potatoes enough; but I hold a family to be in a desperate way when the mother can see the bottom of the pork-barrel. Give me the children that's raised on good sound pork afore all the game in the country. Game's good as a relish, and so's bread; but pork is the staff of life. . . My children I calkerlate to bring up on pork."

Many years before the time to which Cooper referred, Poor Richard asked: "Maids of America, who gave you bad teeth?" and supplied the answer: "Hot soupings and frozen apples." Franklin's question and answer were repeated in a wider sense by many writers, but none was so emphatic as Volney: —

" I will venture to say," declared Volney, "that if a prize were proposed for the scheme of a regimen most calculated to injure the stomach, the teeth, and the health in general, no better could be invented than that of the Americans. In the morning at breakfast they deluge their stomach with a quart of hot water, impregnated with tea, or so slightly with coffee that it is mere colored water; and they swallow, almost without chewing, hot bread, half baked, toast soaked in butter, cheese of the fattest kind, slices of salt or hung beef, ham, etc., all which are nearly insoluble. At dinner they have boiled pastes under the name of puddings, and the fattest are esteemed the most delicious; all their sauces, even for roast beef, are melted butter; their turnips and potatoes swim in hog's lard, butter, or fat; under the name of pie or pumpkin, their pastry is nothing but a greasy paste, never sufficiently baked. To digest these viscous substances they take tea almost instantly after dinner, making it so strong that it is absolutely bitter to the taste, in which state it affects the nerves so powerfully that even the English find it brings on a more

obstinate restlessness than coffee. Supper again intro-
duces salt meats or oysters. As Chastellux says, the
whole day passes in heaping indigestions on one another ; and to give tone to the poor, relaxed, and wearied
stomach, they drink Madeira, rum, French brandy, gin,
or malt spirits, which complete the ruin of the nervous
system."

An American breakfast never failed to interest foreigners, on account of the variety and abundance of
its dishes. On the main lines of travel, fresh meat
and vegetables were invariably served at all meals ;
but Indian corn was the national crop, and Indian
corn was eaten three times a day in another form as
salt pork. The rich alone could afford fresh meat.
Ice-chests were hardly known. In the country fresh
meat could not regularly be got, except in the shape
of poultry or game ; but the hog cost nothing to keep,
and very little to kill and preserve. Thus the ordinary rural American was brought up on salt pork
and Indian corn, or rye ; and the effect of this diet
showed itself in dyspepsia.

One of the traits to which Liancourt alluded marked
more distinctly the stage of social development. By
day or by night, privacy was out of the question. Not
only must all men travel in the same coach, dine at
the same table, at the same time, on the same fare,
but even their beds were in common, without distinction of persons. Innkeepers would not understand
that a different arrangement was possible. When the
English traveller Weld reached Elkton, on the main

road from Philadelphia to Baltimore, he asked the
landlord what accommodation he had. "Don't trouble yourself about that," was the reply; "I have no
less than eleven beds in one room alone." This primitive habit extended over the whole country from
Massachusetts to Georgia, and no American seemed
to revolt against the tyranny of innkeepers.

"At New York I was lodged with two others,
in a back room on the ground floor," wrote, in
1796, the Philadelphian whose complaints have already been mentioned. "What can be the reason
for that vulgar, hoggish custom, common in America, of squeezing three, six, or eight beds into one
room?"

Nevertheless, the Americans were on the whole
more neat than their critics allowed. "You have
not seen the Americans," was Cobbett's reply, in
1819, to such charges; "you have not seen the nice,
clean, neat houses of the farmers of Long Island, in
New England, in the Quaker counties of Pennsylvania; you have seen nothing but the smoke-dried
ultra-montanians." Yet Cobbett drew a sharp contrast between the laborer's neat cottage familiar to
him in Surrey and Hampshire, and the "shell of
boards" which the American occupied, "all around
him as barren as a sea-beach." He added, too, that
"the example of neatness was wanting;" no one
taught it by showing its charm. Felix de Beaujour,
otherwise not an enthusiastic American, paid a warm
compliment to the country in this single respect,

although he seemed to have the cities chiefly in mind : —

" American neatness must possess some very attractive quality, since it seduces every traveller ; and there is no one of them who, in returning to his own country, does not wish to meet again there that air of ease and neatness which rejoiced his sight during his stay in the United States."

Almost every traveller discussed the question whether the Americans were a temperate people, or whether they drank more than the English. Temperate they certainly were not, when judged by a modern standard. Every one acknowledged that in the South and West drinking was occasionally excessive ; but even in Pennsylvania and New England the universal taste for drams proved habits by no means strict. Every grown man took his noon toddy as a matter of course ; and although few were seen publicly drunk, many were habitually affected by liquor. The earliest temperance movement, ten or twelve years later, was said to have had its source in the scandal caused by the occasional intoxication of ministers at their regular meetings. Cobbett thought drinking the national disease ; at all hours of the day, he said, young men, " even little boys, at or under twelve years of age, go into stores and tip off their drams." The mere comparison with England proved that the evil was great, for the English and Scotch were among the largest consumers of beer and alcohol on the globe.

In other respects besides sobriety American manners and morals were subjects of much dispute, and if
judged by the diatribes of travellers like Thomas Moore
and H. W. Bülow, were below the level of Europe.
Of all classes of statistics, moral statistics were least
apt to be preserved. Even in England, social vices
could be gauged only by the records of criminal and
divorce courts ; in America, police was wanting and
a divorce suit almost, if not quite, unknown. Apart
from some coarseness, society must have been pure ;
and the coarseness was mostly an English inheritance.
Among New Englanders, Chief-Justice Parsons was
the model of judicial, social, and religious propriety ;
yet Parsons, in 1808, presented to a lady a copy of
" Tom Jones," with a letter calling attention to the
adventures of Molly Seagrim and the usefulness of
describing vice. Among the social sketches in the
" Portfolio" were many allusions to the coarseness
of Philadelphia society, and the manners common to
tea-parties. " I heard from married ladies," said a
writer in February, 1803, " whose station as mothers
demanded from them a guarded conduct, — from
young ladies, whose age forbids the audience of such
conversation, and who using it modesty must dis-
claim, — indecent allusions, indelicate expressions,
and even at times immoral innuendoes. A loud laugh
or a coarse exclamation followed each of these, and
the young ladies generally went through the form of
raising their fans to their faces."

Yet public and private records might be searched

long, before they revealed evidence of misconduct such as filled the press and formed one of the commonest topics of conversation in the society of England and France. Almost every American family, however respectable, could show some victim to intemperance among its men, but few were mortified by a public scandal due to its women.

If the absence of positive evidence did not prove American society to be as pure as its simple and primitive condition implied, the same conclusion would be reached by observing the earnestness with which critics collected every charge that could be brought against it, and by noting the substance of the whole. Tried by this test, the society of 1800 was often coarse and sometimes brutal, but, except for intemperance, was moral. Indeed, its chief offence, in the eyes of Europeans, was dulness. The amusements of a people were commonly a fair sign of social development, and the Americans were only beginning to amuse themselves. The cities were small and few in number, and the diversions were such as cost little and required but elementary knowledge. In New England, although the theatre had gained a firm foothold in Boston, Puritan feelings still forbade the running of horses.

"The principal amusements of the inhabitants," said Dwight, "are visiting, dancing, music, conversation, walking, riding, sailing, shooting at a mark, draughts, chess, and unhappily, in some of the larger towns, cards and dramatic exhibitions. A considerable amusement is also furnished in many places by the examination and exhibitions of the superior schools ; and a more considerable one by the public exhibitions of colleges. Our countrymen also fish and hunt. Journeys taken for pleasure are very numerous, and are a very favorite object. Boys and young men play at foot-ball, cricket, quoits, and at many other sports of an athletic cast, and in the winter are peculiarly fond of skating. Riding in a sleigh, or sledge, is also a favorite diversion in New England."

President Dwight was sincere in his belief that college commencements and sleigh-riding satisfied the wants of his people ; he looked upon whist as an unhappy dissipation, and upon the theatre as immoral. He had no occasion to condemn horse-racing, for no race-course was to be found in New England. The horse and the dog existed only in varieties little suited for sport. In colonial days New England produced one breed of horses worth preserving and developing, — the Narragansett pacer ; but, to the regret even of the clergy, this animal almost disappeared, and in 1800 New England could show nothing to take its place. The germ of the trotter and the trotting-match, the first general popular amusement, could be seen in almost any country village, where the owners of horses were in the habit of trotting what were called scratch-races, for a quarter or half a mile from the door of the tavern, along the public road. Perhaps this amusement had already a right to be called a New-England habit, showing defined tastes ; but the force of the popular instinct was not fully felt in Massachusetts, or even in New York, although there it was given full play. New York possessed a race-course, and made in 1792 a great stride toward popularity by importing the famous stallion " Messenger " to become the source of endless interest for future generations; but Virginia was the region where the American showed his true character as a lover of sport. Long before the Revolution the race-course was commonly established in Virginia and Maryland; English running-horses of pure blood — descendants of the Darley Arabian and the Godolphin Arabian — were imported, and racing became the chief popular entertainment. The long Revolutionary War, and the general ruin it caused, checked the habit and deteriorated the breed; but with returning prosperity Virginia showed that the instinct was stronger than ever. In 1798 " Diomed," famous as the sire of racers, was imported into the State, and future rivalry between Virginia and New York could be foreseen. In 1800 the Virginia race-course still remained at the head of American popular amusements.

In an age when the Prince of Wales and crowds of English gentlemen attended every prize-fight, and patronized Tom Crib, Dutch Sam, the Jew Mendoza, and the negro Molyneux, an Englishman could hardly have expected that a Virginia race-course should be free from vice; and perhaps travellers showed best the general morality of the people by their practice of dwelling on Virginia vices. They charged the

Virginians with fondness for horse-racing, cock-fight-
ing, betting, and drinking; but the popular habit
which most shocked them, and with which books of
travel filled pages of description, was the so-called
rough-and-tumble fight. The practice was not one
on which authors seemed likely to dwell; yet foreigners like Weld, and Americans like Judge Long-
street in "Georgia Scenes," united to give it a sort of
grotesque dignity like that of a bull-fight, and under
their treatment it became interesting as a popular
habit. The rough-and-tumble fight differed from the
ordinary prize-fight, or boxing-match, by the absence
of rules. Neither kicking, tearing, biting, nor gouging was forbidden by the law of the ring. Brutal as
the practice was, it was neither new nor exclusively
Virginian. The English travellers who described it
as American barbarism, might have seen the same
sight in Yorkshire at the same date. The rough-and-
tumble fight was English in origin, and was brought
to Virginia and the Carolinas in early days, whence
it spread to the Ohio and Mississippi. The habit
attracted general notice because of its brutality in a
society that showed few brutal instincts. Friendly
foreigners like Liancourt were honestly shocked by
it; others showed somewhat too plainly their pleasure
at finding a vicious habit which they could consider
a natural product of democratic society. Perhaps
the description written by Thomas Ashe showed best
not only the ferocity of the fight but also the antipathies of the writer, for Ashe had something of the

artist in his touch, and he felt no love for Americans. The scene was at Wheeling. A Kentuckian and a Virginian were the combatants.

" Bulk and bone were in favor of the Kentuckian; science and craft in that of the Virginian. The former promised himself victory from his power; the latter from his science. Very few rounds had taken place or fatal blows given, before the Virginian contracted his whole form, drew up his arms to his face, with his hands nearly closed in a concave by the fingers being bent to the full extension of the flexors, and summoning up all his energy for one act of desperation, pitched himself into the bosom of his opponent. Before the effects of this could be ascertained, the sky was rent by the shouts of the multitude; and I could learn that the Virginian had expressed as much beauty and skill in his retraction and bound, as if he had been bred in a menagerie and practised action and attitude among panthers and wolves. The shock received by the Kentuckian, and the want of breath, brought him instantly to the ground. The Virginian never lost his hold. Like those bats of the South who never quit the subject on which they fasten till they taste blood, he kept his knees in his enemy's body; fixing his claws in his hair and his thumbs on his eyes, gave them an instantaneous start from their sockets. The sufferer roared aloud, but uttered no complaint. The citizens again shouted with joy."

Ashe asked his landlord whether this habit spread down the Ohio.

" I understood that it did, on the left-hand side, and that I would do well to land there as little as possible.

. . . I again demanded how a stranger was to distinguish a good from a vicious house of entertainment. ' By previous inquiry, or, if that was impracticable, a tolerable judgment could be formed from observing in the landlord a possession or an absence of ears.' "

The temper of the writer was at least as remarkable in this description as the scene he pretended to describe, for Ashe's Travels were believed to have been chiefly imaginary; but no one denied the roughness of the lower classes in the South and Southwest, nor was roughness wholly confined to them. No prominent man in Western society bore himself with more courtesy and dignity than Andrew Jackson of Tennessee, who in 1800 was candidate for the post of major-general of State militia, and had previously served as Judge on the Supreme Bench of his State; yet the fights in which he had been engaged exceeded belief.

Border society was not refined, but among its vices, as its virtues, few were permanent, and little idea could be drawn of the character that would at last emerge. The Mississippi boatman and the squatter on Indian lands were perhaps the most distinctly American type then existing, as far removed from the Old World as though Europe were a dream. Their language and imagination showed contact with Indians. A traveller on the levee at Natchez, in 1808, overheard a quarrel in a flatboat near by : —

"I am a man; I am a horse; I am a team," cried one voice; "I can whip any man in all Kentucky, by

God!" "I am an alligator," cried the other; "half man, half horse; can whip any man on the Mississippi, by God!" "I am a man," shouted the first; "have the best horse, best dog, best gun, and handsomest wife in all Kentucky, by God!" "I am a Mississippi snapping-turtle," rejoined the second; "have bear's claws, alligator's teeth, and the devil's tail; can whip *any* man, by God!"

And on this usual formula of defiance the two fire-eaters began their fight, biting, gouging, and tearing. Foreigners were deeply impressed by barbarism such as this, and orderly emigrants from New England and Pennsylvania avoided contact with Southern drinkers and fighters; but even then they knew that with a new generation such traits must disappear, and that little could be judged of popular character from the habits of frontiersmen. Perhaps such vices deserved more attention when found in the older communities, but even there they were rather survivals of English low-life than products of a new soil, and they were given too much consequence in the tales of foreign travellers.

This was not the only instance where foreigners were struck by what they considered popular traits, which natives rarely noticed. Idle curiosity was commonly represented as universal, especially in the Southern settler who knew no other form of conversation : —

"Frequently have I been stopped by one of them," said Weld, "and without further preface asked where

I was from, if I was acquainted with any news, where bound to, and finally my name. ' Stop, Mister! why, I guess now you be coming from the new State?' ' No, sir.' ' Why, then, I guess as how you be coming from Kentuck?' ' No, sir.' ' Oh, why, then, pray now where might you be coming from?' ' From the low country.' ' Why, you must have heard all the news, then; pray now, Mister, what might the price of bacon be in those parts?' ' Upon my word, my friend, I can't inform you.' ' Ay, ay; I see, Mister, you be'ent one of us. Pray now, Mister, what might your name be?' "

Almost every writer spoke with annoyance of the inquisitorial habits of New England and the impertinence of American curiosity. Complaints so common could hardly have lacked foundation, yet the Americans as a people were never loquacious, but inclined to be somewhat reserved, and they could not recognize the accuracy of the description. President Dwight repeatedly expressed astonishment at the charge, and asserted that in his large experience it had no foundation. Forty years later, Charles Dickens found complaint with Americans for taciturnity. Equally strange to modern experience were the continual complaints in books of travel that loungers and loafers, idlers of every description, infested the taverns, and annoyed respectable travellers both native and foreign. Idling seemed to be considered a popular vice, and was commonly associated with tippling. So completely did the practice disappear in the course of another generation that it could scarcely be recalled as offensive; but in truth less work was done by the average man in 1800 than in aftertimes, for there was actually less work to do. " Good country this for lazy fellows," wrote Wilson from Kentucky; " they plant corn, turn their pigs into the woods, and in the autumn feed upon corn and pork. They lounge about the rest of the year." The roar of the steam-engine had never been heard in the land, and the carrier's wagon was three weeks between Philadelphia and Pittsburg. What need for haste when days counted for so little? Why not lounge about the tavern when life had no better amusement to offer? Why mind one's own business when one's business would take care of itself?

Yet however idle the American sometimes appeared, and however large the class of tavern loafers may have actually been, the true American was active and industrious. No immigrant came to America for ease or idleness. If an English farmer bought land near New York, Philadelphia, or Baltimore, and made the most of his small capital, he found that while he could earn more money than in Surrey or Devonshire, he worked harder and suffered greater discomforts. The climate was trying; fever was common; the crops ran new risks from strange insects, drought, and violent weather; the weeds were annoying; the flies and mosquitoes tormented him and his cattle; laborers were scarce and indifferent; the slow and magisterial ways of England, where everything was made easy, must be exchanged for quick and energetic action; the farmer's own eye must see to every detail, his own hand must hold the plough and the scythe. Life was more exacting, and every such man in America was required to do, and actually did, the work of two such men in Europe. Few English farmers of the conventional class took kindly to American ways, or succeeded in adapting themselves to the changed conditions. Germans were more successful and became rich; but the poorer and more adventurous class, who had no capital, and cared nothing for the comforts of civilization, went West, to find a harder lot. When, after toiling for weeks, they reached the neighborhood of Genessee or the banks of some stream in southern Ohio or Indiana, they put up a rough cabin of logs with an earthen floor, cleared an acre or two of land, and planted Indian corn between the tree-stumps, — lucky if, like the Kentuckian, they had a pig to turn into the woods. Between April and October, Albert Gallatin used to say, Indian corn made the penniless immigrant a capitalist. New settlers suffered many of the ills that would have afflicted an army marching and fighting in a country of dense forest and swamp, with one sore misery besides, — that whatever trials the men endured, the burden bore most heavily upon the women and children. The chance of being shot or scalped by Indians was hardly worth considering when compared with the certainty of malarial fever, or the strange disease called milk-sickness, or the still more depressing home-sickness, or the misery of nervous prostration, which wore out generation after generation of women and children on the frontiers, and left a tragedy in every log-cabin. Not for love of ease did men plunge into the wilderness. Few laborers of the Old World endured a harder lot, coarser fare, or anxieties and responsibilities greater than those of the Western emigrant. Not merely because he enjoyed the luxury of salt pork, whiskey, or even coffee three times a day did the American laborer claim superiority over the European.

A standard far higher than the average was common to the cities; but the city population was so small as to be trifling. Boston, New York, Philadelphia, and Baltimore together contained one hundred and eighty thousand inhabitants; and these were the only towns containing a white population of more than ten thousand persons. In a total population of more than five millions, this number of city people, as Jefferson and his friends rightly thought, was hardly American, for the true American was supposed to be essentially rural. Their comparative luxury was outweighed by the squalor of nine hundred thousand slaves alone.

From these slight notices of national habits no other safe inference could be drawn than that the people were still simple. The path their development might take was one of the many problems with which their future was perplexed. Such few habits as might prove to be fixed, offered little clew to the habits that might be adopted in the process of growth, and speculation was useless where change alone could be considered certain.

If any prediction could be risked, an observer might have been warranted in suspecting that the popular character was likely to be conservative, for as yet this trait was most marked, at least in the older societies of New England, Pennsylvania, and Virginia. Great as were the material obstacles in the path of the United States, the greatest obstacle of all was in the human mind. Down to the close of the eighteenth century no change had occurred in the world which warranted practical men in assuming that great changes were to come. Afterward, as time passed, and as science developed man's capacity to control Nature's forces, old-fashioned conservatism vanished from society, reappearing occasionally, like the stripes on a mule, only to prove its former existence; but during the eighteenth century the progress of America, except in political paths, had been less rapid than ardent reformers wished, and the reaction which followed the French Revolution made it seem even slower than it was. In 1723 Benjamin Franklin landed at Philadelphia, and with his loaf of bread under his arm walked along Market Street toward an immortality such as no American had then conceived. He died in 1790, after witnessing great political revolutions; but the intellectual revolution was hardly as rapid as he must, in his youth, have hoped.

In 1732 Franklin induced some fifty persons to found

a subscription library, and his example and energy set
a fashion which was generally followed. In 1800
the library he founded was still in existence; numerous small subscription libraries on the same model,
containing fifty or a hundred volumes, were scattered
in country towns; but all the public libraries in the
United States — collegiate, scientific, or popular, en-
dowed or unendowed — could hardly show fifty thousand volumes, including duplicates, fully one third
being still theological.

Half a century had passed since Franklin's active
mind drew the lightning from heaven, and decided
the nature of electricity. No one in America had yet
carried further his experiments in the field which he
had made American. This inactivity was commonly
explained as a result of the long Revolutionary War;
yet the war had not prevented population and wealth
from increasing, until Philadelphia in 1800 was far in
advance of the Philadelphia which had seen Franklin's
kite flying among the clouds.

In the year 1753 Franklin organized the postal
system of the American colonies, making it self-
supporting. No record was preserved of the number
of letters then carried in proportion to the population,
but in 1800 the gross receipts for postage were
$320,000, toward which Pennsylvania contributed
most largely, — the sum of $55,000. From letters the
Government received in gross $290,000. The lowest
rate of letter-postage was then eight cents. The
smallest charge for letters carried more than a

hundred miles was twelve and a half cents. If on an average ten letters were carried for a dollar, the whole number of letters was 2,900,000, — about one a year for every grown inhabitant.

Such a rate of progress could not be called rapid even by conservatives, and more than one stanch conservative thought it unreasonably slow. Even in New York, where foreign influence was active and the rewards of scientific skill were comparatively liberal, science hardly kept pace with wealth and population.

Noah Webster, who before beginning his famous dictionary edited the "New York Commercial Advertiser," and wrote on all subjects with characteristic confidence, complained of the ignorance of his countrymen. He claimed for the New Englanders an acquaintance with theology, law, politics, and light English literature; "but as to classical learning, history (civil and ecclesiastical), mathematics, astronomy, chemistry, botany, and natural history, excepting here and there a rare instance of a man who is eminent in some one of these branches, we may be said to have no learning at all, or a mere smattering." Although defending his countrymen from the criticisms of Dr. Priestley, he admitted that " our learning is superficial in a shameful degree, . . . our colleges are disgracefully destitute of books and philosophical apparatus, . . . and I am ashamed to own that scarcely a branch of science can be fully investigated in America for want of books, especially origi-

nal works. This defect of our libraries I have experienced myself in searching for materials for the
History of Epidemic Diseases. . . . As to libraries,
we have no such things. There are not more than
three or four tolerable libraries in America, and
these are extremely imperfect. Great numbers of
the most valuable authors have not found their way
across the Atlantic."

This complaint was made in the year 1800, and was
the more significant because it showed that Webster,
a man equally at home in Philadelphia, New York,
and Boston, thought his country's deficiencies greater
than could be excused or explained by its circumstances. George Ticknor felt at least equal difficulty
in explaining the reason why, as late as 1814, even
good schoolbooks were rare in Boston, and a copy of
Euripides in the original could not be bought at any
book-seller's shop in New England. For some reason,
the American mind, except in politics, seemed to these
students of literature in a condition of unnatural
sluggishness ; and such complaints were not confined
to literature or science. If Americans agreed in any
opinion, they were united in wishing for roads ; but
even on that point whole communities showed an indifference, or hostility, that annoyed their contemporaries. President Dwight was a somewhat extreme
conservative in politics and religion, while the State
of Rhode Island was radical in both respects ; but
Dwight complained with bitterness unusual in his
mouth that Rhode Island showed no spirit of prog-

ress.   The subject of his criticism was an unfinished turnpike-road across the State.

" The people of Providence expended upon this road, as we are informed, the whole sum permitted by the Legislature. This was sufficient to make only those parts which I have mentioned. The turnpike company then applied to the Legislature for leave to expend such an additional sum as would complete the work. The Legislature refused. The principal reason for the refusal, as alleged by one of the members, it is said, was the following: that turnpikes and the establishment of religious worship had their origin in Great Britain, the government of which was a monarchy and the inhabitants slaves; that the people of Massachusetts and Connecticut were obliged by law to support ministers and pay the fare of turnpikes, and were therefore slaves also; that if they chose to be slaves they undoubtedly had a right to their choice, but that free-born Rhode Islanders ought never to submit to be priest-ridden, nòr to pay for the privilege of travelling on the highway. This demonstrative reasoning prevailed, and the road continued in the state which I have mentioned until the year 1805. It was then completed, and free-born Rhode Islanders bowed their necks to the slavery of travelling on a good road."

President Dwight seldom indulged in sarcasm or exaggeration such as he showed in this instance; but he repeated only matters of notoriety in charging some of the most democratic communities with unwillingness to pay for good roads. If roads were to exist, they must be the result of public or private enterprise;

and if the public in certain States would neither
construct roads nor permit corporations to construct
them, the entire Union must suffer for want of communication.   So strong was the popular prejudice
against paying for the privilege of travelling on a
highway that in certain States, like Rhode Island and
Georgia, turnpikes were long unknown, while in Virginia and North Carolina the roads were little better
than where the prejudice was universal.

In this instance the economy of a simple and somewhat rude society accounted in part for indifference ;
in other cases, popular prejudice took a form less
easily understood.   So general was the hostility to
Banks as to offer a serious obstacle to enterprise.
The popularity of President Washington and the usefulness of his administration were impaired by his
support of a national bank and a funding system.
Jefferson's hostility to all the machinery of capital
was shared by a great majority of the Southern people and a large minority in the North.   For seven
years the New York legislature refused to charter
the first banking company in the State ; and when in
1791 the charter was obtained, and the Bank fell into
Federalist hands, Aaron Burr succeeded in obtaining
banking privileges for the Manhattan Company only
by concealing them under the pretence of furnishing
a supply of fresh water to the city of New York.

This conservative habit of mind was more harmful
in America than in other communities, because Americans needed more than older societies the activity

which could alone partly compensate for the relative
feebleness of their means compared with the magni-
tude of their task.   Some instances of sluggishness,
common to Europe and America, were hardly credi-
ble.   For more than ten years in England the steam-
engines of Watt had been working, in common and
successful use, causing a revolution in industry that
threatened to drain the world for England's advantage ; yet Europe during a generation left England
undisturbed to enjoy the monopoly of steam.   France
and Germany were England's rivals in commerce and
manufactures, and required steam for self-defence ;
while the United States were commercial allies of England, and needed steam neither for mines nor manufactures, but their need was still extreme.   Every
American knew that if steam could be successfully
applied to navigation, it must produce an immediate
increase of wealth, besides an ultimate settlement
of the most serious material and political difficulties
of the Union.   Had both the national and State
Governments devoted millions of money to this object, and had the citizens wasted, if necessary, every
dollar in their slowly filling pockets to attain it, they
would have done no more than the occasion warranted, even had they failed ; but failure was not to
be feared, for they had with their own eyes seen the
experiment tried, and they did not dispute its success.
For America this question had been settled as early
as 1789, when John Fitch — a mechanic, without education or wealth, but with the energy of genius — in-

vented engine and paddles of his own, with so much
success that during a whole summer Philadelphians
watched his ferry-boat plying daily against the river
current. No one denied that his boat was rapidly,
steadily, and regularly moved against wind and tide,
with as much certainty and convenience as could be
expected in a first experiment; yet Fitch's company
failed. He could raise no more money; the public
refused to use his boat or to help him build a better;
they did not want it, would not believe in it, and
broke his heart by their contempt. Fitch struggled
against failure, and invented another boat moved by
a screw. The Eastern public still proving indifferent, he wandered to Kentucky, to try his fortune on
the Western waters. Disappointed there, as in Philadelphia and New York, he made a deliberate attempt
to end his life by drink; but the process proving too
slow, he saved twelve opium pills from the physician's
prescription, and was found one morning dead.

Fitch's death took place in an obscure Kentucky inn,
three years before Jefferson, the philosopher president, entered the White House. Had Fitch been the
only inventor thus neglected, his peculiarities and the
defects of his steamboat might account for his failure; but he did not stand alone. At the same moment Philadelphia contained another inventor, Oliver
Evans, a man so ingenious as to be often called the
American Watt. He, too, invented a locomotive steam-
engine which he longed to bring into common use.
The great services actually· rendered by this extraor-

dinary man were not a tithe of those he would gladly
have performed, had he found support and encouragement; but his success was not even so great as that of
Fitch, and he stood aside while Livingston and Fulton,
by their greater resources and influence, forced the
steamboat on a sceptical public.

While the inventors were thus ready, and while
State legislatures were offering mischievous monopo-
lies for this invention, which required only some few
thousand dollars of ready money, the Philosophical
Society of Rotterdam wrote to the American Philosophical Society at Philadelphia, requesting to know
what improvements had been made in the United
States in the construction of steam-engines. The
subject was referred to Benjamin H. Latrobe, the
most eminent engineer in America, and his Report,
presented to the Society in May, 1803, published in
the Transactions, and transmitted abroad, showed
the reasoning on which conservatism rested.

" During the general lassitude of mechanical exertion
which succeeded the American Revolution," said Latrobe,
" the utility of steam-engines appears to have been forgotten; but the subject afterward started into very general notice in a form in which it could not possibly be attended with much success. A sort of mania began to
prevail, which indeed has not yet entirely subsided, for
impelling boats by steam-engines. . . . For a short time
a passage-boat, rowed by a steam-engine, was established between Bordentown and Philadelphia, but it was
soon laid aside. . . . There are indeed general objec-

tions to the use of the steam-engine for impelling boats, from which no particular mode of application can be free. These are, first, the weight of the engine and of the fuel; second, the large space it occupies; third, the tendency of its action to rack the vessel and render it leaky; fourth, the expense of maintenance; fifth, the irregularity of its motion and the motion of the water in the boiler and cistern, and of the fuel-vessel in rough water; sixth, the difficulty arising from the liability of the paddles or oars to break if light, and from the weight, if made strong. Nor have I ever heard of an instance, verified by other testimony than that of the inventor, of a speedy and agreeable voyage having been performed in a steamboat of any construction. I am well aware that there are still many very respectable and ingenious men who consider the application of the steam-engine to the purpose of navigation as highly important and as very practicable, especially on the rapid waters of the Mississippi, and who would feel themselves almost offended at the expression of an opposite opinion. And perhaps some of the objections against it may be obviated. That founded on the expense and weight of the fuel may not for some years exist in the Mississippi, where there is a redundance of wood on the banks; but the cutting and loading will be almost as great an evil."

Within four years the steamboat was running, and Latrobe was its warmest friend. The dispute was a contest of temperaments, a divergence between minds, rather than a question of science; and a few visionaries such as those to whom Latrobe alluded — men like Chancellor Livingston, Joel Barlow, John Stevens, Samuel L. Mitchill, and Robert Fulton —

dragged society forward. What but scepticism could
be expected among a people thus asked to adopt the
steamboat, when as yet the ordinary atmospheric
steam-engine, such as had been in use in Europe for
a hundred years, was practically unknown to them,
and the engines of Watt were a fable? Latrobe's
Report further said that in the spring of 1803, when
he wrote, five steam-engines were at work in the
United States, — one lately set up by the Manhattan
Water Company in New York to supply the city with
water; another in New York for sawing timber; two
in Philadelphia, belonging to the city, for supplying
water and running a rolling and slitting mill; and
one at Boston employed in some manufacture. All
but one of these were probably constructed after
1800, and Latrobe neglected to say whether they
belonged to the old Newcomen type, or to Watt's
manufacture, or to American invention; but he added
that the chief American improvement on the steam-
engine had been the construction of a wooden boiler,
which developed sufficient power to work the Philadelphia pump at the rate of twelve strokes, of six
feet, per minute. Twelve strokes a minute, or one
stroke every five seconds, though not a surprising
power, might have answered its purpose, had not the
wooden boiler, as Latrobe admitted, quickly decom-
posed, and steam-leaks appeared at every bolt-hole.

If so eminent and so intelligent a man as Latrobe,
who had but recently emigrated in the prime of life
from England, knew little about Watt, and nothing

about Oliver Evans, whose experience would have
been well worth communicating to any philosophical
society in Europe, the more ignorant and unscientific
public could not feel faith in a force of which they
knew nothing at all. For nearly two centuries the
Americans had struggled on foot or horseback over
roads not much better than trails, or had floated
down rushing streams in open boats momentarily in
danger of sinking or upsetting. They had at length,
in the Eastern and Middle States, reached the point
of constructing turnpikes and canals. Into these
undertakings they put sums of money relatively
large, for the investment seemed safe and the profits
certain. Steam as a locomotive power was still a
visionary idea, beyond their experience, contrary to
European precedent, and exposed to a thousand risks.
They regarded it as a delusion.

About three years after Latrobe wrote his Report
on the steam-engine, Robert Fulton began to build
the boat which settled forever the value of steam as
a locomotive power. According to Fulton's well-
known account of his own experience, he suffered
almost as keenly as Fitch, twenty years before, under
the want of popular sympathy : —

" When I was building my first steamboat at New
York," he said, according to Judge Story's report, " the
project was viewed by the public either with indifference
or with contempt as a visionary scheme. My friends
indeed were civil, but they were shy. They listened with
patience to my explanations, but with a settled cast of

incredulity upon their countenances.   I felt the full force
of the lamentation of the poet, —

> ' Truths would you teach, or save a sinking land,
>   All fear, none aid you, and few understand.'

As I had occasion to pass daily to and from the building-
yard while my boat was in progress, I have often loitered
unknown near the idle groups of strangers gathering in
little circles, and heard various inquiries as to the object
of this new vehicle.   The language was uniformly that
of scorn, or sneer, or ridicule.   The loud laugh often
rose at my expense; the dry jest; the wise calculation
of losses and expenditures; the dull but endless repetition of the Fulton Folly.   Never did a single encouraging remark, a bright hope, or a warm wish cross my
path."

Possibly Fulton and Fitch, like other inventors,
may have exaggerated the public apathy and contempt; but whatever was the precise force of the
innovating spirit, conservatism possessed the world
by right.   Experience forced on men's minds the
conviction that what had ever been must ever be.
At the close of the eighteenth century nothing had
occurred which warranted the belief that even the
material difficulties of America could be removed.
Radicals as extreme as Thomas Jefferson and Albert
Gallatin were contented with avowing no higher aim
than that America should reproduce the simpler forms
of European republican society without European
vices; and even this their opponents thought visionary.   The United States had thus far made a single

great step in advance of the Old World, — they had
agreed to try the experiment of embracing half a continent in one republican system ; but so little were
they disposed to feel confidence in their success, that
Jefferson himself did not look on this American idea
as vital ; he would not stake the future on so new an
invention. " Whether we remain in one confederacy,"
he wrote in 1804, " or form into Atlantic and Mississippi confederations, I believe not very important to
the happiness of either part." Even over his liberal
mind history cast a spell so strong, that he thought
the solitary American experiment of political confeder-
ation " not very important " beyond the Alleghanies.

The task of overcoming popular inertia in a democratic society was new, and seemed to offer peculiar
difficulties. Without a scientific class to lead the
way, and without a wealthy class to provide the
means of experiment, the people of the United States
were still required, by the nature of their problems,
to become a speculating and scientific nation. They
could do little without changing their old habit of
mind, and without learning to love novelty for novelty's sake. Hitherto their timidity in using money
had been proportioned to the scantiness of their
means. Henceforward they were under every inducement to risk great stakes and frequent losses in
order to win occasionally a thousand fold. In the
colonial state they had naturally accepted old processes as the best, and European experience as final
authority. As an independent people, with half a

continent to civilize, they could not afford to waste time in following European examples, but must devise new processes of their own. A world which assumed that what had been must be, could not be scientific; yet in order to make the Americans a successful people, they must be roused to feel the necessity of scientific training. Until they were satisfied that knowledge was money, they would not insist upon high education; nor until they saw with their own eyes stones turned into gold, and vapor into cattle and corn, would they learn the meaning of science.

CHAPTER III.

WHETHER the United States were to succeed or fail in their economical and political undertakings, the people must still develop some intellectual life of their own, and the character of this development was likely to interest mankind. New conditions and hopes could hardly fail to produce a literature and arts more or less original. Of all possible triumphs, none could equal that which might be won in the regions of thought if the intellectual influence of the United States should equal their social and economical importance. Young as the nation was, it had already produced an American literature bulky and varied enough to furnish some idea of its probable qualities in the future, and the intellectual condition of the literary class in the United States at the close of the eighteenth century could scarcely fail to suggest both the successes and the failures of the same class in the nineteenth.

In intellectual tastes, as in all else, the Union showed well-marked divisions between New England, New York, Pennsylvania, and the Southern States. New England was itself divided between two intellectual centres, — Boston and New Haven. The Massachusetts and Connecticut schools were as old as the colonial existence; and in 1800 both were still alive, if not flourishing.

Society in Massachusetts was sharply divided by politics. In 1800 one half the population, represented under property qualifications by only some twenty thousand voters, was Republican. The other half, which cast about twenty-five thousand votes, included nearly every one in the professional and mercantile classes, and represented the wealth, social position, and education of the Commonwealth; but its strength lay in the Congregational churches and in the cordial union between the clergy, the magistracy, the bench and bar, and respectable society throughout the State. This union created what was unknown beyond New England, — an organized social system, capable of acting at command either for offence or defence, and admirably adapted for the uses of the eighteenth century.

Had the authority of the dominant classes in Massachusetts depended merely on office, the task of overthrowing it would have been as simple as it was elsewhere; but the New England obligarchy struck its roots deep into the soil, and was supported by the convictions of the people. Unfortunately the system was not and could not be quickly adapted to the movement of the age. Its starting-point lay in the educational system, which was in principle excellent; but it was also antiquated. Little change had been made in it since colonial times. The common schools were what they had been from the first; the acad-

emies and colleges were no more changed than the
schools. On an average of ten years, from 1790 to
1800, thirty-nine young men annually took degrees
from Harvard College ; while during the ten years,
1766–1776, that preceded the Revolutionary War,
forty-three bachelors of arts had been annually sent
into the world, and even in 1720–1730 the average
number had been thirty-five. The only sign of change
was that in 1720–1730 about one hundred and forty
graduates had gone into the Church, while in 1790–1800
only about eighty chose this career. At the earlier
period the president, a professor of theology, one of
mathematics, and four tutors gave instruction to the
under-graduates. In 1800 the president, the professor of theology, the professor of mathematics, and
a professor of Hebrew, created in 1765, with the four
tutors did the same work. The method of instruction
had not changed in the interval, being suited to
children fourteen years of age ; the instruction itself
was poor, and the discipline was indifferent. Harvard College had not in eighty years made as much
progress as was afterward made in twenty. Life
was quickening within it as within all mankind, —
the spirit and vivacity of the coming age could not
be wholly shut out ; but none the less the college resembled a priesthood which had lost the secret of its
mysteries, and patiently stood holding the flicker-
ing torch before cold altars, until God should vouch-
safe a new dispensation of sunlight.

Nevertheless, a medical school with three professors

had been founded in 1783, and every year gave degrees to an average class of two doctors of medicine. Science had already a firm hold on the college, and a large part of the conservative clergy were distressed by the liberal tendencies which the governing body betrayed. This was no new thing. The college always stood somewhat in advance of society, and never joined heartily in dislike for liberal movements ; but unfortunately it had been made for an instrument, and had never enjoyed the free use of its powers. Clerical control could not be thrown off, for if the college was compelled to support the clergy, on the other hand the clergy did much to support the college ; and without the moral and material aid of this clerical body, which contained several hundred of the most respected and respectable citizens, clad in every town with the authority of spiritual magistrates, the college would have found itself bankrupt in means and character. The graduates passed from the college to the pulpit, and from the pulpit attempted to hold the college, as well as their own congregations, facing toward the past. " Let us guard against the insidious encroachments of *innovation*," they preached, — " that evil and beguiling spirit which is now stalking to and fro through the earth, seeking whom he may destroy." These words were spoken by Jedediah Morse, a graduate of Yale in 1783, pastor of the church at Charlestown, near Boston, and still known in biographical dictionaries as " the father of American geography." They were contained in the Election Sermon of this worthy and useful man, delivered June 6, 1803 ; but the sentiment was not peculiar to him, or confined to the audience he was then addressing, — it was the burden of a thousand discourses enforced by a formidable authority.

The power of the Congregational clergy, which had lasted unbroken until the Revolution, was originally minute and inquisitory, equivalent to a police authority. During the last quarter of the century the clergy themselves were glad to lay aside the more odious watchfulness over their parishes, and to welcome social freedom within limits conventionally fixed ; but their old authority had not wholly disappeared. In country parishes they were still autocratic. Did an individual defy their authority, the minister put his three-cornered hat on his head, took his silver-topped cane in his hand, and walked down the village street, knocking at one door and another of his best parishioners, to warn them that a spirit of license and of French infidelity was abroad, which could be repressed only by a strenuous and combined effort. Any man once placed under this ban fared badly if he afterward came before a bench of magistrates. The temporal arm vigorously supported the ecclesiastical will. Nothing tended so directly to make respectability conservative, and conservatism a fetich of respectability, as this union of bench and pulpit. The democrat had no caste ; he was not respectable ; he was a Jacobin, — and no such character was

admitted into a Federalist house.   Every dissolute
intriguer, loose-liver, forger, false-coiner, and prison-
bird ; every hair-brained, loud-talking demagogue ;
every speculator, scoffer, and atheist, — was a fol-
lower of Jefferson ; and Jefferson was himself the
incarnation of their theories.

A literature belonging to this subject exists, —
stacks of newspapers and sermons, mostly dull, and
wanting literary merit.   In a few of them Jefferson
figured under the well-remembered disguises of Puritan politics : he was Ephraim, and had mixed himself among the people ; had apostatized from his God
and religion ; gone to Assyria, and mingled himself
among the heathen ; " gray hairs are here and there
upon him, yet he knoweth not ; " or he was Jeroboam,
who drave Israel from following the Lord, and made
them sin a great sin.   He had doubted the authority
of revelation, and ventured to suggest that petrified
shells found embedded in rocks fifteen thousand feet
above sea-level could hardly have been left there by
the Deluge, because if the whole atmosphere were
condensed as water, its weight showed that the seas
would be raised only fifty-two and a half feet.   Scep-
tic as he was, he could not accept the scientific theory
that the ocean-bed had been uplifted by natural forces ;
but although he had thus instantly deserted this battery raised against revelation, he had still expressed
the opinion that a universal deluge was *equally* un-
satisfactory as an explanation, and had avowed preference for a profession of ignorance rather than a

belief in error.   He had said, " It does me no injury
for my neighbors to say there are twenty gods, or no
god," and that all the many forms of religious faith
in the Middle States were " good enough, and sufficient to preserve peace and order."   He was notoriously a deist ; he probably ridiculed the doctrine of
total depravity ; and he certainly would never have
part or portion in the blessings of the New Covenant,
or be saved because of grace.

No abler or more estimable clergyman lived than
Joseph Buckminster, the minister of Portsmouth, in
New Hampshire, and in his opinion Jefferson was
bringing a judgment upon the people.

" I would not be understood to insinuate," said he in
his sermon on Washington's death, " that contemners of
religious duties, and even men void of religious principle,
may not have an attachment to their country and a desire
for its civil and political prosperity, — nay, that they
may not even expose themselves to great dangers, and
make great sacrifices to accomplish this object ; but by
their impiety . . . they take away the heavenly defence
and security of a people, and render it necessary for him
who ruleth among the nations in judgment to testify his
displeasure against those who despise his laws and con-
temn his ordinances."

Yet the congregational clergy, though still greatly
respected, had ceased to be leaders of thought.   Theological literature no longer held the prominence
it had enjoyed in the days of Edwards and Hopkins.
The popular reaction against Calvinism, felt rather

than avowed, stopped the development of doctrinal
theology; and the clergy, always poor as a class,
with no weapons but their intelligence and purity of
character, commonly sought rather to avoid than to
challenge hostility. Such literary activity as existed
was not clerical but secular. Its field was the Boston
press, and its recognized literary champion was
Fisher Ames.

The subject of Ames's thought was exclusively political. At that moment every influence combined to
maintain a stationary condition in Massachusetts politics. The manners and morals of the people were
pure and simple; their society was democratic; in
the worst excesses of their own revolution they had
never become savage or bloodthirsty; their experience
could not explain, nor could their imagination excuse,
wild popular excesses; and when in 1793 the French
nation seemed mad with the frenzy of its recovered
liberties, New England looked upon the bloody and
blasphemous work with such horror as religious citizens could not but feel. Thenceforward the mark
of a wise and good man was that he abhorred the
French Revolution, and believed democracy to be
its cause. Like Edmund Burke, they listened to no
argument: " It is a vile, illiberal school, this French
Academy of the sans-culottes; there is nothing in it
that is fit for a gentleman to learn." The answer to
every democratic suggestion ran in a set phrase,
" Look at France ! " This idea became a monomania
with the New England leaders, and took exclusive

hold of Fisher Ames, their most brilliant writer and
talker, until it degenerated into a morbid illusion.
During the last few months of his life, even so late
as 1808, this dying man could scarcely speak of his
children without expressing his fears of their future
servitude to the French. He believed his alarms to
be shared by his friends. "Our days," he wrote,
"are made heavy with the pressure of anxiety, and
our nights restless with visions of horror. We listen
to the clank of chains, and overhear the whispers of
assassins. We mark the barbarous dissonance of
mingled rage and triumph in the yell of an infuriated
mob ; we see the dismal glare of their burnings, and
scent the loathsome steam of human victims offered
in sacrifice." In theory the French Revolution was
not an argument or a proof, but only an illustration,
of the workings of divine law ; and what had happened in France must sooner or later happen in
America if the ignorant and vicious were to govern
the wise and good.

The bitterness against democrats became intense
after the month of May, 1800, when the approach-
ing victory of Jefferson was seen to be inevitable.
Then for the first time the clergy and nearly all the
educated and respectable citizens of New England
began to extend to the national government the
hatred which they bore to democracy. The expressions of this mixed antipathy filled volumes. "Our
country," wrote Fisher Ames in 1803, "is too big
for union, too sordid for patriotism, too democratic

for liberty. What is to become of it, he who made it best knows. Its vice will govern it, by practising upon its folly. This is ordained for democracies." He explained why this inevitable fate awaited it. " A democracy cannot last. Its nature ordains that its next change shall be into a military despotism, — of all known governments perhaps the most prone to shift its head, and the slowest to mend its vices. The reason is that the tyranny of what is called the people, and that by the sword, both operate alike to debase and corrupt, till there are neither men left with the spirit to desire liberty, nor morals with the power to sustain justice. Like the burning pestilence that destroys the human body, nothing can subsist by its dissolution but vermin." George Cabot, whose political opinions were law to the wise and good, held the same convictions. " Even in New England," wrote Cabot in 1804, " where there is among the body of the people more wisdom and virtue than in any other part of the United States, we are full of errors which no reasoning could eradicate, if there were a Lycurgus in every village. We are democratic altogether, and I hold democracy in its natural operation to be the government of the worst."

Had these expressions of opinion been kept to the privacy of correspondence, the public could have ignored them ; but so strong were the wise and good in their popular following, that every newspaper seemed to exult in denouncing the people. They urged the use of force as the protection of wisdom and virtue. A paragraph from Dennie's " Portfolio," reprinted by all the Federalist newspapers in 1803, offered one example among a thousand of the infatuation which possessed the Federalist press, neither more extravagant nor more treasonable than the rest: —

" A democracy is scarcely tolerable at any period of national history. Its omens are always sinister, and its powers are unpropitious. It is on its trial here, and the issue will be civil war, desolation, and anarchy. No wise man but discerns its imperfections, no good man but shudders at its miseries, no honest man but proclaims its fraud, and no brave man but draws his sword against its force. The institution of a scheme of policy so radically contemptible and vicious is a memorable example of what the villany of some men can devise, the folly of others receive, and both establish in spite of reason, reflection, and sensation."

The Philadelphia grand jury indicted Dennie for this paragraph as a seditious libel, but it was not more expressive than the single word uttered by Alexander Hamilton, who owed no small part of his supremacy to the faculty of expressing the prejudices of his followers more tersely than they themselves could do. Compressing the idea into one syllable, Hamilton, at a New York dinner, replied to some democratic sentiment by striking his hand sharply on the table and saying, " Your people, sir, — your people is a great *beast!*"

The political theories of these ultra-conservative

New Englanders did not require the entire exclusion
of all democratic influence from government. " While
I hold," said Cabot, " that a government altogether
popular is in effect a government of the populace, I
maintain that no government can bé relied on that
has not a material portion of the democratic mixture
in its composition." Cabot explained what should be
the true portion of democratic mixture : " If no man
in New England could vote for legislators who was
not possessed in his own right of two thousand dollars' value *in land*, we could do something better."
The Constitution of Massachusetts already restricted
the suffrage to persons " having a freehold estate
within the commonwealth of an annual income of
three pounds, or any estate of the value of sixty
pounds." A further restriction to freeholders whose
estate was worth two thousand dollars would hardly
have left a material mixture of any influence which
democrats would have recognized as theirs.

Meanwhile even Cabot and his friends Ames and
Colonel Hamilton recognized that the reform they
wished could be effected only with the consent of the
people ; and firm in the conviction that democracy
must soon produce a crisis, as in Greece and Rome,
in England and France, when political power must
revert to the wise and good, or to the despotism of
a military chief, they waited for the catastrophe
they foresaw. History and their own experience
supported them. They were right, so far as human
knowledge could make them so ; but the old spirit of

Puritan obstinacy was more evident than reason or experience in the simple-minded, overpowering conviction with which the clergy and serious citizens of Massachusetts and Connecticut, assuming that the people of America were in the same social condition as the contemporaries of Catiline and the adherents of Robespierre, sat down to bide their time until the tempest of democracy should drive the frail government so near destruction that all men with one voice should call on God and the Federalist prophets for help. The obstinacy of the race was never better shown than when, with the sunlight of the nineteenth century bursting upon them, these resolute sons of granite and ice turned their faces from the sight, and smiled in their sardonic way at the folly or wickedness of men who could pretend to believe the world improved because henceforth the ignorant and vicious were to rule the United States and govern the churches and schools of New England.

Even Boston, the most cosmopolitan part of New England, showed no tendency in its educated classes to become American in thought or feeling. Many of the ablest Federalists, and among the rest George Cabot, Theophilus Parsons, and Fisher Ames, shared few of the narrower theological prejudices of their time, but were conservatives of the English type, whose alliance with the clergy betrayed as much policy as religion, and whose intellectual life was wholly English. Boston made no strong claim to intellectual prominence. Neither clergy, lawyers,

physicians, nor literary men were much known beyond the State.   Fisher Ames enjoyed a wider fame ;
but Ames's best political writing was saturated with
the despair of the tomb to which his wasting body
was condemned.   Five years had passed since he
closed his famous speech on the British Treaty with
the foreboding that if the treaty were not carried
into effect, " even I, slender and almost broken as my
hold upon life is, may outlive the government and
constitution of my country."   Seven years more were
to pass in constant dwelling upon the same theme, in
accents more and more despondent, before the long-
expected grave closed over him, and his warning
voice ceased to echo painfully on the air.   The number of his thorough-going admirers was small, if his
own estimate was correct.   " There are," he said,
" not many, perhaps not five hundred, even among
the Federalists, who yet allow themselves to view
the progress of licentiousness as so speedy, so sure,
and so fatal as the deplorable experience of our
country shows that it is, and the evidence of history
and the constitution of human nature demonstrate
that it must be."   These five hundred, few as they
were, comprised most of the clergy and the State
officials, and overawed large numbers more.

Ames was the mouthpiece in the press of a remarkable group, of which George Cabot was the recognized
chief in wisdom, and Timothy Pickering the most
active member in national politics.   With Ames,
Cabot, and Pickering, joined in confidential relations,

was Theophilus Parsons, who in the year 1800 left
Newburyport for Boston.   Parsons was an abler man
than either Cabot, Ames, or Pickering, and his influence was great in holding New England fast to an
independent course which could end only in the overthrow of the Federal constitution which these men
had first pressed upon an unwilling people ; but though
gifted with strong natural powers, backed by laborious
study and enlivened by the ready and somewhat
rough wit native to New England, Parsons was not
bold on his own account ; he was felt rather than
seen, and although ever ready in private to advise
strong measures, he commonly let others father them
before the world.

These gentlemen formed the Essex Junto, so called
from the county of Essex where their activity was
first felt.   According to Ames, not more than five
hundred men fully shared their opinions ; but Massachusetts society was so organized as to make their
influence great, and experience foretold that as the
liberal Federalists should one by one wander to the
Democratic camp where they belonged, the conservatism of those who remained would become
more bitter and more absolute as the Essex Junto
represented a larger and larger proportion of their
numbers.

Nevertheless, the reign of old-fashioned conservatism was near its end.   The New England Church
was apparently sound ; even Unitarians and Baptists
were recognized as parts of one fraternity.   Except

a few Roman and Anglican bodies, all joined in the
same worship, and said little on points of doctrinal
difference. No one had yet dared to throw a fire-
brand into the temple; but Unitarians were strong
among the educated and wealthy class, while the tendencies of a less doctrinal religious feeling were shaping themselves in Harvard College. William Ellery
Channing took his degree in 1798, and in 1800 was a
private tutor in Virginia. Joseph Stevens Buckminster, thought by his admirers a better leader than
Channing, graduated in 1800, and was teaching
boys to construe their Latin exercises at Exeter
Academy. Only the shell of orthodoxy was left, but
respectable society believed this shell to be necessary as an example of Christian unity and a safe-
guard against more serious innovations. No one
could fail to see that the public had lately become
restive under its antiquated discipline. The pulpits
still fulminated against the fatal tolerance which
within a few years had allowed theatres to be opened
in Boston, and which scandalized God-fearing men
by permitting public advertisements that " Hamlet "
and " Othello " were to be performed in the town
founded to protest against worldly pageants. Another innovation was more strenuously resisted. Only
within the last thirty years had Sunday travel been
allowed even in England; in Massachusetts and Connecticut it was still forbidden by law, and the law
was enforced. Yet not only travellers, but inn-keep-
ers and large numbers of citizens connived at Sun-

day travel, and it could not long be prevented. The clergy saw their police authority weakening year by year, and understood, without need of many words, the tacit warning of the city congregations that in this world they must be allowed to amuse themselves, even though they were to suffer for it in the next.

The longing for amusement and freedom was a reasonable and a modest want. Even the young theologians, the Buckminsters and Channings, were hungry for new food. Boston was little changed in appearance, habits, and style from what it had been under its old king. When young Dr. J. C. Warren returned from Europe about the year 1800, to begin practice in Boston, he found gentlemen still dressed in colored coats and figured waistcoats, short breeches buttoning at the knee, long boots with white tops, ruffled shirts and wristbands, a white cravat filled with what was called a " pudding," and for the elderly, cocked hats, and wigs which once every week were sent to the barber's to be dressed, — so that every Saturday night the barbers' boys were seen carrying home piles of wig-boxes in readiness for Sunday's church. At evening parties gentlemen appeared in white small-clothes, silk stockings and pumps, with a colored or white waistcoat. There were few hackney-coaches, and ladies walked to evening entertainments. The ancient minuet was danced as late as 1806. The waltz was not yet tolerated.

Fashionable society was not without charm. In summer Southern visitors appeared, and admired the town, with its fashionable houses perched on the hill-sides, each in its own garden, and each looking sea-ward over harbor and islands. Boston was then what Newport afterward became, and its only rival as a summer watering-place in the North was Ballston, whither society was beginning to seek health before finding it a little farther away at Saratoga. Of intellectual amusement there was little more at one place than at the other, except that the Bostonians devoted themselves more seriously to church-going and to literature. The social instinct took shape in varied forms, but was highly educated in none; while the typical entertainment in Boston, as in New York, Philadelphia, and Charleston, was the state dinner, — not the light, feminine triviality which France introduced into an amusement-loving world, but the serious dinner of Sir Robert Walpole and Lord North, where gout and plethora waited behind the chairs; an effort of animal endurance.

There was the arena of intellectual combat, if that could be called combat where disagreement in principle was not tolerated. The talk of Samuel Johnson and Edmund Burke was the standard of excellence to all American society that claimed intellectual rank, and each city possessed its own circle of Federalist talkers. Democrats rarely figured in these entertainments, at least in fashionable private houses. "There was no exclusiveness," said a lady who long outlived the time; "but I should as soon have expected to see a cow in a drawing-room as a Jacobin."

In New York, indeed, Colonel Burr and the Livingstons may have held their own, and the active-minded
Dr. Mitchill there, like Dr. Eustis in Boston, was
an agreeable companion.   Philadelphia was comparatively cosmopolitan; in Baltimore the Smiths were a
social power; and Charleston, after deserting Federal
principles in 1800, could hardly ignore Democrats;
but Boston society was still pure.   The clergy took a
prominent part in conversation, but Fisher Ames was
the favorite of every intelligent company; and when
Gouverneur Morris, another brilliant talker, visited
Boston, Ames was pitted against him.

The intellectual wants of the community grew
with the growing prosperity; but the names of half-
a-dozen persons could hardly be mentioned whose
memories survived by intellectual work made public
in Massachusetts between 1783 and 1800.   Two or
three local historians might be numbered, including Jeremy Belknap, the most justly distinguished.
Jedediah Morse the geographer was well known;
but not a poet, a novelist, or a scholar could be
named.   Nathaniel Bowditch did not publish his
" Practical Navigator " till 1800, and not till then
did Dr. Waterhouse begin his struggle to introduce
vaccination.   With the exception of a few Revolutionary statesmen and elderly clergymen, a political
essayist like Ames, and lawyers like Samuel Dexter
and Theophilus Parsons, Massachusetts could show
little that warranted a reputation for genius; and, in
truth, the intellectual prominence of Boston began

as the conservative system died out, starting with
the younger Buckminster several years after the
century opened.

The city was still poorer in science. Excepting
the medical profession, which represented nearly all
scientific activity, hardly a man in Boston got his
living either by science or art. When in the year
1793 the directors of the new Middlesex Canal Corporation, wishing to bring the Merrimac River to
Boston Harbor, required a survey of an easy route
not thirty miles long, they could find no competent
civil engineer in Boston, and sent to Philadelphia
for an Englishman named Weston, engaged on the
Delaware and Schuylkill Canal.

Possibly a few Bostonians could read and even
speak French; but Germany was nearly as unknown
as China, until Madame de Staël published her famous
work in 1814. Even then young George Ticknor, in-
cited by its account of German university education,
could find neither a good teacher nor a dictionary,
nor a German book in the shops or public libraries
of the city or at the college in Cambridge. He had
discovered a new world.

Pope, Addison, Akenside, Beattie, and Young were
still the reigning poets. Burns was accepted by a
few; and copies of a volume were advertised by book-
sellers, written by a new poet called Wordsworth.
America offered a fair demand for new books, and
anything of a light nature published in England was
sure to cross the ocean. Wordsworth crossed with

the rest, and his " Lyrical Ballads " were reprinted in 1802, not in Boston or New York, but in Philadelphia, where they were read and praised. In default of other amusements, men read what no one could have endured had a choice of amusements been open. Neither music, painting, science, the lecture-room, nor even magazines offered resources that could rival what was looked upon as classical literature. Men had not the alternative of listening to political discussions, for stump-speaking was a Southern practice not yet introduced into New England, where such a political canvass would have terrified society with dreams of Jacobin license. The clergy and the bar took charge of politics; the tavern was the club and the forum of political discussion; but for those who sought other haunts, and especially for women, no intellectual amusement other than what was called " belles-lettres " existed to give a sense of occupation to an act¦ve mind. This keen and innovating people, hungry for the feast that was almost served, the Walter Scotts and Byrons so near at hand, tried meanwhile to nourish themselves with husks.

Afraid of Shakspeare and the drama, trained to the standards of Queen Anne's age, and ambitious beyond reason to excel, the New Englanders attempted to supply their own wants. Massachusetts took no lead in the struggle to create a light literature, if such poetry and fiction could be called light. In Connecticut the Muses were most obstinately wooed; and there, after the Revolutionary War, a persistent

effort was made to give prose the form of poetry.
The chief of the movement was Timothy Dwight,
a man of extraordinary qualities, but one on whom
almost every other mental gift had been conferred
in fuller measure than poetical genius.   Twenty-five
years had passed since young Dwight, fresh from
Yale College, began his career by composing an epic
poem, in eleven books and near ten thousand lines,
called "The Conquest of Canaan."   In the fervor
of patriotism, before independence was secured or
the French Revolution imagined, he pictured the
great Hebrew leader Joshua preaching the Rights
of Man, and prophesying the spread of his "sons"
over America: —

> "Then o'er wide lands, as blissful Eden bright,
>   Type of the skies, and seats of pure delight,
>   Our sons with prosperous course shall stretch their sway,
>   And claim an empire spread from sea to sea;
>   In one great whole th' harmonious tribes combine,
>   Trace Justice' path, and choose their chiefs divine;
>   On Freedom's base erect the heavenly plan,
>   Teach laws to reign, and save the Rights of Man.
>   Then smiling Art shall wrap the fields in bloom,
>   Fine the rich ore, and guide the useful loom;
>   Then lofty towers in golden pomp arise,
>   Then spiry cities meet auspicious skies;
>   The soul on Wisdom's wing sublimely soar,
>   New virtues cherish and new truths explore;
>   Through Time's long tract our name celestial run,
>   Climb in the east and circle with the sun;
>   And smiling Glory stretch triumphant wings
>   O'er hosts of heroes and o'er tribes of kings."

A world of eighteenth-century thought, peopled with personifications, lay buried in the ten thousand lines of President Dwight's youthful poem. Perhaps in the year 1800, after Jefferson's triumph, Dwight would have been less eager that his hero should save the Rights of Man; by that time the phrase had acquired a flavor of French infidelity which made it unpalatable to good taste. Yet the same Jeffersonian spirit ran through Dwight's famous national song, which was also written in the Revolutionary War : —

> "Columbia, Columbia, to glory arise,
>   The queen of the world and child of the skies!
>
>   .   .   .   .
>   Thy heroes the rights of mankind shall defend,
>   And triumph pursue them, and glory attend.
>
>   .   .   .   .
>   While the ensigns of union in triumph unfurled
>   Hush the tumult of war and give peace to the world."

"Peace to the world" was the essence of Jeffersonian principles, worth singing in something better than jingling metre and indifferent rhyme; but President Dwight's friends in 1800 no longer sang this song. More and more conservative as he grew older, he published in 1797 an orthodox " Triumph of Infidelity," introduced by a dedication to Voltaire. His rebuke to mild theology was almost as severe as that to French deism : —

> "There smiled the smooth divine, unused to wound
>   The sinner's heart with Hell's alarming sound."

His poetical career reached its climax in 1794 in a clerical Connecticut pastoral in seven books, called " Greenfield Hill." Perhaps his verses were not above the level of the Beatties and Youngs he imitated ; but at least they earned for President Dwight no mean reputation in days when poetry was at its lowest ebb, and made him the father of a school.

One quality gave respectability to his writing apart from genius. He loved and believed in his country. Perhaps the uttermost depths of his nature were stirred only by affection for the Connecticut Valley ; but after all where was human nature more respectable than in that peaceful region ? What had the United States then to show in scenery and landscape more beautiful or more winning than that country of meadow and mountain ? Patriotism was no ardent feeling among the literary men of the time, whose general sentiment was rather expressed by Cliffton's lines : —

> " In these cold shades, beneath these shifting skies,
> Where Fancy sickens, and where Genius dies,
> Where few and feeble are the Muse's strains,
> And no fine frenzy riots in the veins,
> There still are found a few to whom belong
> The fire of virtue and the soul of song."

William Cliffton, a Pennsylvania Friend, who died in 1799 of consumption, in his twenty-seventh year, knew nothing of the cold shades and shifting skies which chilled the genius of European poets ; he knew only that America cared little for such genius and fancy as he could offer, and he rebelled against the neglect. He was better treated than Wordsworth, Keats, or Shelley ; but it was easy to blame the public for dulness and indifference, though readers were kinder than authors had a right to expect. Even Cliffton was less severe than some of his contemporaries. A writer in the " Boston Anthology," for January, 1807, uttered in still stronger words the prevailing feeling of the literary class : —

" We know that in this land, where the spirit of democracy is everywhere diffused, we are exposed as it were to a poisonous atmosphere, which blasts everything beautiful in nature, and corrodes everything elegant in art ; we know that with us ' the rose-leaves fall ungathered,' and we believe that there is little to praise and nothing to admire in most of the objects which would first present themselves to the view of a stranger."

Yet the American world was not unsympathetic toward Cliffton and his rivals, though they strained prose through their sieves of versification, and showed open contempt for their audience. Toward President Dwight the public was even generous ; and he returned the generosity with parental love and condescension which shone through every line he wrote. For some years his patriotism was almost as enthusiastic as that of Joel Barlow. He was among the numerous rivals of Macaulay· and Shelley for the honor of inventing the stranger to sit among the

ruins of St. Paul's; and naturally America supplied
the explorer who was to penetrate the forest of London and indulge his national self-complacency over
ruined temples and towers.

> "Some unknown wild, some shore without a name,
>   In all thy pomp shall then majestic shine
>   As silver-headed Time's slow years decline.
>   Not ruins only meet th' inquiring eye;
>   Where round yon mouldering oak vain brambles twine,
>   The filial stem, already towering high,
> Erelong shall stretch his arms and nod in yonder sky."

From these specimens of President Dwight's poetry
any critic, familiar with the time, could infer that his
prose was sensible and sound.   One of the few books
of travel which will always retain value for New Englanders was written by President Dwight to describe
his vacation rambles; and although in his own day
no one would have ventured to insult him by calling
these instructive volumes amusing, the quaintness
which here and there gave color to the sober narrative had a charm of its own.   How could the contrast be better expressed between volatile Boston and
orthodox New Haven than in Dwight's quiet reproof,
mixed with paternal tenderness?   The Bostonians, he
said, were distinguished by a lively imagination, ardor,
and sensibility; they were "more like the Greeks
than the Romans;" admired where graver people
would only approve; applauded or hissed where another audience would be silent; their language was

frequently hyperbolical, their pictures highly colored; the tea shipped to Boston was destroyed, — in New York and Philadelphia it was stored; education in Boston was superficial, and Boston women showed the effects of this misfortune, for they practised accomplishments only that they might be admired, and were taught from the beginning to regard their dress as a momentous concern.

Under Dwight's rule the women of the Connecticut Valley were taught better; but its men set to the Bostonians an example of frivolity without a parallel, and they did so with the connivance of President Dwight and under the lead of his brother Theodore. The frivolity of the Hartford wits, as they were called, was not so light as that of Canning and the "Anti-Jacobin," but had it been heavier than the "Conquest of Canaan" itself, it would still have found no literary rivalry in Boston. At about the time when Dwight composed his serious epic, another tutor at Yale, John Trumbull, wrote a burlesque epic in Hudibrastic verse, "McFingal," which his friend Dwight declared to be not inferior to "Hudibras" in wit and humor, and in every other respect superior. When "Hudibras" was published, more than a hundred years before, Mr. Pepys remarked: "It hath not a good liking in me, though I had tried but twice or three times reading to bring myself to think it witty." After the lapse of more than another century, the humor of neither poem may seem worth imitation; but to Trumbull in 1784 Butler was a modern classic, for the standard of

taste between 1663 and 1784 changed less than in any
twenty years of the following century. " McFingal "
was a success, and laid a solid foundation for the
coming school of Hartford wits. Posterity ratified
the verdict of Trumbull's admirers by preserving for
daily use a few of his lines quoted indiscriminately
with Butler's best : —

> " What has posterity done for us ? "
> " Optics sharp it needs, I ween,
>   To see what is not to be seen."
> " A thief ne'er felt the halter draw
>   With good opinion of the law."

Ten years after the appearance of " McFingal,"
and on the strength of its success, Trumbull, Lemuel
Hopkins, Richard Alsop, Theodore Dwight, Joel Barlow, and others began a series of publications, " The
Anarchiad," " The Echo," " The Guillotine," and the
like, in which they gave tongue to their wit and
sarcasm. As Alsop described the scene, —

> " Begrimed with blood where erst the savage fell,
>   Shrieked the wild war-whoop with infernal yell,
>   The Muses sing; lo, Trumbull wakes the lyre.
>   .   .   .   .
>   Majestic Dwight, sublime in epic strain,
>   Paints the fierce horrors of the crimson plain ;
>   And in Virgilian Barlow's tuneful lines
>   With added splendor great Columbus shines."

Perhaps the Muses would have done better by not
interrupting the begrimed savage; for Dwight, Trum-

bull, Alsop, and Hopkins, whatever their faults, were
Miltonic by the side of Joel Barlow. Yet Barlow
was a figure too important in American history to
be passed without respectful attention. He expressed
better than any one else that side of Connecticut
character which roused at the same instant the laughter and the respect of men. Every human influence
twined about his career and lent it interest; every
forward movement of his time had his sympathy, and
few steps in progress were made which he did not
assist. His ambition, above the lofty ambition of
Jefferson, made him aspire to be a Connecticut Mæ-
cenas and Virgil in one; to patronize Fulton and
employ Smirke; counsel Jefferson and contend with
Napoleon. In his own mind a figure such as the
world rarely saw, — a compound of Milton, Rousseau,
and the Duke of Bridgewater, — he had in him so
large a share of conceit, that tragedy, which would
have thrown a solemn shadow over another man's
life, seemed to render his only more entertaining.
As a poet, he undertook to do for his native land
what Homer had done for Greece and Virgil for
Rome, Milton for England and Camoens for Portugal, — to supply America with a great epic, without which no country could be respectable ; and
his " Vision of Columbus," magnified afterward into
the " Columbiad," with a magnificence of typography and illustration new to the United States,
remained a monument of his ambition. In this
vision Columbus was shown a variety of coming

celebrities, including all the heroes of the Revolutionary War : —

> " Here stood stern Putnam, scored with ancient scars,
>   The living records of his country's wars;
>   Wayne, like a moving tower, assumes his post,
>   Fires the whole field, and is himself a host;
>   Undaunted Stirling, prompt to meet his foes,
>   And Gates and Sullivan for action rose;
>   Macdougal, Clinton, guardians of the State,
>   Stretch the nerved arm to pierce the depth of fate;
>   Moultrie and Sumter lead their banded powers;
>   Morgan in front of his bold riflers towers,
>   His host of keen-eyed marksmen, skilled to pour
>   Their slugs unerring from the twisted bore;
>   No sword, no bayonet they learn to wield,
>   They gall the flank, they skirt the battling field,
>   Cull out the distant foe in full horse speed,
>   Couch the long tube and eye the silver bead,
>   Turn as he turns, dismiss the whizzing lead,
>   And lodge the death-ball in his heedless head."

More than seven thousand lines like these furnished constant pleasure to the reader, the more because the " Columbiad " was accepted by the public in a spirit as serious as that in which it was composed. The Hartford wits, who were bitter Federalists, looked upon Barlow as an outcast from their fold, a Jacobin in politics, and little better than a French atheist in religion; but they could not deny that his poetic garments were of a piece with their own. Neither could they without great ingratitude repudiate his poetry as they did his politics, for they themselves figured with Manco Capac, Montezuma,

Raleigh, and Pocahontas before the eyes of Columbus ; and the world bore witness that Timothy Dwight,
" Heaven in his eye and rapture on his tongue," tuned
his " high harp " in Barlow's inspired verses. Europe
was as little disposed as America to cavil; and the
Abbé Grégoire assured Barlow in a printed letter
that this monument of genius and typography would
immortalize the author and silence the criticisms
of Pauw and other writers on the want of talent
in America.

That the " Columbiad " went far to justify those
criticisms was true ; but on the other hand it proved
something almost equivalent to genius. Dwight,
Trumbull, and Barlow, whatever might be their
differences, united in offering proof of the bound-
less ambition which marked the American character.
Their aspirations were immense, and sooner or later
such restless craving was sure to find better expression. Meanwhile Connecticut was a province by itself, a part of New England rather than of the United
States. The exuberant patriotism of the Revolution
was chilled by the steady progress of democratic principles in the Southern and Middle States, until at
the election of Jefferson in 1800 Connecticut stood
almost alone with no intellectual companion except
Massachusetts, while the breach between them and
the Middle States seemed to widen day by day. That
the separation was only superficial was true ; but the
connection itself was not yet deep. An extreme
Federalist partisan like Noah Webster did not cease

working for his American language and literature because of the triumph of Jeffersonian principles elsewhere; Barlow became more American when his friends gained power; the work of the colleges went on unbroken; but prejudices, habits, theories, and laws remained what they had been in the past, and in Connecticut the influence of nationality was less active than ten, twenty, or even thirty years before. Yale College was but a reproduction of Harvard with stricter orthodoxy, turning out every year about thirty graduates, of whom nearly one fourth went into the Church. For the last ten years the number tended rather to diminish than to increase.

Evidently an intellectual condition like that of New England could not long continue. The thoughts and methods of the eighteenth century held possession of men's minds only because the movement of society was delayed by political passions. Massachusetts, and especially Boston, already contained a younger generation eager to strike into new paths, while forcibly held in the old ones. The more decidedly the college graduates of 1800 disliked democracy and its habits of thought, the more certain they were to compensate for political narrowness by freedom in fields not political. The future direction of the New England intellect seemed already suggested by the impossibility of going further in the line of President Dwight and Fisher Ames. Met by a barren negation on that side, thought was driven to some new channel; and the United States were the more concerned in the result because, with the training and literary habits of New Englanders and the new models already established in Europe for their guidance, they were likely again to produce something that would command respect.

CHAPTER IV.

BETWEEN New England and the Middle States was a gap like that between Scotland and England. The conceptions of life were different. In New England society was organized on a system, — a clergy in alliance with a magistracy; universities supporting each, and supported in turn, — a social hierarchy, in which respectability, education, property, and religion united to defeat and crush the unwise and vicious. In New York wisdom and virtue, as understood in New England, were but lightly esteemed. From an early moment no small number of those who by birth, education, and property were natural leaders of the wise and virtuous, showed themselves ready to throw in their lot with the multitude. Yet New York, much more than New England, was the home of natural leaders and family alliances. John Jay, the governor; the Schuylers, led by Philip Schuyler and his son-in-law Alexander Hamilton; the Livingstons, led by Robert R. Livingston the chancellor, with a promising younger brother Edward nearly twenty years his junior, and a brother-in-law John Armstrong, whose name and relationship will be prominent in this narrative, besides Samuel Osgood, Morgan Lewis, and Smith Thompson, other

connections by marriage with the great Livingston
stock; the Clintons, headed by Governor George
Clinton, and supported by the energy of De Witt his
nephew, thirty years of age, whose close friend Ambrose Spencer was reckoned as one of the family;
finally, Aaron Burr, of pure Connecticut Calvinistic
blood, whose two active lieutenants, William P. Van
Ness and John Swartwout, were socially well connected and well brought up, — all these Jays, Schuylers, Livingstons, Clintons, Burrs, had they lived in
New England, would probably have united in the
support of their class, or abandoned the country; but
being citizens of New York they quarrelled. On one
side Governor Jay, General Schuyler, and Colonel
Hamilton were true to their principles. Rufus King,
the American minister in London, by birth a New
Englander, adhered to the same connection. On the
other hand, George Clinton, like Samuel Adams in
Boston, was a Republican by temperament, and his
protest against the Constitution made him leader of
the Northern Republicans long before Jefferson was
mentioned as his rival. The rest were all backsliders
from Federalism, — and especially the Livingston faction, who, after carefully weighing arguments and
interests, with one accord joined the mob of free-
thinking democrats, the " great beast " of Alexander
Hamilton. Aaron Burr, who prided himself on the
inherited patrician quality of his mind and manners,
coldly assuming that wisdom and virtue were powerless in a democracy, followed Chancellor Livingston

into the society of Cheetham and Paine. Even the influx of New Englanders into the State could not save the Federalists ; and in May, 1800, after a sharp struggle, New York finally enrolled itself on the side of Jefferson and George Clinton.

Fortunately for society, New York possessed no church to overthrow, or traditional doctrines to root out, or centuries of history to disavow. Literature of its own it had little ; of intellectual unity, no trace. Washington Irving was a boy of seventeen wandering along the banks of the river he was to make famous ; Fenimore Cooper was a boy of eleven playing in the primitive woods of Otsego, or fitting himself at Albany for entrance to Yale College ; William Cullen Bryant was a child of six in the little village of Cummington, in western Massachusetts.

Political change could as little affect the educational system as it could affect history, church, or literature. In 1795, at the suggestion of Governor Clinton, an attempt had been made by the New York legislature to create a common-school system, and a sum of fifty thousand dollars was for five years annually applied to that object ; but in 1800 the appropriation was exhausted, and the thirteen hundred schools which had been opened were declining. Columbia College, with a formidable array of unfilled professorships, and with fifteen or twenty annual graduates, stood apart from public affairs, although one of its professors, Dr. Samuel L. Mitchill, gave scientific reputation to the whole State. Like the poet Barlow,

Mitchill was a universal genius, — a chemist, botanist, naturalist, physicist, and politician, who, to use the words of a shrewd observer, supported the Republican party because Jefferson was its leader, and supported Jefferson because he was a philosopher. Another professor of Columbia College, Dr. David Hosack, was as active as Dr. Mitchill in education, although he contented himself with private life, and did not, like Mitchill, reach the dignity of congressman and senator.

Science and art were still less likely to be harmed by a democratic revolution. For scientific work accomplished before 1800 New York might claim to excel New England ; but the result was still small. A little botany and mineralogy, a paper on the dispute over yellow fever or vaccination, was the utmost that medicine could show ; yet all the science that existed was in the hands of the medical faculty. Botany, chemistry, mineralogy, midwifery, and surgery were so closely allied that the same professor might regard them all as within the range of his instruction ; and Dr. Mitchill could have filled in succession, without much difficulty, every chair in Columbia College as well as in the Academy of Fine Arts about to be established. A surgeon was assumed to be an artist. The Capitol at Washington was designed, in rivalry with a French architect, by Dr. William Thornton, an English physician, who in the course of two weeks' study at the Philadelphia Library gained enough knowledge of architecture to draw incorrectly an

exterior elevation. When Thornton was forced to
look for some one to help him over his difficulties,
Jefferson could find no competent native American,
and sent for Latrobe. Jefferson considered himself a
better architect than either of them, and had he
been a professor of materia medica at Columbia College, the public would have accepted his claim as
reasonable.

The intellectual and moral character of New York
left much to be desired ; but on the other hand, had
society adhered stiffly to what New England thought
strict morals, the difficulties in the path of national
development would have been increased. Innovation
was the most useful purpose which New York could
serve in human interests, and never was a city better
fitted for its work. Although the great tide of prosperity had hardly begun to flow, the political character
of city and State was already well defined in 1800 by
the election which made Aaron Burr vice-president
of the United States, and brought De Witt Clinton into public life as Burr's rival. De Witt Clinton was
hardly less responsible than Burr himself for lowering
the standard of New York politics, and indirectly that
of the nation ; but he was foremost in creating the
Erie Canal. Chancellor Livingston was frequently
charged with selfishness as great as that of Burr and
Clinton ; but he built the first steamboat, and gave
immortality to Fulton. Ambrose Spencer's politics
were inconsistent enough to destroy the good name
of any man in New England ; but he became a chief-

justice of ability and integrity. Edward Livingston was a defaulter under circumstances of culpable carelessness, as the Treasury thought; but Gallatin, who dismissed him from office, lived to see him become the author of a celebrated code of civil law, and of the still more celebrated Nullification Proclamation. John Armstrong's character was so little admired that his own party could with difficulty be induced to give him high office; yet the reader will judge how Armstrong compared in efficiency of public service with the senators who distrusted him.

New York cared but little for the metaphysical subtleties of Massachusetts and Virginia, which convulsed the nation with spasms almost as violent as those that, fourteen centuries before, distracted the Eastern Empire in the effort to establish the double or single nature of Christ. New York was indifferent whether the nature of the United States was single or multiple, whether they were a nation or a league. Leaving this class of questions to other States which were deeply interested in them, New York remained constant to no political theory. There society, in spite of its aristocratic mixture, was democratic by instinct; and in abandoning its alliance with New England in order to join Virginia and elect Jefferson to the Presidency, it pledged itself to principles of no kind, least of all to Virginia doctrines. The Virginians aimed at maintaining a society so simple that purity should suffer no danger, and corruption gain no foothold; and never did America witness a stranger

union than when Jefferson, the representative of ideal
purity, allied himself with Aaron Burr, the Livingstons and Clintons, in the expectation of fixing the
United States in a career of simplicity and virtue.
George Clinton indeed, a States-rights Republican of
the old school, understood and believed the Virginia
doctrines; but as for Aaron Burr, Edward Livingston,
De Witt Clinton, and Ambrose Spencer,— young men
whose brains were filled with dreams of a different
sort,— what had such energetic democrats to do with
the plough, or what share had the austerity of Cato
and the simplicity of Ancus Martius in their ideals?
The political partnership between the New York Republicans and the Virginians was from the first that
of a business firm; and no more curious speculation
could have been suggested to the politicians of 1800
than the question whether New York would corrupt
Virginia, or Virginia would check the prosperity of
New York.

In deciding the issue of this struggle, as in every
other issue that concerned the Union, the voice which
spoke in most potent tones was that of Pennsylvania.
This great State, considering its political importance,
was treated with little respect by its neighbors; and
yet had New England, New York, and Virginia been
swept out of existence in 1800, democracy could have
better spared them all than have lost Pennsylvania.
The only true democratic community then existing
in the eastern States, Pennsylvania was neither picturesque nor troublesome. The State contained no

hierarchy like that of New England ; no great families like those of New York ; no oligarchy like the planters of Virginia and South Carolina. "In Pennsylvania," said Albert Gallatin, "not only we have neither Livingstons nor Rensselaers, but from the suburbs of Philadelphia to the banks of the Ohio I do not know a single family that has any extensive influence. An equal distribution of property has rendered every individual independent, and there is among us true and real equality." This was not all. The value of Pennsylvania to the Union lay not so much in the democratic spirit of society as in the rapidity with which it turned to national objects. Partly for this reason the State made an insignificant figure in politics. As the nation grew, less and less was said in Pennsylvania of interests distinct from those of the Union. Too thoroughly democratic to fear democracy, and too much nationalized to dread nationality, Pennsylvania became the ideal American State, easy, tolerant, and contented. If its soil bred little genius, it bred still less treason. With twenty different religious creeds, its practice could not be narrow, and a strong Quaker element made it humane. If the American Union succeeded, the good sense, liberality, and democratic spirit of Pennsylvania had a right to claim credit for the result; and Pennsylvanians could afford to leave power and patronage to their neighbors, so long as their own interests were to decide the path of administration.

The people showed little of that acuteness which prevailed to the eastward of the Hudson. Pennsylvania was never smart, yet rarely failed to gain her objects, and never committed serious follies. To politics the Pennsylvanians did not take kindly. Perhaps their democracy was so deep an instinct that they knew not what to do with political power when they gained it; as though political power were aristocratic in its nature, and democratic power a contradiction in terms. On this ground rested the reputation of Albert Gallatin, the only Pennsylvanian who made a mark on the surface of national politics. Gallatin's celebrated financial policy carried into practice the doctrine that the powers of government, being necessarily irresponsible, and therefore hostile to liberty, ought to be exercised only within the narrowest bounds, in order to leave democracy free to develop itself without interference in its true social, intellectual, and economical strength. Unlike Jefferson and the Virginians, Gallatin never hesitated to claim for government all the powers necessary for whatever object was in hand; but he agreed with them in checking the practical use of power, and this he did with a degree of rigor which has been often imitated but never equalled. The Pennsylvanians followed Gallatin's teachings. They indulged in endless factiousness over offices, but they never attempted to govern, and after one brief experience they never rebelled. Thus holding abstract politics at arm's length, they supported the national government with a sagacious sense that their own interests were those of the United States.

Although the State was held by the New Englanders and Virginians in no high repute for quickness of intellect, Philadelphia in 1800 was still the intellectual centre of the nation. For ten years the city had been the seat of national government, and at the close of that period had gathered a more agreeable society, fashionable, literary, and political, than could be found anywhere, except in a few capital cities of Europe. This Quaker city of an ultra-democratic State startled travellers used to luxury, by its extravagance and display. According to the Duc de Liancourt, writing in 1797, —

"The profusion and luxury of Philadelphia on great days, at the tables of the wealthy, in their equipages, and the dresses of their wives and daughters, are extreme. I have seen balls on the President's birthday where the splendor of the rooms and the variety and richness of the dresses did not suffer in comparison with Europe ; and it must be acknowledged that the beauty of the American ladies has the advantage in the comparison. The young women of Philadelphia are accomplished in different degrees, but beauty is general with them. They want the ease and fashion of French women, but the brilliancy of their complexion is infinitely superior. Even when they grow old they are still handsome ; and it would be no exaggeration to say, in the numerous assemblies of Philadelphia it is impossible to meet with what is called a plain woman. As to the young men, they for the most part seem to belong to another species."

For ten years Philadelphia had attracted nearly all the intelligence and cultivation that could be detached from their native stocks. Stagnation was impossible in this rapid current of men and ideas. The Philadelphia press showed the effect of such unusual movement. There Cobbett vociferated libels against democrats. His career was cut short by a blunder of his own; for he quitted the safe field of politics in order to libel the physicians, and although medical practice was not much better than when it had been satirized by Le Sage some eighty years before, the physicians had not become less sensitive. If ever medical practice deserved to be libelled, the bleeding which was the common treatment not only for fevers but for consumption, and even for old age, warranted all that could be said against it; but Cobbett found to his cost that the Pennsylvanians were glad to bleed, or at least to seize the opportunity for silencing the libeller. In 1800 he returned to England; but the style of political warfare in which he was so great a master was already established in the Philadelphia press. An Irish-American named Duane, who had been driven from England and India for expressing opinions too liberal for the time and place, came to Philadelphia and took charge of the opposition newspaper, the "Aurora," which became in his hands the most energetic and slanderous paper in America. In the small society of the time libels rankled, and Duane rivalled Cobbett in the boldness with which he slandered. Another point of resemblance existed between the two men. At a later stage in his career Duane, like Cobbett, disregarded friend as well as foe; he then attacked all who offended him, and denounced his party leaders as bitterly as he did his opponents; but down to the year 1800 he reserved his abuse for his enemies, and the " Aurora " was the nearest approach to a modern newspaper to be found in the country.

Judged by the accounts of his more reputable enemies, Duane seemed beneath forbearance; but his sins, gross as they were, found abettors in places where such conduct was less to be excused. He was a scurrilous libeller; but so was Cobbett; so was William Coleman, who in 1801 became editor of the New York " Evening Post " under the eye of Alexander Hamilton; so was the refined Joseph Dennie, who in the same year established at Philadelphia the " Portfolio," a weekly paper devoted to literature, in which for years to come he was to write literary essays, diversified by slander of Jefferson. Perhaps none of these habitual libellers deserved censure so much as Fisher Ames, the idol of respectability, who cheered on his party to vituperate his political opponents. He saw no harm in showing " the knaves," Jefferson and Gallatin, " the cold-thinking villains who lead, ' whose black blood runs temperately bad,' " the motives of " their own base hearts. . . . The vain, the timid, and trimming must be made by examples to see that scorn smites and blasts and withers like lightning the knaves that mislead them."

Little difference could be seen between the two parties in their use of such weapons, except that democrats claimed a right to slander opponents because
they were monarchists and aristocrats, while Federalists thought themselves bound to smite and wither
with scorn those who, as a class, did not respect
established customs.

Of American newspapers there was no end; but
the education supposed to have been widely spread
by eighteenth-century newspapers was hardly to be
distinguished from ignorance. The student of history
might search forever these storehouses of political
calumny for facts meant to instruct the public in any
useful object. A few dozen advertisements of shipping and sales; a marine list; rarely or never a
price-list, unless it were European; copious extracts
from English newspapers, and long columns of political disquisition, — such matter filled the chief city
newspapers, from which the smaller sheets selected
what their editors thought fit. Reporters and regular
correspondents were unknown. Information of events
other than political — the progress of the New York
or Philadelphia water-works, of the Middlesex Canal,
of Fitch's or Fulton's voyages, or even the commonest
details of a Presidential inauguration — could rarely
be found in the press. In such progress as newspapers
had made Philadelphia took the lead, and in 1800
was at the height of her influence. Not until 1801
did the extreme Federalists set up the "Evening
Post" under William Coleman, in New York, where

at about the same time the Clinton interest put an English refugee named Cheetham in charge of their new paper, the " American Citizen and Watchtower," while Burr's friends established the " Morning Chronicle," edited by Dr. Peter Irving. Duane's importance was greatly reduced by this outburst of journalism in New York, and by the rise of the " National Intelligencer " at Washington, semi-official organ of Jefferson's administration. After the year 1800 the " Aurora " languished ; but between 1795 and 1800 it was the leading newspaper of the United States, and boasted in 1802 of a circulation of four thousand copies, at least half of which its rivals declared to be imaginary.

Although Philadelphia was the literary as well as the political capital of America, nothing proved the existence of a highly intellectual society. When Joseph Dennie, a graduate of Harvard College, quitted Boston and established his " Portfolio " in Philadelphia in 1801, he complained as bitterly as the Pennsylvanian Cliffton against the land " where Genius sickens and where Fancy dies ; " but he still thought Philadelphia more tolerable than any other city in the United States. With a little band of literary friends he passed his days in defying the indifference of his countrymen. " In the society of Mr. Dennie and his friends at Philadelphia I passed the few agreeable moments which my tour through the States afforded me," wrote in 1804 the British poet whom all the world united in calling by the familiar name

of Tom Moore. " If I did not hate as I ought the
rabble to which they are opposed, I could not value
as I do the spirit with which they defy it; and in
learning from them what Americans *can be*, I but see
with the more indignation what Americans *are*."

> " Yet, yet forgive me, O you sacred few,
>   Whom late by Delaware's green banks I knew ;
>   Whom, known and loved, through many a social eve
>   'T was bliss to live with, and 't was pain to leave.
>   Oh, but for *such*, Columbia's days were done !
>   Rank without ripeness, quickened without sun,
>   Crude at the surface, rotten at the core,
>   Her fruits would fall before her spring were o'er."

If Columbia's days were to depend on " *such*," they
were scarcely worth prolonging; for Dennie's genius
was but the thin echo of an English classicism thin at
its best. Yet Moore's words had value, for they gave
a lifelike idea of the "sacred few " who sat with him,
drinking deep, and reviling America because she
could not produce poets like Anacreon and artists
like Phidias, and still more because Americans cared
little for Addisonian essays. An adventurer called
John Davis, who published in London a book of
American travels, mentioned in it that he too met
the Philadelphia authors. " Dennie passed his morn-
ings in the shop of Mr. Dickens, which I found the
rendezvous of the Philadelphia sons of literature, —
Blair [Linn], author of a poem called the ' Powers
of Genius ; ' Ingersoll, known by a tragedy of which I
forget the title ; Stock, celebrated for his dramatic

criticisms." C. J. Ingersoll did in fact print a tragedy called " Edwy and Elgiva," which was acted in 1801, and John Blair Linn's " Powers of Genius " appeared in the same year; but Dennie's group boasted another member more notable than these. Charles Brockden Brown, the first American novelist of merit, was a Philadelphian. Davis called upon Brown. " He occupied a dismal room in a dismal street. I asked him whether a view of Nature would not be more propitious to composition, or whether he should not write with more facility were his window to command the prospect of the Lake of Geneva. ' Sir,' said he, ' good pens, thick paper, and ink well diluted would facilitate my composition more than the prospect of the broadest expanse of water or mountains rising against the clouds.' "

Pennsylvania was largely German and the Moravians were not without learning, yet no trace of German influence showed itself in the educated and literary class. Schiller was at the end of his career, and Goethe at the zenith of his powers; but neither was known in Pennsylvania, unless it might be by translations of the " Robbers " or the " Sorrows of Werther." As for deeper studies, search in America would be useless for what was rare or unknown either in England or France. Kant had closed and Hegel was beginning his labors; but the Western nations knew no more of German thought than of Egyptian hieroglyphics, and America had not yet reached the point of understanding that metaphysics

apart from theology could exist at all. Locke was
a college text-book, and possibly a few clergymen
had learned to deride the idealism of Berkeley; but
as an interest which concerned life, metaphysics, apart
from Calvinism, had no existence in America, and
was to have none for another generation. The literary labors of Americans followed easier paths, and
such thought as prevailed was confined within a
narrow field, — yet within this limit Pennsylvania
had something to show, even though it failed to
please the taste of Dennie and Moore.

Not far from the city of Philadelphia, on the banks
of the Schuylkill, lived William Bartram, the naturalist, whose "Travels" through Florida and the
Indian country, published in 1791, were once praised
by Coleridge, and deserved reading both for the
matter and the style. Not far from Bartram, and his
best scholar, was Alexander Wilson, a Scotch poet of
more than ordinary merit, gifted with a dogged enthusiasm, which in spite of obstacles gave to America
an ornithology more creditable than anything yet accomplished in art or literature. Beyond the mountains, at Pittsburg, another author showed genuine
and original qualities. American humor was not
then so marked as it afterward became, and good-
nature was rarer; but H. H. Brackenridge set an
example of both in a book once universally popular
throughout the South and West. A sort of prose
"Hudibras," it had the merit of leaving no sting, for
this satire on democracy was written by a democrat

and published in the most democratic community of America. "Modern Chivalry" told the adventures of a militia captain, who riding about the country with a raw Irish servant, found this red-headed, ignorant bog-trotter, this Sancho Panza, a much more popular person than himself, who could only with difficulty be restrained from becoming a clergyman, an Indian chief, a member of the legislature, of the philosophical society, and of Congress. At length his employer got for him the appointment of excise officer in the Alleghanies, and was gratified at seeing him tarred and feathered by his democratic friends. "Modern Chivalry" was not only written in good last-century English, none too refined for its subject, but was more thoroughly American than any book yet published, or to be published until the "Letters of Major Jack Downing" and the "Georgia Scenes" of forty years later. Never known, even by title, in Europe, and little enjoyed in the seaboard States, where bog-trotters and weavers had no such prominence, Judge Brackenridge's book filled the place of Don Quixote on the banks of the Ohio and along the Mississippi.

Another man whose literary merits were not to be overlooked, had drifted to Philadelphia because of its varied attractions. If in the last century America could boast of a poet who shared some of the delicacy if not the grandeur of genius, it was Philip Freneau ; whose verses, poured out for the occasion, ran freely, good and bad, but the bad, as was natural, much more

freely than the good.   Freneau proved his merit by an
experience unique in history.   He was twice robbed
by the greatest English poets of his day.   Among his
many slight verses were some pleasing lines called
" The Indian Burying Ground " : —

> " His bow for action ready bent,
>   And arrows with a head of stone,
> Can only mean that life is spent,
>   And not the finer essence gone.
>
> " By midnight moons, o'er moistening dews,
>   In vestments for the chase arrayed,
> The hunter still the deer pursues,
>   The hunter and the deer, — a shade."

The last line was taken by the British poet Campbell
for his own poem called " O'Connor's Child," and
Freneau could afford to forgive the theft which thus
called attention to the simple grace of his melody;
but although one such compliment might fall to the
lot of a common man, only merit could explain a
second accident of the same kind.   Freneau saw a
greater genius than Campbell borrow from his modest
capital.   No one complained of Walter Scott for taking whatever he liked wherever he chose, to supply
that flame of genius which quickened the world; but
Freneau had the right to claim that Scott paid him
the highest compliment one poet could pay to another.
In the Introduction to the third canto of " Marmion "
stood and still stands a line taken directly from the
verse in Freneau's poem on the Heroes of Eutaw : —

> " They took the spear — but left the shield."

All these men — Wilson, Brackenridge, Freneau — were democrats, and came not within the Federalist circle where Moore could alone see a hope for Columbia; yet the names of Federalists also survived in literature.   Alexander Graydon's pleasant Memoirs could never lose interest.   Many lawyers, clergymen, and physicians left lasting records.   Dallas was bringing out his reports; Duponceau was laboring over jurisprudence and languages; William Lewis, William Rawle, and Judge Wilson were high authorities at the bar; Dr. Wistar was giving reputation to the Philadelphia Medical School, and the famous Dr. Physic was beginning to attract patients from far and near as the best surgeon in America.   Gilbert Stuart, the best painter in the country, came to Philadelphia, and there painted portraits equal to the best that England or France could produce, — for Reynolds and Gainsborough were dead, and Sir Thomas Lawrence ruled the fashion of the time.   If Franklin and Rittenhouse no longer lived to give scientific fame to Philadelphia, their liberal and scientific spirit survived.   The reputation of the city was not confined to America, and the accident that made a Philadelphian, Benjamin West, President of the Royal Academy in succession to Sir Joshua Reynolds, was a tacit compliment, not undeserved, to the character of the American metropolis.

There manners were milder and more humane than elsewhere.   Societies existed for lessening the hardships of the unfortunate.   A society labored for the abolition of slavery without exciting popular passion, although New York contained more than twenty thousand slaves, and New Jersey more than twelve thousand. A society for alleviating the miseries of prisons watched the progress of experiments in the model jail, which stood alone of its kind in America. Elsewhere the treatment of criminals was such as it had ever been. In Connecticut they were still confined under-ground, in the shafts of an abandoned copper-mine. The Memoirs of Stephen Burroughs gave some idea of the prisons and prison discipline of Massachusetts. The Pennsylvania Hospital was also a model, for it contained a department for the insane, the only one of the sort in America except the Virginia Lunatic Asylum at Williamsburg. Even there the treatment of these beings, whom a later instinct of humanity thought peculiarly worthy of care and lavish expenditure, was harsh enough, — strait-jackets, whippings, chains, and dark-rooms being a part of the prescribed treatment in every such hospital in the world ; but where no hospitals existed, as in New England, New York, and elsewhere, the treatment was apt to be far worse. No horror of the Middle Ages wrung the modern conscience with a sense of disgust more acute than was felt in remembering the treatment of the insane even within recent times. Shut in attics or cellars, or in cages outside a house, without warmth, light, or care, they lived in filth, with nourishment such as was thrown to dogs. Philadelphia led the way in humanitarian efforts which relieved

man from incessant contact with these cruel and
coarsening associations.

The depth of gratitude due to Pennsylvania as the
model democratic society of the world was so great
as to risk overestimating what had been actually done.
As yet no common-school system existed. Academies and colleges were indifferent. New Jersey was
no better provided than Pennsylvania. The Englishman Weld, a keen if not a friendly critic, visited
Princeton, —

" A large college," he said, " held in much repute by the
neighboring States. The number of students amounts to
upwards of seventy; from their appearance, however,
and the course of studies they seem to be engaged in,
like all the other American colleges I ever saw, it better
deserves the title of a grammar-school than of a college.
The library which we were shown is most wretched, consisting for the most part of old theological books not
even arranged with any regularity. An orrery contrived
by Mr. Rittenhouse stands at one end of the apartment,
but it is quite out of repair, as well as a few detached
parts of a philosophical apparatus enclosed in the same
glass-case. At the opposite end of the room are two
small cupboards which are shown as the museum. These
contain a couple of small stuffed alligators and a few singular fishes in a miserable state of preservation, from
their being repeatedly tossed about."

Philadelphia made no claim to a wide range of
intellectual interests. As late as 1811, Latrobe, by
education an architect and by genius an artist, wrote
to Volney in France, —

" Thinking only of the profession and of the affluence which it yields in Europe to all who follow it, you forget that I am an engineer in America; that I am neither a mechanic nor a merchant, nor a planter of cotton, rice, or tobacco. You forget — for you know it as well as I do — that with us the labor of the hand has precedence over that of the mind; that an engineer is considered only as an overseer of men who dig, and an architect as one that watches others who hew stone or wood."

The labor of the hand had precedence over that of the mind throughout the United States. If this was true in the city of Franklin, Rittenhouse, and West, the traveller who wandered farther toward the south felt still more strongly the want of intellectual variety, and found more cause for complaint.

CHAPTER V.

BETWEEN Pennsylvania and Virginia stretched no barrier of mountains or deserts. Nature seemed to mean that the northern State should reach toward the Chesapeake, and embrace its wide system of coasts and rivers. The Susquehanna, crossing Pennsylvania from north to south, rolled down wealth which in a few years built the city of Baltimore by the surplus of Pennsylvania's resources. Any part of Chesapeake Bay, or of the streams which flowed into it, was more easily accessible to Baltimore than any part of Massachusetts or Pennsylvania to New York. Every geographical reason argued that the Susquehanna, the Potomac, and the James should support one homogeneous people; yet the intellectual difference between Pennsylvania and Virginia was already more sharply marked than that between New England and the Middle States.

The old Virginia society was still erect, priding itself on its resemblance to the society of England, which had produced Hampden and Chatham. The Virginia gentleman, wherever met, was a country gentleman or a lawyer among a society of planters. The absence of city life was the sharpest characteristic of Virginia, even compared with South Carolina.

In the best and greatest of Virginians, the virtues which always stood in most prominence were those of the field and farm, — the simple and straightforward mind, the notions of courage and truth, the absence of mercantile sharpness and quickness, the rusticity and open-handed hospitality, which could exist only where the struggle for life was hardly a struggle at all. No visitor could resist the charm of kindly sympathy which softened the asperities of Virginian ambition. Whether young Albert Gallatin went there, hesitating between Europe and America, or the still younger William Ellery Channing, with all New England on his active conscience, the effect was the same : —

" I blush for my own people," wrote Channing from Richmond in 1799, " when I compare the selfish prudence of a Yankee with the generous confidence of a Virginian. Here I find great vices, but greater virtues than I left behind me. There is one single trait which attaches me to the people I live with more than all the virtues of New England, — they *love money less* than we do ; they are more disinterested ; their patriotism is not tied to their purse-strings. Could I only take from the Virginians their sensuality and their slaves, I should think them the greatest people in the world. As it is, with a few great virtues, they have innumerable vices."

Even forty years afterward, so typical a New Englander as the poet Bryant acknowledged that " whatever may be the comparison in other respects, the South certainly has the advantage over us in point of manners." Manners were not all their charm; for the Virginians at the close of the eighteenth century were inferior to no class of Americans in the sort of education then supposed to make refinement. The Duc de Liancourt bore witness : —

" In spite of the Virginian love for dissipation, the taste for reading is commoner there among men of the first class than in any other part of America ; but the populace is perhaps more ignorant there than elsewhere."

Those whom Liancourt called "men of the first class" were equal to any standard of excellence known to history. Their range was narrow, but within it they were supreme. The traditions of high breeding were still maintained, and a small England, much as it existed in the time of the Commonwealth, was perpetuated in the Virginia of 1800. Social position was a birthright, not merely of the well born, but of the highly gifted. Nearly all the great lawyers of Virginia were of the same social stock as in New England, — poor and gifted men, welcomed into a landed aristocracy simple in tastes and genial in temper. Chief-Justice Marshall was such a man, commanding respect and regard wherever he was seen, — perhaps most of all from New Englanders, who were least familiar with the type. George Mason was an ideal republican, — a character as strong in its way as Washington or Marshall. George Wythe the Chancellor stood in the same universal esteem; and even his young clerk Henry Clay, "the mill-boy of the slashes," who had lately left Chancellor Wythe's office to set up one of his own at Lexington in Kentucky, inherited that Virginia geniality which, as it ripened with his years, made him an idol among Northern and Western multitudes who knew neither the source nor secret of his charm. Law and politics were the only objects of Virginian thought; but within these bounds the Virginians achieved triumphs. What could America offer in legal literature that rivalled the judicial opinions of Chief-Justice Marshall? What political essay equalled the severe beauty of George Mason's Virginia Bill of Rights? What single production of an American pen reached the fame of Thomas Jefferson's Declaration of Independence? "The Virginians are the best orators I ever heard," wrote the young Channing; although Patrick Henry, the greatest of them all, was no longer alive.

Every one admitted that Virginia society was ill at ease. In colonial days it rested on a few great props, the strongest being its close connection with England; and after this had been cut away by the Revolutionary War, primogeniture, the Church, exemption of land from seizure for debt, and negro slavery remained to support the oligarchy of planters. The momentum given by the Declaration of Independence enabled Jefferson and George Wythe to sweep primogeniture from the statute book. After an interval of several years, Madison carried the law which severed Church from State. There the movement ended. All the great Virginians would gladly have gone on, but the current began to flow against them. They suggested a bill for emancipation, but could find no one to father it in the legislature, and they shrank from the storm it would excite.

President Washington, in 1796, in a letter already quoted, admitted that land in Virginia was lower in price than land of the same quality in Pennsylvania. For this inferiority he suggested, among other reasons, the explanation that Pennsylvania had made laws for the gradual abolition of slavery, and he declared nothing more certain than that Virginia must adopt similar laws at a period not remote. Had the Virginians seen a sure prospect that such a step would improve their situation, they would probably have taken it; but the slave-owners were little pleased at the results of reforms already effected, and they were in no humor for abolishing more of their old institutions. The effects of disestablishing the Church were calculated to disgust them with all reform. From early times the colony had been divided into parishes, and each parish owned a church building. The system was the counterpart of that established in New England. The church lands, glebes, and endowments were administered by the clergyman, wardens, and vestry. Good society in Virginia recognized no other religion than was taught in this branch of English episcopacy. " Sure I am of one thing," was the remark in the Virginia legislature of an old-fashioned Federalist, with powdered hair, three-cornered hat, long queue, and white top-boots, — " Sure I am of one thing, that no *gentleman* would choose any road to heaven but the Episcopal." Every plantation was attached to a parish, and the earliest associations of every well-bred man and woman in Virginia were connected with the Church service. In spite of all this, no sooner had Madison and his friends taken away the support of the State than the Church perished. They argued that freedom of religion worked well in Pennsylvania, and therefore must succeed in Virginia; but they were wrong. The Virginia gentry stood by and saw their churches closed, the roofs rot, the aisles and pews become a refuge for sheep and foxes, the tombstones of their ancestry built into strange walls or turned into flagging to be worn by the feet of slaves. By the year 1800, Bishop Madison found his diocese left so nearly bare of clergy and communicants that after a few feeble efforts to revive interest he abandoned the struggle, and contented himself with the humbler task of educating boys at the ancient College of William and Mary in the deserted colonial capital of Williamsburg. There the English traveller Weld visited him about the year 1797, and gave a curious picture of his establishment : —

" The Bishop," he said, " is president of the college, and has apartments in the buildings. Half-a-dozen or more of the students, the eldest about twelve years old, dined at his table one day that I was there. Some were without shoes or stockings, others without coats. During dinner they constantly rose to help themselves at the sideboard. A couple of dishes of salted meat and some oyster-soup formed the whole of the dinner."

Such a state of society was picturesque, but not encouraging. An aristocracy so lacking in energy and self-confidence was a mere shell, to be crushed, as one might think, by a single vigorous blow. Nevertheless, Jefferson and Madison, after striking it again and again with the full force of Revolutionary violence, were obliged to desist, and turned their reforming axes against the Church and hierarchy of New England. There they could do nothing but good, for the society of New England was sound, whatever became of the Church or of slavery; but in Virginia the gap which divided gentry from populace was enormous; and another gap, which seemed impassable, divided the populace from the slaves. Jefferson's reforms crippled and impoverished the gentry, but did little for the people, and for the slaves nothing.

Nowhere in America existed better human material than in the middle and lower classes of Virginians. As explorers, adventurers, fighters, — wherever courage, activity, and force were wanted, — they had no equals; but they had never known discipline, and were beyond measure jealous of restraint. With all their natural virtues and indefinite capacities for good, they were rough and uneducated to a degree that shocked their own native leaders. Jefferson tried in vain to persuade them that they needed schools. Their character was stereotyped, and development impossible; for even Jefferson, with all his liberality of ideas, was Virginian enough to discourage the introduction of manufactures and the gathering of masses in cities, without which no new life could grow. Among the common people, intellectual activity was confined to hereditary commonplaces of politics, resting on the axiom that Virginia was the typical society of a future Arcadian America. To escape the tyranny of Cæsar by perpetuating the simple and isolated lives of their fathers was the sum of their political philosophy; to fix upon the national government the stamp of their own idyllic conservatism was the height of their ambition.

Debarred from manufactures, possessed of no shipping, and enjoying no domestic market, Virginian energies necessarily knew no other resource than agriculture. Without church, university, schools, or literature in any form that required or fostered intellectual life, the Virginians concentrated their thoughts almost exclusively upon politics; and this concentration produced a result so distinct and lasting, and in character so respectable, that American history would lose no small part of its interest in losing the Virginia school.

No one denied that Virginia, like Massachusetts, in the War of Independence, believed herself competent to follow independently of other provinces whatever path seemed good. The Constitution of Virginia did not, like that of Massachusetts, authorize the governor to " be the commander-in-chief of the army

and navy," in order "to take and surprise, by all
ways and means whatsoever, all and every such
person or persons (with their ships, arms, ammu-
nition, and other goods) as shall in a hostile manner invade or attempt the invading, conquering, or
annoying this Commonwealth;" but although Massachusetts expressed the power in language more de-
tailed, Virginia held to its essence with equal tenacity.
When experience showed the necessity of "creating a
more perfect union," none of the great States were
unanimous for the change. Massachusetts and New
York were with difficulty induced to accept the Constitution of 1787. Their final assent was wrung from
them by the influence of the cities and of the commercial class; but Virginia contained no cities and
few merchants. The majority by which the State
Convention of Virginia, after an obstinate contest,
adopted the Constitution, was influenced by pure patriotism as far as any political influence could be called
pure; but the popular majority was probably hostile
to the Constitution, and certainly remained hostile to
the exercise of its powers. From the first the State
took an attitude of opposition to the national government, which became more and more decided, until in
1798 it found expression in a formal announcement,
through the legislature and governor, that the limit of
further obedience was at hand. The General Assembly adopted Resolutions promising support to the
government of the United States in all measures
warranted by the Constitution, but declaring the pow-

ers of the federal government " no further valid than
they are authorized by the grants enumerated in that
compact; and that in case of a deliberate, palpable,
and dangerous exercise of other powers, not granted
by said compact, the States who are parties thereto
have the right, and are in duty bound, to interpose,
for arresting the progress of the evil and for maintaining within their respective limits the authorities, rights,
and liberties appertaining to them."

Acting immediately on this view, the General
Assembly did interpose by declaring certain laws,
known as the Alien and Sedition Laws, unconstitutional, and by inviting the other States to concur, in
confidence " that the necessary and proper measures
will be taken by each for co-operating with this State
in maintaining unimpaired the authorities, rights,
and liberties reserved to the States respectively or to
the people."

These Virginia Resolutions, which were drawn by
Madison, seemed strong enough to meet any possible aggression from the national government; but
Jefferson, as though not quite satisfied with these,
recommended the Kentucky legislature to adopt still
stronger. The draft of the Kentucky Resolutions,
whether originally composed or only approved by
him, representing certainly his own convictions, declared that " where powers are assumed which have
not been delegated a nullification of the Act is the
rightful remedy," and " that every State has a natural
right, in cases not within the compact, to nullify of

their own authority all assumptions of power by others within their limits." Jefferson did not doubt " that the co-States, recurring to their natural right in cases not made federal, will concur in declaring these acts void and of no force, and will each take measures of its own for providing that neither these acts, nor any others of the federal government not plainly and intentionally authorized by the Constitution, shall be exercised within their respective territories."

In the history of Virginia thought, the personal opinions of Jefferson and Madison were more interesting, if not more important, than the official opinion of State legislatures. Kentucky shrank from using language which seemed unnecessarily violent, but still declared, with all the emphasis needed, that the national government was not " the exclusive or final judge of the extent of the powers delegated to itself, since that would have made its discretion, and not the Constitution, the measure of its powers," but that each party had an equal right to judge for itself as to an infraction of the compact, and the proper redress ; that in the case of the Alien and Sedition Laws the compact had been infringed, and that these Acts, being unconstitutional and therefore void, " may tend to drive these States into revolution and blood ; " finally, the State of Kentucky called for an expression of sentiment from other States, like Virginia not doubting " that the co-States, recurring to their natural right in cases not made federal, will concur in declaring these Acts void and of no force."

These famous Resolutions of Virginia and Kentucky, historically the most interesting of all the intellectual products of the Virginia school, were adopted in 1798 and 1799. In 1800, Jefferson their chief author was chosen President of the United States, and Madison became his Secretary of State. Much discussion then and afterward arose over the Constitutional theory laid down by Virginia and Kentucky, and thus apparently adopted by the Union; but in such cases of disputed powers that theory was soundest which was backed by the strongest force, for the sanction of force was the most necessary part of law. The United States government was at that time powerless to enforce its theories; while, on the other hand, Virginia had all the power necessary for the object desired. The Republican leaders believed that the State was at liberty to withdraw from the Union if it should think that an infraction of the Constitution had taken place; and Jefferson in 1798 preferred to go on by way of Resolution rather than by way of Secession, not because of any doubt as to the right, but because, "if we now reduce our Union to Virginia and North Carolina, immediately the conflict will be established between those two States, and they will end by breaking into their simple units." In other letters he explained that the Kentucky Resolutions were intended " to leave the matter in such a train as that we may not be committed absolutely to push the matter to extremities, and yet may be free to push as far as events will render prudent." Union was a question of expediency, not of obligation. This was the conviction of the true Virginia school, and of Jefferson's opponents as well as his supporters; of Patrick Henry, as well as John Taylor of Caroline and John Randolph of Roanoke.

The Virginia and Kentucky Resolutions, giving form to ideas that had not till then been so well expressed, left a permanent mark in history, and fixed for an indefinite time the direction and bounds of Virginia politics; but if New England could go no further in the lines of thought pursued by Fisher Ames and Timothy Dwight, Virginia could certainly expect no better results from those defined by Jefferson and Madison. The science of politics, if limited by the Resolutions of Virginia and Kentucky, must degenerate into an enumeration of powers reserved from exercise. Thought could find little room for free development where it confined its action to narrowing its own field.

This tendency of the Virginia school was the more remarkable because it seemed little suited to the tastes and instincts of the two men who gave it expression and guided its course. By common consent Thomas Jefferson was its intellectual leader. According to the admitted standards of greatness, Jefferson was a great man. After all deductions on which his enemies might choose to insist, his character could not be denied elevation, versatility, breadth, insight, and delicacy; but neither as a politician nor as a political philosopher did he seem at ease in the

atmosphere which surrounded him. As a leader of
democracy he appeared singularly out of place. As
reserved as President Washington in the face of
popular familiarities, he never showed himself in
crowds. During the last thirty years of his life he was
not seen in a Northern city, even during his Presidency; nor indeed was he seen at all except on horseback, or by his friends and visitors in his own house.
With manners apparently popular and informal, he
led a life of his own, and allowed few persons to
share it. His tastes were for that day excessively refined. His instincts were those of a liberal European
nobleman, like the Duc de Liancourt, and he built for
himself at Monticello a château above contact with
man. The rawness of political life was an incessant
torture to him, and personal attacks made him keenly
unhappy. His true delight was in an intellectual life
of science and art. To read, write, speculate in new
lines of thought, to keep abreast of the intellect of
Europe, and to feed upon Homer and Horace, were
pleasures more to his mind than any to be found in a
public assembly. He had some knowledge of mathematics, and a little acquaintance with classical art;
but he fairly revelled in what he believed to be beautiful, and his writings often betrayed subtile feeling
for artistic form, — a sure mark of intellectual sen-
suousness. He shrank from whatever was rough or
coarse, and his yearning for sympathy was almost
feminine. That such a man should have ventured
upon the stormy ocean of politics was surprising, the

more because he was no orator, and owed nothing to any magnetic influence of voice or person. Never effective in debate, for seventeen years before his Presidency he had not appeared in a legislative body except in the chair of the Senate. He felt a nervous horror for the contentiousness of such assemblies, and even among his own friends he sometimes abandoned for the moment his strongest convictions rather than support them by an effort of authority.

If Jefferson appeared ill at ease in the position of a popular leader, he seemed equally awkward in the intellectual restraints of his own political principles. His mind shared little in common with the provincialism on which the Virginia and Kentucky Resolutions were founded. His instincts led him to widen rather than to narrow the bounds of every intellectual exercise; and if vested with political authority, he could no more resist the temptation to stretch his powers than he could abstain from using his mind on any subject merely because he might be drawn upon ground supposed to be dangerous. He was a deist, believing that men could manage their own salvation without the help of a state church. Prone to innovation, he sometimes generalized without careful analysis. He was a theorist, prepared to risk the fate of mankind on the chance of reasoning far from certain in its details. His temperament was sunny and sanguine, and the atrabilious philosophy of New England was intolerable to him. He was curiously vulnerable, for he seldom wrote a page without exposing himself to attack. He was superficial in his knowledge, and a martyr to the disease of omniscience. Ridicule of his opinions and of himself was an easy task, in which his Federalist opponents delighted, for his English was often confused, his assertions inaccurate, and at times of excitement he was apt to talk with indiscretion ; while with all his extraordinary versatility of character and opinions, he seemed during his entire life to breathe with perfect satisfaction nowhere except in the liberal, literary, and scientific air of Paris in 1789.

Jefferson aspired beyond the ambition of a nationality, and embraced in his view the whole future of man. That the United States should become a nation like France, England, or Russia, should conquer the world like Rome, or develop a typical race like the Chinese, was no part of his scheme. He wished to begin a new era. Hoping for a time when the world's ruling interests should cease to be local and should become universal ; when questions of boundary and nationality should become insignificant ; when armies and navies should be reduced to the work of police, and politics should consist only in non-intervention, — he set himself to the task of governing, with this golden age in view. Few men have dared to legislate as though eternal peace were at hand, in a world torn by wars and convulsions and drowned in blood ; but this was what Jefferson aspired to do. Even in such dangers, he believed that Americans might safely set an example which the Christian

world should be led by interest to respect and at
length to imitate. As he conceived a true American
policy, war was a blunder, an unnecessary risk; and
even in case of robbery and aggression the United
States, he believed, had only to stand on the defensive in order to obtain justice in the end. He would
not consent to build up a new nationality merely to
create more navies and armies, to perpetuate the
crimes and follies of Europe; the central government
at Washington should not be permitted to indulge
in the miserable ambitions that had made the Old
World a hell, and frustrated the hopes of humanity.

With these humanitarian ideas which passed beyond the bounds of nationality, Jefferson held other
views which seemed narrower than ordinary provincialism. Cities, manufactures, mines, shipping, and
accumulation of capital led, in his opinion, to corruption and tyranny.

"Generally speaking," said he, in his only elaborate
work, the Notes on Virginia, "the proportion which the
aggregate of the other classes of citizens bears in any
State to that of its husbandmen is the proportion of its
unsound to its healthy parts, and is a good enough barom-
eter whereby to measure its degree of corruption. . . .
Those who labor in the earth are the chosen people of
God if ever he had a chosen people, whose breasts he
has made his peculiar deposit for substantial and genuine
virtue."

This doctrine was not original with Jefferson, but
its application to national affairs on a great scale

was something new in the world, and the theory itself
clashed with his intellectual instincts of liberality
and innovation.

A school of political thought, starting with postu-
lates like these, was an interesting study, and would
have been more interesting had Jefferson's friends
undertaken to develop his ideas in the extent he held
them. Perhaps this was impossible. At all events,
Madison, although author of the Virginia Resolutions, showed little earnestness in carrying out their
principles either as a political or as a literary task ;
and John Taylor of Caroline, the only consistent
representative of the school, began his writings only
when political power had established precedents inconsistent with their object.

With such simple conceptions as their experience
gave them in politics, law, and agriculture, the Virginians appeared to be satisfied ; and whether satisfied
or not, they were for the time helpless to produce other
literature, science, or art. From the three States
lying farther south, no greater intellectual variety
could be expected. In some respects North Carolina,
though modest in ambition and backward in thought,
was still the healthiest community south of the
Potomac. Neither aristocratic like Virginia and
South Carolina, nor turbulent like Georgia, nor
troubled by a sense of social importance, but above
all thoroughly democratic, North Carolina tolerated
more freedom of political action and showed less family and social influence, fewer vested rights in political

power, and less tyranny of slaveholding interests and terrors than were common elsewhere in the South. Neither cultivated nor brilliant in intellect, nor great in thought, industry, energy, or organization, North Carolina was still interesting and respectable. The best qualities of the State were typified in its favorite representative, Nathaniel Macon.

The small society of rice and cotton planters at Charleston, with their cultivated tastes and hospitable habits, delighted in whatever reminded them of European civilization. They were travellers, readers, and scholars; the society of Charleston compared well in refinement with that of any city of its size in the world, and English visitors long thought it the most agreeable in America. In the southern wilderness which stretched from the Appomattox to the St. Mary's, Charleston was the only oasis. The South Carolinians were ambitious for other distinctions than those which could be earned at the bar or on the plantation. From there Washington Allston went to study at Harvard College, and after taking his degree in the same class with young Buckminster, sailed in the same year, 1800, for Europe with his friend Malbone, to learn to express in color and form the grace and dignity of his imagination. In South Carolina were felt the instincts of city life. During two or three weeks of the winter, the succession of dinners, balls, and races at Charleston rivalled the gayety of Philadelphia itself; and although the city was dull during the rest of the year, it was not deserted even in the heat of summer, for the sea-breeze made it a watering-place, like Boston, and the deadly fevers sure to kill the white man who should pass a night on one bank of the Ashley River were almost unknown on the other. In the summer, therefore, the residents remained or returned; the children got their schooling, and business continued. For this reason South Carolina knew less of the country hospitality which made Virginia famous; city life had the larger share in existence, although in the hot weather torpor and languor took the place of gayety. In certain respects Charleston was more Northern in habits than any town of the North. In other warm countries, the summer evening was commonly the moment when life was best worth living; music, love-making, laughter, and talk turned night into day; but Charleston was Puritanic in discipline. Every night at ten o'clock the slamming of window-blinds and locking of doors warned strangers and visitors to go not only to their houses, but to their beds. The citizens looked with contempt on the gayety of Spanish or Italian temper. Beneath all other thoughts, the care of the huge slave population remained constant. The streets were abandoned at an early hour to the patrol, and no New England village was more silent.

Confident as the Carolinian was in the strength of the slave-system, and careless as he seemed and thought himself to be on that account, the recent fate of St. Domingo gave him cause for constant anxiety; but even without anxiety, he would have been grave.

The gentry of the lower country belonged to the same
English class which produced the gentry of Virginia
and Massachusetts. The austerity of the Puritan
may have been an exaggerated trait, but among the
Middletons, Pinckneys, Rutledges, and Lowndeses the
seriousness of the original English stock was also not
without effect in the habit of their minds. They
showed it in their treatment of the slave-system, but
equally in their churches and houses, their occupations
and prejudices, their races and sports, the character
of their entertainments, the books they read, and the
talk at their tables. No gentleman belonged to any
church but the Anglican, or connected himself with
trade. No court departed from the practice and precedents of English law, however anomalous they
might be. Before the Revolution large numbers of
young men had been educated in England, and their
influence was still strong in the society of Charleston.
The younger generation inherited similar tastes. Of
this class the best-known name which will appear in
this narrative was that of William Lowndes; and no
better example could be offered of the serious temper
which marked Carolinian thought, than was given by
the career of this refined and highly educated gentleman, almost the last of his school.

Charleston was more cosmopolitan than any part
of Virginia, and enjoyed also a certain literary reputation on account of David Ramsay, whose works
were widely read; and of Governor Drayton, whose
" Letters written during a Tour through the Northern

and Eastern States," and " View of South Carolina,"
gave an idea of the author as well as of the countries
he described.   Charleston also possessed a library of
three or four thousand well-selected books, and maintained a well-managed theatre.   The churches were
almost as strictly attended as those in Boston.   The
fashionable wine-party was even more common, and
perhaps the guests took pride in drinking deeper than
they would have been required to do in New York or
Philadelphia.

Politics had not mastered the thought of South
Carolina so completely as that of Virginia, and the
natural instincts of Carolinian society should have led
the gentry to make common cause with the gentry of
New England and the Middle States against democratic innovations.   The conservative side in politics
seemed to be that which no Carolinian gentleman
could fail to support.   The oligarchy of South Carolina, in defiance of democratic principles, held the
political power of the State, and its interests could
never harmonize with those of a theoretic democracy,
or safely consent to trust the national government
in the hands of Jefferson and his friends, who had
founded their power by breaking down in Virginia an
oligarchy closely resembling that of the Carolinian
rice-planters.   Yet in 1800 enough of these gentlemen, under the lead of Charles Pinckney, deserted
their Northern friends, to secure the defeat of the
Federalist candidates, and to elect Jefferson as President.   For this action, no satisfactory reason was

ever given. Of all States in the Union, South Carolina, under its actual system of politics, was the last which could be suspected of democratic tendencies.

Such want of consistency seemed to show some peculiarity of character. Not every educated and privileged class has sacrificed itself to a social sentiment, least of all without understanding its object. The eccentricity was complicated by another peculiar element of society. In South Carolina the interesting union between English tastes and provincial prejudices, which characterized the wealthy planters of the coast, was made more striking by contrast with the character of the poor and hardy yeomanry of the upper country. The seriousness of Charleston society changed to severity in the mountains. Rude, ignorant, and in some of its habits half barbarous, this population, in the stiffness of its religious and social expression, resembled the New England of a century before rather than the liberality of the Union. Largely settled by Scotch and Irish emigrants, with the rigid Presbyterian doctrine and conservatism of their class, they were democratic in practice beyond all American democrats, and were more conservative in thought than the most aristocratic Europeans. Though sharply divided both socially and by interest from the sea-coast planters, these up-country farmers had one intellectual sympathy with their fellow-citizens in Charleston, — a sympathy resting on their common dislike for change, on the serious element which lay at the root of their common characters ; and this marriage of two widely divergent minds produced one of the most extraordinary statesmen of America. In the year 1800 John Caldwell Calhoun, a boy of eighteen, went from the upper country to his brother-in-law's academy in Georgia. Grown nearly to manhood without contact with the world, his modes of thought were those of a Connecticut Calvinist; his mind was cold, stern, and metaphysical; but he had the energy and ambition of youth, the political fervor of Jeffersonian democracy, and little sympathy with slavery or slave-owners. At this early age he, like many other Republicans, looked on slavery as a " scaffolding," to be taken down when the building should be complete. A radical democrat, less liberal, less cultivated, and much less genial than Jefferson, Calhoun was the true heir to his intellectual succession; stronger in logic, bolder in action. Upon him was to fall the duty of attempting to find for Carolina an escape from the logical conclusions of those democratic principles which Jefferson in 1800 claimed for his own, but which in the full swing of his power, and to the last day of his life, he shrank from pressing to their results.

Viewed from every side by which it could be approached, the society of South Carolina, more than that of any other portion of the Union, seemed to bristle with contradictions. The elements of intellectual life existed without a sufficient intellectual atmosphere. Society, colonial by origin and dependent by the conditions of its existence, was striving to exist without external support. Whether it would stand or fall, and whether, either standing or falling, it could contribute any new element to American thought, were riddles which, with so many others, American history was to answer.

CHAPTER VI.

NEARLY every foreign traveller who visited the United States during these early years, carried away an impression sober if not sad. A thousand miles of desolate and dreary forest, broken here and there by settlements; along the sea-coast a few flourishing towns devoted to commerce; no arts, a provincial literature, a cancerous disease of negro slavery, and differences of political theory fortified within geographical lines, — what could be hoped for such a country except to repeat the story of violence and brutality which the world already knew by heart, until repetition for thousands of years had wearied and sickened mankind? Ages must probably pass before the interior could be thoroughly settled; even Jefferson, usually a sanguine man, talked of a thousand years with acquiescence, and in his first Inaugural Address, at a time when the Mississippi River formed the Western boundary, spoke of the country as having "room enough for our descendants to the hundredth and thousandth generation." No prudent person dared to act on the certainty that when settled, one government could comprehend the whole; and when the day of separation should arrive, and America should have her Prussia, Austria, and Italy, as she already had her England, France, and Spain, what else could follow but a return to the old conditions of local jealousies, wars, and corruption which had made a slaughter-house of Europé?

The mass of Americans were sanguine and self-confident, partly by temperament, but partly also by reason of ignorance; for they knew little of the difficulties which surrounded a complex society. The Duc de Liancourt, like many critics, was struck by this trait. Among other instances, he met with one in the person of a Pennsylvania miller, Thomas Lea, "a sound American patriot, persuading himself that nothing good is done, and that no one has any brains, except in America; that the wit, the imagination, the genius of Europe are already in decrepitude;" and the duke added: "This error is to be found in almost all Americans, — legislators, administrators, as well as millers, and is less innocent there." In the year 1796 the House of Representatives debated whether to insert in the Reply to the President's Speech a passing remark that the nation was "the freest and most enlightened in the world," — a nation as yet in swaddling-clothes, which had neither literature, arts, sciences, nor history; nor even enough nationality to be sure that it was a nation. The moment was peculiarly ill-chosen for such a claim, because Europe was on the verge of an outburst of genius. Goethe and Schiller, Mozart and Haydn, Kant and Fichte, Cavendish and Herschel were making way for Walter Scott, Wordsworth, and

Shelley, Heine and Balzac, Beethoven and Hegel, Oersted and Cuvier, great physicists, biologists, geologists, chemists, mathematicians, metaphysicians, and historians by the score. Turner was painting his earliest landscapes, and Watt completing his latest steam-engine; Napoleon was taking command of the French armies, and Nelson of the English fleets; investigators, reformers, scholars, and philosophers swarmed, and the influence of enlightenment, even amid universal war, was working with an energy such as the world had never before conceived. The idea that Europe was in her decrepitude proved only ignorance and want of enlightenment, if not of freedom, on the part of Americans, who could only excuse their error by pleading that notwithstanding these objections, in matters which for the moment most concerned themselves Europe was a full century behind America. If they were right in thinking that the next necessity of human progress was to lift the average man upon an intellectual and social level with the most favored, they stood at least three generations nearer than Europe to their common goal. The destinies of the United States were certainly staked, without reserve or escape, on the soundness of this doubtful and even improbable principle, ignoring or overthrowing the institutions of church, aristocracy, family, army, and political intervention, which long experience had shown to be needed for the safety of society. Europe might be right in thinking that without such safeguards society must come to an end;

but even Europeans must concede that there was a chance, if no greater than one in a thousand, that America might, at least for a time, succeed. If this stake of temporal and eternal welfare stood on the winning card; if man actually should become more virtuous and enlightened, by mere process of growth, without church or paternal authority; if the average human being could accustom himself to reason with the logical processes of Descartes and Newton! — what then?

Then, no one could deny that the United States would win a stake such as defied mathematics. With all the advantages of science and capital, Europe must be slower than America to reach the common goal. American society might be both sober and sad, but except for negro slavery it was sound and healthy in every part. Stripped for the hardest work, every muscle firm and elastic, every ounce of brain ready for use, and not a trace of superfluous flesh on his nervous and supple body, the American stood in the world a new order of man. From Maine to Florida, society was in this respect the same, and was so organized as to use its human forces with more economy than could be approached by any society of the world elsewhere. Not only were artificial barriers carefully removed, but every influence that could appeal to ordinary ambition was applied. No brain or appetite active enough to be conscious of stimulants could fail to answer the intense incentive. Few human beings, however sluggish, could long resist the

temptation to acquire power; and the elements of
power were to be had in America almost for the asking. Reversing the old-world system, the American
stimulant increased in energy as it reached the lowest
and most ignorant class, dragging and whirling them
upward as in the blast of a furnace. The penniless and
homeless Scotch or Irish immigrant was caught and
consumed by it; for every stroke of the axe and the
hoe made him a capitalist, and made gentlemen of
his children. Wealth was the strongest agent for
moving the mass of mankind; but political power
was hardly less tempting to the more intelligent and
better-educated swarms of American-born citizens,
and the instinct of activity, once created, seemed
heritable and permanent in the race.

Compared with this lithe young figure, Europe was
actually in decrepitude. Mere class distinctions,
the *patois* or dialect of the peasantry, the fixity of
residence, the local costumes and habits marking a
history that lost itself in the renewal of identical generations, raised from birth barriers which paralyzed
half the population. Upon this mass of inert matter
rested the Church and the State, holding down activity of thought. Endless wars withdrew many hundred thousand men from production, and changed
them into agents of waste; huge debts, the evidence
of past wars and bad government, created interests to
support the system and fix its burdens on the laboring class; courts, with habits of extravagance that
shamed common-sense, helped to consume private

economics. All this might have been borne; but behind this stood aristocracies, sucking their nourishment from industry, producing nothing themselves, employing little or no active capital or intelligent labor, but pressing on the energies and ambition of society with the weight of an incubus. Picturesque and entertaining as these social anomalies were, they were better fitted for the theatre or for a museum of historical costumes than for an active workshop preparing to compete with such machinery as America would soon command. From an economical point of view, they were as incongruous as would have been the appearance of a mediæval knight in helmet and armor, with battle-axe and shield, to run the machinery of Arkwright's cotton-mill; but besides their bad economy they also tended to prevent the rest of society from gaining a knowledge of its own capacities. In Europe, the conservative habit of mind was fortified behind power. During nearly a century Voltaire himself — the friend of kings, the wit and poet, historian and philosopher of his age — had carried on, in daily terror, in exile and excommunication, a protest against an intellectual despotism contemptible even to its own supporters. Hardly was Voltaire dead, when Priestley, as great a man if not so great a wit, trying to do for England what Voltaire tried to do for France, was mobbed by the people of Birmingham and driven to America. Where Voltaire and Priestley failed, common men could not struggle; the weight of society stifled their thought. In America the balance between conservative and liberal forces was close; but in Europe conservatism held the physical power of government.   In Boston a young Buckminster might be checked for a time by his father's prayers or commands in entering the path that led toward freer thought; but youth beckoned him on, and every reward that society could offer was dangled before his eyes.   In London or Paris, Rome, Madrid, or Vienna, he must have sacrificed the worldly prospects of his life.

Granting that the American people were about to risk their future on a new experiment, they naturally wished to throw aside all burdens of which they could rid themselves.   Believing that in the long run interest, not violence, would rule the world, and that the United States must depend for safety and success on the interests they could create, they were tempted to look upon war and preparations for war as the worst of blunders; for they were sure that every dollar capitalized in industry was a means of overthrowing their enemies more effective than a thousand dollars spent on frigates or standing armies. The success of the American system was, from this point of view, a question of economy.   If they could relieve themselves from debts, taxes, armies, and government interference with industry, they must succeed in outstripping Europe in economy of production; and Americans were even then partly aware that if their machine were not so weakened by these economies as to break down in the working, it must of necessity break down every rival. If their theory was sound, when the day of competition should arrive, Europe might choose between American and Chinese institutions, but there would be no middle path ; she might become a confederated democracy, or a wreck.

Whether these ideas were sound or weak, they seemed self-evident to those Northern democrats who, like Albert Gallatin, were comparatively free from slave-owning theories, and understood the practical forces of society. If Gallatin wished to reduce the interference of government to a minimum, and cut down expenditures to nothing, he aimed not so much at saving money as at using it with the most certain effect. The revolution of 1800 was in his eyes chiefly political, because it was social ; but as a revolution of society, he and his friends hoped to make it the most radical that had occurred since the downfall of the Roman empire. Their ideas were not yet cleared by experience, and were confused by many contradictory prejudices, but wanted neither breadth nor shrewdness.

Many apparent inconsistencies grew from this undeveloped form of American thought, and gave rise to great confusion in the different estimates of American character that were made both at home and abroad.

That Americans should not be liked was natural ; but that they should not be understood was more significant by far. After the downfall of the French republic they had no right to expect a kind word

from Europe, and during the next twenty years
they rarely received one. The liberal movement of
Europe was cowed, and no one dared express democratic sympathies until the Napoleonic tempest had
passed. With this attitude Americans had no right
to find fault, for Europe cared less to injure them
than to protect herself. Nevertheless, observant readers could not but feel surprised that none of the
numerous Europeans who then wrote or spoke about
America seemed to study the subject seriously. The
ordinary traveller was apt to be little more reflec-
tive than a bee or an ant, but some of these critics
possessed powers far from ordinary ; yet Talleyrand
alone showed that had he but seen America a few
years later than he did, he might have suggested
some sufficient reason for apparent contradictions
that perplexed him in the national character. The
other travellers — great and small, from the Duc de
Liancourt to Basil Hall, a long and suggestive list —
were equally perplexed. They agreed in observing the
contradictions, but all, including Talleyrand, saw only
sordid motives. Talleyrand expressed extreme astonishment at the apathy of Americans in the face of
religious sectarians ; but he explained it by assuming
that the American ardor of the moment was absorbed in money-making. The explanation was evidently insufficient, for the Americans were capable
of feeling and showing excitement, even to their
great pecuniary injury, as they frequently proved ;
but in the foreigner's range of observation, love of

money was the most conspicuous and most common trait of American character. "There is, perhaps, no civilized country in the world," wrote Félix de Beaujour, soon after 1800, " where there is less generosity in the souls, and in the heads fewer of those illusions which make the charm or the consolation of life. Man here weighs everything, calculates everything, and sacrifices everything to his interest." An Englishman named Fearon, in 1818, expressed the same idea with more distinctness : " In going to America, I would say generally, the emigrant must expect to find, not an economical or cleanly people; not a social or generous people; not a people of enlarged ideas ; not a people of liberal opinions, or toward whom you can express your thoughts free as air ; not a people friendly to the advocates of liberty in Europe; not a people who understand liberty from investigation and principle ; not a people who comprehend the meaning of the words ' honor ' and ' generosity.' " Such quotations might be multiplied almost without limit. Rapacity was the accepted explanation of American peculiarities ; yet every traveller was troubled by inconsistencies that required explanations of a different kind. " It is not in order to hoard that the Americans are rapacious," observed Liancourt as early as 1796. The extravagance, or what economical Europeans thought extravagance, with which American women were allowed and encouraged to spend money, was as notorious in 1790 as a century later ; the recklessness with which Americans often risked their money, and the liberality with which they used it, were marked even then, in comparison with the ordinary European habit. Europeans saw such contradictions, but made no attempt to reconcile them. No foreigner of that day — neither poet, painter, nor philosopher — could detect in American life anything higher than vulgarity; for it was something beyond the range of their experience, which education and culture had not framed a formula to express. Moore came to Washington, and found there no loftier inspiration than any Federalist rhymester of Dennie's school.

> " Take Christians, Mohawks, democrats and all,
> From the rude wigwam to the Congress hall, —
> From man the savage, whether slaved or free,
> To man the civilized, less tame than he:
> 'T is one dull chaos, one unfertile strife
> Betwixt half-polished and half-barbarous life;
> Where every ill the ancient world can brew
> Is mixed with every grossness of the new;
> Where all corrupts, though little can entice,
> And nothing 's known of luxury but vice."

Moore's two small volumes of Epistles, printed in 1807, contained much more so-called poetry of the same tone, — poetry more polished and less respectable than that of Barlow and Dwight; while, as though to prove that the Old World knew what grossness was, he embalmed in his lines the slanders which the Scotch libeller Callender invented against Jefferson : —

> " The weary statesman for repose hath fled
> From halls of council to his negro's shed ;
> Where, blest, he woos some black Aspasia's grace,
> And dreams of freedom in his slave's embrace."

To leave no doubt of his meaning, he explained in a footnote that his allusion was to the President of the United States ; and yet even Moore, trifler and butterfly as he was, must have seen, if he would, that between the morals of politics and society in America and those then prevailing in Europe, there was no room for comparison, — there was room only for contrast.

Moore was but an echo of fashionable England in his day. He seldom affected moral sublimity ; and had he in his wanderings met a race of embodied angels, he would have sung of them or to them in the slightly erotic notes which were so well received in the society he loved to frequent and flatter. His remarks upon American character betrayed more temper than truth ; but even in this respect he expressed only the common feeling of Europeans, which was echoed by the Federalist society of the United States. Englishmen especially indulged in unbounded invective against the sordid character of American society, and in shaping their national policy on this contempt they carried their theory into practice with so much energy as to produce its own refutation. To their astonishment and anger, a day came when the Americans, in defiance of self-interest and in contradiction of all the qualities ascribed to them, insisted

on declaring war; and readers of this narrative will
be surprised at the cry of incredulity, not unmixed
with terror, with which Englishmen started to their
feet when they woke from their delusion on seeing
what they had been taught to call the meteor flag of
England, which had burned terrific at Copenhagen
and Trafalgar, suddenly waver and fall on the bloody
deck of the " Guerriere."   Fearon and Beaujour,
with a score of other contemporary critics, could see
neither generosity, economy, honor, nor ideas of any
kind in the American breast; yet the obstinate repetition of these denials itself betrayed a lurking fear
of the social forces whose strength they were candid
enough to record.   What was it that, as they complained, turned the European peasant into a new
man within half an hour after landing at New York?
Englishmen were never at a loss to understand the
poetry of more prosaic emotions.   Neither they nor
any of their kindred failed in later times to feel the
" large excitement " of the country boy, whose " spirit
leaped within him to be gone before him," when the
lights of London first flared in the distance; yet none
seemed ever to feel the larger excitement of the
American immigrant.   Among the Englishmen who
criticised the United States was one greater than
Moore, — one who thought himself at home only in
the stern beauty of a moral presence.   Of all poets,
living or dead, Wordsworth felt most keenly what
he called the still, sad music of humanity; yet the
highest conception he could create of America was

not more poetical than that of any Cumberland beggar he might have met in his morning walk : —

> " Long-wished-for sight, the Western World appeared ;
> And when the ship was moored, I leaped ashore
> Indignantly, — resolved to be a man,
> Who, having o'er the past no power, would live
> No longer in subjection to the past,
> With abject mind — from a tyrannic lord
> Inviting penance, fruitlessly endured.
> So, like a fugitive whose feet have cleared
> Some boundary which his followers may not cross
> In prosecution of their deadly chase,
> Respiring, I looked round.   How bright the sun,
> The breeze how soft !   Can anything produced
> In the Old World compare, thought I, for power
> And majesty, with this tremendous stream
> Sprung from the desert ?   And behold a city
> Fresh, youthful, and aspiring ! . . .
> > > > Sooth to say,
> On nearer view, a motley spectacle
> Appeared, of high pretensions — unreproved
> But by the obstreperous voice of higher still ;
> Big passions strutting on a petty stage,
> Which a detached spectator may regard
> Not unamused.   But ridicule demands
> Quick change of objects ; and to laugh alone,
> . . . in the very centre of the crowd
> To keep the secret of a poignant scorn,
> > > > . . . is least fit
> For the gross spirit of mankind."

Thus Wordsworth, although then at his prime, indulging in what sounded like a boast that he alone had felt the sense sublime of something interfused, whose dwelling is the light of setting suns, and the round ocean, and the living air, and the blue sky, and in the mind of man, — even he, to whose moods the heavy and the weary weight of all this unintelligible world was lightened by his deeper sympathies with nature and the soul, could do no better, when he stood in the face of American democracy, than " keep the secret of a poignant scorn."

Possibly the view of Wordsworth and Moore, of Weld, Dennie, and Dickens was right. The American democrat possessed little art of expression, and did not watch his own emotions with a view of uttering them either in prose or verse; he never told more of himself than the world might have assumed without listening to him. Only with diffidence could history attribute to such a class of men a wider range of thought or feeling than they themselves cared to proclaim. Yet the difficulty of denying or even ignoring the wider range was still greater, for no one questioned the force or the scope of an emotion which caused the poorest peasant in Europe to see what was invisible to poet and philosopher, — the dim outline of a mountain-summit across the ocean, rising high above the mist and mud of American democracy. As though to call attention to some such difficulty, European and American critics, while affirming that Americans were a race without illusions or enlarged ideas, declared in the same breath that Jefferson was a visionary whose theories would cause the heavens to fall upon them. Year after year, with endless iteration, in every accent of contempt, rage, and despair, they repeated this charge against Jefferson. Every foreigner and Federalist agreed that he was a man of illusions, dangerous to society and unbounded in power of evil; but if this view of his character was right, the same visionary qualities seemed also to be a national trait, for every one admitted that Jefferson's opinions, in one form or another, were shared by a majority of the American people.

Illustrations might be carried much further, and might be drawn from every social class and from every period in national history. Of all presidents, Abraham Lincoln has been considered the most typical representative of American society, chiefly because his mind, with all its practical qualities, also inclined, in certain directions, to idealism. Lincoln was born in 1809, the moment when American character stood in lowest esteem. Ralph Waldo Emerson, a more distinct idealist, was born in 1803. William Ellery Channing, another idealist, was born in 1780. Men like John Fitch, Oliver Evans, Robert Fulton, Joel Barlow, John Stevens, and Eli Whitney were all classed among visionaries. The whole society of Quakers belonged in the same category. The records of the popular religious sects abounded in examples of idealism and illusion to such an extent that the masses seemed hardly to find comfort or hope in any authority, however old or well established. In religion as in politics, Americans seemed to require a system which gave play to their imagination and their hopes.

Some misunderstanding must always take place when the observer is at cross-purposes with the society he describes.   Wordsworth might have convinced himself by a moment's thought that no country could act on the imagination as America acted upon the instincts of the ignorant and poor, without some quality that deserved better treatment than poignant scorn ; but perhaps this was only one among innumerable cases in which the unconscious poet breathed an atmosphere which the self-conscious poet could not penetrate.   With equal reason he might have taken the opposite view, — that the hard, practical, money-getting American democrat, who had neither generosity nor honor nor imagination, and who inhabited cold shades where fancy sickened and where genius died, was in truth living in a world of dream, and acting a drama more instinct with poetry than all the avatars of the East, walking in gardens of emerald and rubies, in ambition already ruling the world and guiding Nature with a kinder and wiser hand than had ever yet been felt in human history.   From this point his critics never approached him, — they stopped at a stone's throw ; and at the moment when they declared that the man's mind had no illusions, they added that he was a knave or a lunatic.   Even on his practical and sordid side, the American might easily have been represented as a victim to illusion. If the Englishman had lived as the American speculator did, — in the future, — the hyperbole of enthusiasm would have seemed less monstrous.   " Look

at my wealth!" cried the American to his foreign
visitor. "See these solid mountains of salt and iron,
of lead, copper, silver, and gold! See these magnificent cities scattered broadcast to the Pacific!
See my cornfields rustling and waving in the summer breeze from ocean to ocean, so far that the
sun itself is not high enough to mark where the
distant mountains bound my golden seas! Look at
this continent of mine, fairest of created worlds, as
she lies turning up to the sun's never-failing caress
her broad and exuberant breasts, overflowing with
milk for her hundred million children! See how
she glows with youth, health, and love!" Perhaps
it was not altogether unnatural that the foreigner,
on being asked to see what needed centuries to produce, should have looked about him with bewilder-
ment and indignation. "Gold! cities! cornfields!
continents! Nothing of the sort! I see nothing
but tremendous wastes, where sickly men and women
are dying of home-sickness or are scalped by sav-
ages! mountain-ranges a thousand miles long, with
no means of getting to them, and nothing in them
when you get there! swamps and forests choked
with their own rotten ruins! nor hope of better for a
thousand years! Your story is a fraud, and you
are a liar and swindler!"

Met in this spirit, the American, half perplexed
and half defiant, retaliated by calling his antagonist
a fool, and by mimicking his heavy tricks of manner.
For himself he cared little, but his dream was his

whole existence.   The men who denounced him admitted that they left him in his forest-swamp quaking
with fever, but clinging in the delirium of death to
the illusions of his dazzled brain.   No class of men
could be required to support their convictions with a
steadier faith, or pay more devotedly with their persons for the mistakes of their judgment.   Whether
imagination or greed led them to describe more than
actually existed, they still saw no more than any inventor or discoverer must have seen in order to give
him the energy of success.   They said to the rich as
to the poor, " Come and share our limitless riches!
Come and help us bring to light these unimaginable
stores of wealth and power!"   The poor came, and
from them were seldom heard complaints of decep-
tion or delusion.   Within a moment, by the mere
contact of a moral atmosphere, they saw the gold
and jewels, the summer cornfields and the glowing
continent.   The rich for a long time stood aloof, —
they were timid and narrow-minded ; but this was
not all, — between them and the American democrat
was a gulf.

The charge that Americans were too fond of money
to win the confidence of Europeans was a curious inconsistency ; yet this was a common belief.   If the
American deluded himself and led others to their
death by baseless speculations ; if he buried those he
loved in a gloomy forest where they quaked and died
while he persisted in seeing there a splendid, healthy,
and well-built city, — no one could deny that he sac-

rificed wife and child to his greed for gain, that the
dollar was his god, and a sordid avarice his demon.
Yet had this been the whole truth, no European capitalist would have hesitated to make money out of his
grave; for, avarice against avarice, no more sordid or
meaner type existed in America than could be shown
on every 'Change in Europe.   With much more reason Americans might have suspected that in America Englishmen found everywhere a silent influence,
which they found nowhere in Europe, and which had
nothing to do with avarice or with the dollar, but, on
the contrary, seemed likely at any moment to sacrifice the dollar in a cause and for an object so illusory
that most Englishmen could not endure to hear it
discussed.   European travellers who passed through
America noticed that everywhere, in the White House
at Washington and in log-cabins beyond the Alleghanies, except for a few Federalists, every American,
from Jefferson and Gallatin down to the poorest
squatter, seemed to nourish an idea that he was doing
what he could to overthrow the tyranny which the
past had fastened on the human mind.   Nothing
was easier than to laugh at the ludicrous expressions
of this simple-minded conviction, or to cry out against
its coarseness, or grow angry with its prejudices; to
see its nobler side, to feel the beatings of a heart un-
derneath the sordid surface of a gross humanity, was
not so easy.   Europeans seemed seldom or never conscious that the sentiment could possess a noble side,
but found only matter for complaint in the remark

that every American democrat believed himself to
be working for the overthrow of tyranny, aristocracy,
hereditary privilege, and priesthood, wherever they existed. Even where the American did not openly proclaim this conviction in words, he carried so dense an
atmosphere of the sentiment with him in his daily
life as to give respectable Europeans an uneasy sense
of remoteness.

Of all historical problems, the nature of a national
character is the most difficult and the most important.
Readers will be troubled, at almost every chapter of
the coming narrative, by the want of some formula
to explain what share the popular imagination bore
in the system pursued by government. The acts
of the American people during the administrations
of Jefferson and Madison were judged at the time by
no other test. According as bystanders believed
American character to be hard, sordid, and free
from illusion, they were severe and even harsh in
judgment. This rule guided the governments of
England and France. Federalists in the United
States, knowing more of the circumstances, often
attributed to the democratic instinct a visionary
quality which they regarded as sentimentality, and
charged with many bad consequences. If their view
was correct, history could occupy itself to no better
purpose than in ascertaining the nature and force of
the quality which was charged with results so serious ;
but nothing was more elusive than the spirit of American democracy. Jefferson, the literary representa-

tive of the class, spoke chiefly for Virginians, and
dreaded so greatly his own reputation as a visionary that he seldom or never uttered his whole thought.
Gallatin and Madison were still more cautious. The
press in no country could give shape to a mental condition so shadowy. The people themselves, although
millions in number, could not have expressed their
finer instincts had they tried, and might not have
recognized them if expressed by others.

In the early days of colonization, every new settlement represented an idea and proclaimed a mission.
Virginia was founded by a great, liberal movement
aiming at the spread of English liberty and empire.
The Pilgrims of Plymouth, the Puritans of Boston,
the Quakers of Pennsylvania, all avowed a moral
purpose, and began by making institutions that consciously reflected a moral idea. No such character
belonged to the colonization of 1800. From Lake
Erie to Florida, in long, unbroken line, pioneers were
at work, cutting into the forests with the energy of
so many beavers, and with no more express moral purpose than the beavers they drove away. The civilization they carried with them was rarely illumined
by an idea; they sought room for no new truth, and
aimed neither at creating, like the Puritans, a government of saints, nor, like the Quakers, one of love and
peace; they left such experiments behind them, and
wrestled only with the hardest problems of frontier
life. No wonder that foreign observers, and even the
educated, well-to-do Americans of the sea-coast, could

seldom see anything to admire in the ignorance and
brutality of frontiersmen, and should declare that virtue and wisdom no longer guided the United States!
What they saw was not encouraging. To a new society, ignorant and semi-barbarous, a mass of dema-
gogues insisted on applying every stimulant that could
inflame its worst appetites, while at the same instant
taking away every influence that had hitherto helped
to restrain its passions. Greed for wealth, lust for
power, yearning for the blank void of savage freedom such as Indians and wolves delighted in, — these
were the fires that flamed under the caldron of American society, in which, as conservatives believed, the
old, well-proven, conservative crust of religion, government, family, and even common respect for age,
education, and experience was rapidly melting away,
and was indeed already broken into fragments, swept
about by the seething mass of scum ever rising in
greater quantities to the surface.

Against this Federalist and conservative view of
democratic tendencies, democrats protested in a
thousand forms, but never in any mode of expression
which satisfied them all, or explained their whole
character. Probably Jefferson came nearest to the
mark, for he represented the hopes of science as well
as the prejudices of Virginia; but Jefferson's writings
may be searched from beginning to end without revealing the whole measure of the man, far less of the
movement. Here and there in his letters a suggestion
was thrown out, as though by chance, revealing larger

hopes, — as in 1815, at a moment of despondency, he wrote: "I fear from the experience of the last twenty-five years that morals do not of necessity advance hand in hand with the sciences." In 1800, in the flush of triumph, he believed that his task in the world was to establish a democratic republic, with the sciences for an intellectual field, and physical and moral advancement keeping pace with their advance. Without an excessive introduction of more recent ideas, he might be imagined to define democratic progress, in the somewhat affected precision of his French philosophy: "Progress is either physical or intellectual. If we can bring it about that men are on the average an inch taller in the next generation than in this; if they are an inch larger round the chest; if their brain is an ounce or two heavier, and their life a year or two longer, — that is progress. If fifty years hence the average man shall invariably argue from two ascertained premises where he now jumps to a conclusion from a single supposed revelation, — that is progress! I expect it to be made here, under our democratic stimulants, on a great scale, until every man is potentially an athlete in body and an Aristotle in mind." To this doctrine the New Englander replied, "What will you do for moral progress?" Every possible answer to this question opened a chasm. No doubt Jefferson held the faith that men would improve morally with their physical and intellectual growth; but he had no idea of any moral improvement other than that which came by nature. He could not tolerate a priesthood, a state church, or revealed religion. Conservatives, who could tolerate no society without such pillars of order, were, from their point of view, right in answering, " Give us rather the worst despotism of Europe, — there our souls at least may have a chance of salvation !" To their minds vice and virtue were not relative, but fixed terms. The Church was a divine institution. How could a ship hope to reach port when the crew threw overboard sails, spars, and compass, unshipped their rudder, and all the long day thought only of eating and drinking. Nay, even should the new experiment succeed in a worldly sense, what was a man profited if he gained the whole world, and lost his own soul ? The Lord God was a jealous God, and visited the sins of the parents upon the children ; but what worse sin could be conceived than for a whole nation to join their chief in chanting the strange hymn with which Jefferson, a new false prophet, was deceiving and betraying his people : " It. does me no injury for my neighbor to say there are twenty Gods or no God !"

On this ground conservatism took its stand, as it had hitherto done with success in every similar emergency in the world's history, and fixing its eyes on moral standards of its own, refused to deal with the subject as further open to argument. The two parties stood facing opposite ways, and could see no common ground of contact.

Yet even then one part of the American social

system was proving itself to be rich in results. The average American was more intelligent than the average European, and was becoming every year still more active-minded as the new movement of society caught him up and swept him through a life of more varied experiences. On all sides the national mind responded to its stimulants. Deficient as the American was in the machinery of higher instruction; remote, poor; unable by any exertion to acquire the training, the capital, or even the elementary text-books he needed for a fair development of his natural powers, — his native energy and ambition already responded to the spur applied to them. Some of his triumphs were famous throughout the world; for Benjamin Franklin had raised high the reputation of American printers, and the actual President of the United States, who signed with Franklin the treaty of peace with Great Britain, was the son of a small farmer, and had himself kept a school in his youth. In both these cases social recognition followed success; but the later triumphs of the American mind were becoming more and more popular. John Fitch was not only one of the poorest, but one of the least-educated Yankees who ever made a name; he could never spell with tolerable correctness, and his life ended as it began, — in the lowest social obscurity. Eli Whitney was better educated than Fitch, but had neither wealth, social influence, nor patron to back his ingenuity. In the year 1800 Eli Terry, another Connecticut Yankee of the same class, took into his

employ two young men to help him make wooden
clocks, and this was the capital on which the greatest
clock-manufactory in the world began its operations.
In 1797 Asa Whittemore, a Massachusetts Yankee,
invented a machine to make cards for carding wool,
which "operated as if it had a soul," and became
the foundation for a hundred subsequent patents.   In
1790 Jacob Perkins, of Newburyport, invented a machine capable of cutting and turning out two hundred
thousand nails a day; and then invented a process
for transferring engraving from a very small steel
cylinder to copper, which revolutionized cotton-print-
ing.   The British traveller Weld, passing through
Wilmington, stopped, as Liancourt had done before
him, to see the great flour-mills on the Brandywine.
"The improvements," he said, "which have been
made in the machinery of the flour-mills in America
are very great.   The chief of these consist in a new
application of the screw, and the introduction of what
are called elevators, the idea of which was evidently
borrowed from the chain-pump."   This was the invention of Oliver Evans, a native of Delaware, whose
parents were in very humble life, but who was himself, in spite of every disadvantage, an inventive genius of the first order.   Robert Fulton, who in 1800
was in Paris with Joel Barlow, sprang from the same
source in Pennsylvania.   John Stevens, a native of
New York, belonged to a more favored class, but followed the same impulses.   All these men were the
outcome of typical American society, and all their

inventions transmuted the democratic instinct into a practical and tangible shape. Who would undertake to say that there was a limit to the fecundity of this teeming source? Who that saw only the narrow, practical, money-getting nature of these devices could venture to assert that as they wrought their end and raised the standard of millions, they would not also raise the creative power of those millions to a higher plane? If the priests and barons who set their names to Magna Charta had been told that in a few centuries every swine-herd and cobbler's apprentice would write and read with an ease such as few kings could then command, and reason with better logic than any university could then practise, the priest and baron would have been more incredulous than any man who was told in 1800 that within another five centuries the ploughboy would go a-field whistling a sonata of Beethoven, and figure out in quaternions the relation of his furrows. The American democrat knew so little of art that among his popular illusions he could not then nourish artistic ambition; but leaders like Jefferson, Gallatin, and Barlow might without extravagance count upon a coming time when diffused ease and education should bring the masses into familiar contact with higher forms of human achievement, and their vast creative power, turned toward a nobler culture, might rise to the level of that democratic genius which found expression in the Parthenon; might revel in the delights of a new Buonarotti and a richer Titian; might create for

five hundred million people the America of thought
and art which alone could satisfy their omnivorous
ambition.

Whether the illusions, so often affirmed and so
often denied to the American people, took such forms
or not, these were in effect the problems that lay before American society: Could it transmute its social power into the higher forms of thought? Could
it provide for the moral and intellectual needs of
mankind?   Could it take permanent political shape?
Could it give new life to religion and art?   Could it
create and maintain in the mass of mankind those
habits of mind which had hitherto belonged to men
of science alone?   Could it physically develop the
convolutions of the human brain?   Could it produce, or was it compatible with, the differentiation
of a higher variety of the human race? Nothing
less than this was necessary for its complete success.

CHAPTER VII.

THE man who mounted the steps of the Capitol, March 4, 1801, to claim the place of an equal between Pitt and Bonaparte, possessed a character which showed itself in acts; but person and manner can be known only by contemporaries, and the liveliest description was worth less than a moment of personal contact. Jefferson was very tall, six feet two-and-a-half inches in height; sandy-complexioned; shy in manner, seeming cold; awkward in attitude, and with little in his bearing that suggested command. Senator Maclay of Pennsylvania described him in 1790, when he had returned from France to become Secretary of State, and appeared before a Committee of the Senate to answer questions about foreign relations.

" Jefferson is a slender man," wrote the senator;[1] "has rather the air of stiffness in his manner. His clothes seem too small for him. He sits in a lounging manner, on one hip commonly, and with one of his shoulders elevated much above the other. His face has a sunny aspect. His whole figure has a loose, shackling air. He had a rambling, vacant look, and nothing of

[1] Sketches of Debate in the First Senate, by William Maclay, p. 212.

that firm collected deportment which I expected would
dignify the presence of a secretary or minister. I looked
for gravity, but a laxity of manner seemed shed about
him. He spoke almost without ceasing ; but even his
discourse partook of his personal demeanor. It was
loose and rambling ; and yet he scattered information
wherever he went, and some even brilliant sentiments
sparkled from him."

Maclay was one of the earliest members of the
Republican party, and his description was not un-
friendly. Augustus Foster, Secretary of the British
Legation, described Jefferson as he appeared in
1804 : [1] —

"He was a tall man, with a very red freckled face,
and gray neglected hair ; his manners good-natured,
frank, and rather friendly, though he had somewhat of a
cynical expression of countenance. He wore a blue coat,
a thick gray-colored hairy waistcoat, with a red under-
waistcoat lapped over it, green velveteen breeches with
pearl buttons, yarn stockings, and slippers down at the
heels, — his appearance being very much like that of a
tall, large-boned farmer."

In the middle of the seventeenth century the celebrated Cardinal de Retz formed a judgment of the
newly-elected Pope from his remark, at a moment
when minds were absorbed in his election, that he
had for two years used the same pen. "It is only
a trifle," added De Retz, " but I have often observed
that the smallest things are sometimes better marks

[1] The Quarterly Review (London, 1841), p. 24.

than the greatest." Perhaps dress could never be considered a trifle. One of the greatest of modern writers first made himself famous by declaring that society was founded upon *cloth;* and Jefferson, at moments of some interest in his career as President, seemed to regard his peculiar style of dress as a matter of political importance, while the Federalist newspapers never ceased ridiculing the corduroy small-clothes, red-plush waistcoat, and sharp-toed boots with which he expressed his contempt for fashion.

For eight years this tall, loosely built, somewhat stiff figure, in red waistcoat and yarn stockings, slippers down at the heel, and clothes that seemed too small for him, may be imagined as Senator Maclay described him, sitting on one hip, with one shoulder high above the other, talking almost without ceasing to his visitors at the White House. His skin was thin, peeling from his face on exposure to the sun, and giving it a tettered appearance. This sandy face, with hazel eyes and sunny aspect; this loose, shackling person; this rambling and often brilliant conversation, belonged to the controlling influences of American history, more necessary to the story than three-fourths of the official papers, which only hid the truth. Jefferson's personality during these eight years appeared to be the government, and impressed itself, like that of Bonaparte, although by a different process, on the mind of the nation. In the village simplicity of Washington he was more than a king,

for he was alone in social as well as in political pre-
eminence. Except the British Legation, no house in
Washington was open to general society; the whole
mass of politicians, even the Federalists, were dependent on Jefferson and " The Palace " for amusement;
and if they refused to go there, they " lived like bears,
brutalized and stupefied." [1]

Jefferson showed his powers at their best in his
own house, where among friends as genial and cheer-
ful as himself his ideas could flow freely, and could
be discussed with sympathy. Such were the men
with whom he surrounded himself by choice, and
none but such were invited to enter his Cabinet.
First and oldest of his political associates was James
Madison, about to become Secretary of State, whose
character also described itself, and whose personality
was as distinct as that of his chief. A small man,
quiet, somewhat precise in manner, pleasant, fond
of conversation, with a certain mixture of ease and
dignity in his address, Madison had not so much as
Jefferson of the commanding attitude which imposed
respect on the world. " He has much more the appearance of what I have imagined a Roman cardinal
to be," wrote Senator Mills of Massachusetts in 1815.[2]
An imposing presence had much to do with political
influence, and Madison labored under serious disadvantage in the dryness of his personality. Political

[1] The Quarterly Review (London, 1841), p. 23.
[2] Massachusetts Historical Society's Proceedings, vol. xix. 1881–
1882.

opponents of course made fun of him. "As to Jemmy Madison, — oh, poor Jemmy! — he is but a withered little apple-john," wrote Washington Irving in 1812, instinctively applying the Knickerbocker view of history to national concerns.

"In his dress," said one who knew him,[1] "he was not at all eccentric or given to dandyism, but always appeared neat and genteel, and in the costume of a well-bred and tasty old-school gentleman. I have heard in early life he sometimes wore light-colored clothes; but from the time I first knew him . . . never any other color than black, his coat being cut in what is termed dress-fashion; his breeches short, with buckles at the knees, black silk stockings, and shoes with strings, or long fair top-boots when out in cold weather, or when he rode on horseback, of which he was fond. . . . He wore powder on his hair, which was dressed full over the ears, tied behind, and brought to a point above the forehead, to cover in some degree his baldness, as may be noticed in all the likenesses taken of him."

Madison had a sense of humor, felt in his conversation, and detected in the demure cast of his flexile lips, but leaving no trace in his published writings. Small in stature, in deportment modest to the point of sensitive reserve, in address simple and pleasing, in feature rather thoughtful and benevolent than strong, he was such a man as Jefferson, who so much disliked contentious and self-asserting manners, loved

[1] Grigsby's Convention of 1776, p. 85.

to keep by his side. Sir Augustus Foster liked Mr.
Madison, although in 1812 Madison sent him out of
the country : —

"I thought Mr. Jefferson more of a statesman and
man of the world than Mr. Madison, who was rather too
much the disputatious pleader; yet the latter was better
informed, and moreover a social, jovial, and good-
humored companion, full of anecdote, sometimes rather
of a loose description, but oftener of a political and historical interest. He was a little man with small features,
rather wizened when I saw him, but occasionally lit up
with a good-natured smile. He wore a black coat, stockings with shoes buckled, and had his hair powdered, with
a tail."

The third aristocrat in this democratic triumvirate
was Albert Gallatin, marked by circumstances even
more than by the President's choice for the post of
Secretary of the Treasury. Like the President and
the Secretary of State, Gallatin was born and bred a
gentleman; in person and manners he was well fitted
for the cabinet-table over which Jefferson presided.
Gallatin possessed the personal force which was somewhat lacking in his two friends. His appearance
impressed by-standers with a sense of strength. His
complexion was dark; his eyes were hazel and full of
expression; his hair black, and like Madison he was
becoming bald. From long experience, at first among
the democrats of western Pennsylvania, and afterward as a leader in the House of Representatives, he
had lost all shyness in dealing with men. His long

prominent nose and lofty forehead showed character, and his eyes expressed humor. A slight foreign
accent betrayed his Genevan origin.   Gallatin was
also one of the best talkers in America, and perhaps
the best-informed man in the country; for his laborious mind had studied America with infinite care, and
he retained so much knowledge of European affairs
as to fit him equally for the State Department or the
Treasury.   Three more agreeable men than Jefferson,
Madison, and Gallatin were never collected round the
dinner-table of the White House; and their difference
in age was enough to add zest to their friendship; for
Jefferson was born in 1743, Madison in 1751, and
Gallatin in 1761.   While the President was nearly
sixty years old, his Secretary of the Treasury had the
energy and liberality of forty.

Jefferson was the first President inaugurated at
Washington, and the ceremony, necessarily simple,
was made still simpler for political reasons.   The
retiring President was not present at the installation
of his successor.   In Jefferson's eyes a revolution had
taken place as vast as that of 1776; and if this was
his belief, perhaps the late President was wise to
retire from a stage where everything was arranged
to point a censure upon his principles, and where he
would have seemed, in his successor's opinion, as
little in place as George III. would have appeared
at the installation of President Washington.   The
collapse of government which marked the last weeks
of February, 1801, had been such as to leave of the

old Cabinet only Samuel Dexter of Massachusetts,
the Secretary of the Treasury, and Benjamin Stoddert of Maryland, the Secretary of the Navy, still in
office. John Marshall, the late Secretary of State,
had been appointed, six weeks before, Chief-Justice
of the Supreme Court.

In this first appearance of John Marshall as Chief-
Justice, to administer the oath of office, lay the
dramatic climax of the inauguration. The retiring
President, acting for what he supposed to be the best
interests of the country, by one of his last acts of
power, deliberately intended to perpetuate the principles of his administration, placed at the head of the
judiciary, for life, a man as obnoxious to Jefferson as
the bitterest New England Calvinist could have been;
for he belonged to that class of conservative Virginians whose devotion to President Washington, and
whose education in the common law, caused them to
hold Jefferson and his theories in antipathy. The
new President and his two Secretaries were political
philanthropists, bent on restricting the powers of the
national government in the interests of human liberty. The Chief-Justice, a man who in grasp of mind
and steadiness of purpose had no superior, perhaps
no equal, was bent on enlarging the powers of government in the interests of justice and nationality.
As they stood face to face on this threshold of their
power, each could foresee that the contest between
them would end only with life.

If Jefferson and his two friends were the most

aristocratic of democrats, John Marshall was of all aristocrats the most democratic in manners and appearance.

" A tall, slender figure," wrote Joseph Story in 1808,[1] " not graceful or imposing, but erect and steady. His hair is black, his eyes small and twinkling, his forehead rather low; but his features are in general harmonious. His manners are plain yet dignified, and an unaffected modesty diffuses itself through all his actions. His dress is very simple yet neat; his language chaste, but hardly elegant; it does not flow rapidly, but it seldom wants precision. In conversation he is quite familiar, but is occasionally embarrassed by a hesitancy and drawling. . . . I love his laugh, — it is too hearty for an intriguer; and his good temper and unwearied patience are equally agreeable on the bench and in the study."

The unaffected simplicity of Marshall's life was delightful to all who knew him, for it sprang from the simplicity of his mind. Never self-conscious, his dignity was never affected by his situation. Bishop Meade,[2] who was proud of the Chief-Justice as one of his flock, being in a street near Marshall's house one morning between daybreak and sunrise, met the Chief-Justice on horseback, with a bag of clover-seed lying before him, which he was carrying to his little farm at seed-time. Simple as American life was, his habits were remarkable for modest plainness; and only the character of his mind, which seemed to have

[1] Life of Story, i. 166.
[2] Old Churches of Virginia, ii. 222.

no flaw, made his influence irresistible upon all who were brought within its reach.

Nevertheless this great man nourished one weakness. Pure in life; broad in mind, and the despair of bench and bar for the unswerving certainty of his legal method; almost idolized by those who stood nearest him, and loving warmly in return, — this excellent and amiable man clung to one rooted prejudice: he detested Thomas Jefferson. He regarded with quiet, unspoken, but immovable antipathy the character and doings of the philosopher standing before him, about to take the oath to preserve, protect, and defend the Constitution. No argument or entreaty affected his conviction that Jefferson was not an honest man. "By weakening the office of President he will increase his personal power," were Marshall's words, written at this time;[1] "the morals of the author of the letter to Mazzei cannot be pure." Jefferson in return regarded Marshall with a repugnance tinged by a shade of some deeper feeling, almost akin to fear. "The judge's inveteracy is profound," he once wrote,[2] "and his mind of that gloomy malignity which will never let him forego the opportunity of satiating it on a victim."

Another person, with individuality not less marked, took the oath of office the same day. When the Sen-

[1] Marshall to Hamilton, Jan. 1, 1801 ; Hamilton's Works, vi. 502.

[2] Jefferson to Gallatin, Sept. 27, 1810; Gallatin's Writings, i. 492.

ate met at ten o'clock on the morning of March 4, 1801, Aaron Burr stood at the desk, and having duly sworn to support the Constitution, took his seat in the chair as Vice-President. This quiet, gentlemanly, and rather dignified figure, hardly taller than Madison, and dressed in much the same manner, impressed with favor all who first met him. An aristocrat imbued in the morality of Lord Chesterfield and Napoleon Bonaparte, Colonel Burr was the chosen head of Northern democracy, idol of the wards of New York city, and aspirant to the highest offices he could reach by means legal or beyond the law; for as he pleased himself with saying, after the manner of the First Consul of the French Republic, "Great souls care little for small morals." Among the other party leaders who have been mentioned, — Jefferson, Madison, Gallatin, Marshall, — not one was dishonest. The exaggerations or equivocations that Jefferson allowed himself, which led to the deep-rooted conviction of Marshall that he did not tell the truth and must therefore be dangerous, amounted to nothing when compared with the dishonesty of a corrupt man. Had the worst political charges against Jefferson been true, he would not have been necessarily corrupt. The self-deception inherent in every struggle for personal power was not the kind of immorality which characterized Colonel Burr. Jefferson, if his enemies were to be believed, might occasionally make misstatements of fact; yet he was true to the faith of his life, and would rather have abdicated his office and foregone his honors than have compassed even an imaginary wrong against the principles he professed. His life, both private and public, was pure. His associates, like Madison, Gallatin, and Monroe, were men upon whose reputations no breath of scandal rested. The standard of morality at Washington, both in private society and in politics, was respectable. For this reason Colonel Burr was a new power in the government; for being in public and in private life an adventurer of the same school as scores who were then seeking fortune in the antechambers of Bonaparte and Pitt, he became a loadstone for every other adventurer who frequented New York or whom the chances of politics might throw into office. The Vice-President wielded power, for he was the certain centre of corruption.

Thus when the doors of the Senate chamber were thrown open, and the new President of the United States appeared on the threshold; when the Vice-President rose from his chair, and Jefferson sat down in it, with Aaron Burr on his right hand and John Marshall on his left, the assembled senators looked up at three men who profoundly disliked and distrusted each other.

John Davis, one of many Englishmen who were allowed by Burr to attach themselves to him on the chance of some future benefit to be derived from them, asserted in a book of American travels published in London two years afterward, that he was present at the inauguration, and that Jefferson rode

on horseback to the Capitol, and after hitching his
horse to the palings, went in to take the oath. This
story, being spread by the Federalist newspapers,
was accepted by the Republicans and became a legend
of the Capitol. In fact Davis was not then at
Washington, and his story was untrue. Afterward
as President, Jefferson was in the habit of going
on horseback, rather than in a carriage, wherever
business called him, and the Federalists found fault
with him for doing so. " He makes it a point," they
declared,[1] " when he has occasion to visit the Capitol
to meet the representatives of the nation on public
business, to go on a single horse, which he leads
into the shed and hitches to a peg." Davis wished
to write a book that should amuse Englishmen, and
in order to give an air of truth to invention, he
added that he was himself present at the ceremony.
Jefferson was then living as Vice-President at Con-
rad's boarding-house, within a stone's throw of the
Capitol. He did not mount his horse only to ride
across the square and dismount in a crowd of observers. Doubtless he wished to offer an example of republican simplicity, and he was not unwilling to
annoy his opponents ; but the ceremony was conducted with proper form.

Edward Thornton, then in charge of the British
Legation at Washington, wrote to Lord Grenville,
then Foreign Secretary in Pitt's administration, a
despatch enclosing the new President's Inaugural

[1] Evening Post, April 20, 1802.

Address, with comments upon its democratic tendencies; and after a few remarks on this subject, he added: [1] —

" The same republican spirit which runs through this performance, and which in many passages discovers some bitterness through all the sentiments of conciliation and philanthropy with which it is overcharged, Mr. Jefferson affected to display in performing the customary ceremonies. He came from his own lodgings to the House where the Congress convenes, and which goes by the name of the Capitol, on foot, in his ordinary dress, escorted by a body of militia artillery from the neighboring State, and accompanied by the Secretaries of the Navy and the Treasury, and a number of his political friends in the House of Representatives. He was received by Mr. Burr, the Vice-President of the United States, who arrived a day or two ago at the seat of government, and who was previously admitted this morning to the chair of the Senate; and was afterward complimented at his own lodgings by the very few foreign agents who reside at this place, by the members of Congress, and other public officials."

Only the north wing of the Capitol had then been so far completed as to be occupied by the Senate, the courts, and the small library of Congress. The centre rose not much above its foundations; and the south wing, some twenty feet in height, contained a temporary oval brick building, commonly called the " Oven," in which the House of Representatives sat

[1] Thornton to Grenville, March 4, 1801 ; MSS. British Archives.

in some peril of their lives, for had not the walls been strongly shored up from without, the structure would have crumbled to pieces. Into the north wing the new President went, accompanied by the only remaining secretaries, Dexter and Stoddert, and by his friends from the House. Received by Vice-President Burr, and seated in the chair between Burr and Marshall, after a short pause Jefferson rose, and in a somewhat inaudible voice began his Inaugural Address.

Time, which has laid its chastening hand on many reputations, and has given to many once famous formulas a meaning unsuspected by their authors, has not altogether spared Jefferson's first Inaugural Address, although it was for a long time almost as well known as the Declaration of Independence; yet this Address was one of the few State Papers which should have lost little of its interest by age. As the starting-point of a powerful political party, the first Inaugural was a standard by which future movements were measured, and it went out of fashion only when its principles were universally accepted or thrown aside. Even as a literary work, it possessed a certain charm of style peculiar to Jefferson, a flavor of Virginia thought and manners, a Jeffersonian ideality calculated to please the ear of later generations forced to task their utmost powers in order to carry the complex trains of their thought.

The chief object of the Address was to quiet the passions which had been raised by the violent agita-

tion of the past eight years. Every interest of the
new Administration required that the extreme Federalists should be disarmed. Their temper was such
as to endanger both Administration and Union; and
their power was still formidable, for they controlled
New England and contested 'New York. To them,
Jefferson turned: —

"Let us unite with one heart and one mind," he en-
treated; "let us restore to social intercourse that harmony
and affection without which liberty and even life itself
are but dreary things. And let us reflect, that, having
banished from our land that religious intolerance under
which mankind so long bled and suffered, we have yet
gained little if we countenance a political intolerance as
despotic, as wicked, and capable of as bitter and bloody
persecutions. During the throes and convulsions of the
ancient world, during the agonizing spasms of infuriated
man, seeking through blood and slaughter his long-lost
liberty, it was not wonderful that the agitation of the
billows should reach even this distant and peaceful shore;
that this should be more felt and feared by some than by
others; that this should divide opinions as to measures
of safety. But every difference of opinion is not a difference of principle. We are all Republicans, we are all
Federalists."

The Federalist newspapers never ceased laughing
at the "spasms" so suddenly converted into "billows,"
and at the orthodoxy of Jefferson's Federalism; but
perhaps his chief fault was to belittle the revolution
which had taken place. In no party sense was it

true that all were Republicans or all Federalists.
As will appear, Jefferson himself was far from meaning what he seemed to say. He wished to soothe the
great body of his opponents, and if possible to win
them over ; but he had no idea of harmony or affection other than that which was to spring from his own
further triumph ; and in representing that he was
in any sense a Federalist, he did himself a wrong.

"I know, indeed," he continued, "that some honest
men fear that a republican government cannot be strong ;
that this government is not strong enough. But would
the honest patriot, in the full tide of successful experiment, abandon a government which has so far kept us
free and firm, on the theoretic and visionary fear that
this government, the world's best hope, may by possibility want energy to preserve itself? I trust not. I believe this, on the contrary, the strongest government on
earth. I believe it is the only one where every man, at
the call of the laws, would fly to the standard of the law,
and would meet invasions of the public order as his own
personal concern. Sometimes it is said that man cannot
be trusted with the government of himself. Can he then
be trusted with the government of others? Or have we
found angels in the forms of kings to govern him? Let
history answer this question!"

That the government, the world's best hope, had
hitherto kept the country free and firm, in the full
tide of successful experiment, was a startling compliment to the Federalist party, coming as it did
from a man who had not been used to compliment

his political opponents; but Federalists, on the other
hand, might doubt whether this government would
continue to answer the same purpose when administered for no other avowed object than to curtail its
powers.   Clearly, Jefferson credited government with
strength which belonged to society; and if he meant to
practise upon this idea, by taking the tone of "the
strongest government on earth" in the face of Bonaparte and Pitt, whose governments were strong in a
different sense, he might properly have developed this
idea at more length, for it was likely to prove deeply
interesting.   Moreover, history, if asked, must at that
day have answered that no form of government,
whether theocratic, autocratic, aristocratic, democratic, or mixed, had ever in Western civilization
lasted long, without change or need of change.   History was not the witness to which Republicans could
with entire confidence appeal, even against kings.

The Address next enumerated the advantages which
America enjoyed, and those which remained to be
acquired : —

"With all these blessings, what more is necessary to
make us a happy and prosperous people?   Still one thing
more, fellow-citizens, — a wise and frugal government,
which shall restrain men from injuring one another,
which shall leave them otherwise free to regulate their
own pursuits of industry and improvement, and shall not
take from the mouth of labor the bread it has earned.
This is the sum of good government, and this is necessary
to close the circle of our felicities."

A government restricted to keeping the peace, which should raise no taxes except for that purpose, seemed to be simply a judicature and a police. Jefferson gave no development to the idea further than to define its essential principles, and those which were to guide his Administration. Except the Kentucky and Virginia Resolutions of 1798, this short passage was the only official gloss ever given to the Constitution by the Republican party; and for this reason students of American history who would understand the course of American thought should constantly carry in mind not only the Constitutions of 1781 and of 1787, but also the Virginia and Kentucky Resolutions, and the following paragraph of Jefferson's first Inaugural Address : —

"I will compress them," said the President, "within the narrowest compass they will bear, stating the general principle, but not all its limitations. Equal and exact justice to all men, of whatever state or persuasion, religious or political; peace, commerce, and honest friendship with all nations, entangling alliances with none; the support of the State governments in all their rights, as the most competent administrations for our domestic concerns and the surest bulwarks against anti-republican tendencies; the preservation of the general government in its whole Constitutional vigor, as the sheet-anchor of our peace at home and safety abroad; a jealous care of the right of election by the People,— a mild and safe corrective of abuses which are lopped by the sword of revolution where peaceable remedies are unprovided; absolute acquiescence in the decisions of the majority, —

the vital principle of republics, from which there is no appeal but to force, the vital principle and immediate parent of despotism ; a well-disciplined militia, — our best reliance in peace and for the first moments of war, till regulars may relieve them ; the supremacy of the civil over the military authority ; economy in the public expense, that labor may be lightly burdened ; the honest payment of our debts, and sacred preservation of the public faith ; encouragement of agriculture, and of commerce as its handmaid ; the diffusion of information, and arraignment of all abuses at the bar of public reason ; freedom of religion, freedom of the press, and freedom of person under the protection of the *habeas corpus;* and trial by juries impartially selected ; — these principles form the bright constellation which has gone before us and guided our steps through an age of revolution and reformation.   The wisdom of our sages and the blood of our heroes have been devoted to their attainment ; they should be the creed of our political faith, the text of civic instruction, the touchstone by which to try the services of those we trust ; and should we wander from them in moments of error or alarm, let us hasten to retrace our steps and to regain the road which alone leads to peace, liberty, and safety."

From the metaphors in which these principles appeared as a constellation, a creed, a text, a touchstone, and a road, the world learned that they had already guided the American people through an age of revolution.   In fact, they were mainly the principles of President Washington, and had they been announced by a Federalist President, would have created little remonstrance or surprise.   In Jefferson's mouth they sounded less familiar, and certain phrases seemed even out of place.

Among the cardinal points of republicanism thus proclaimed to the world was one in particular, which as a maxim of government seemed to contradict cherished convictions and the fixed practice of the Republican party. "Absolute acquiescence" was required " in the decisions of the majority, — the vital principle of republics, from which there is no appeal but to force, the vital principle and immediate parent of despotism." No principle was so thoroughly entwined in the roots of Virginia republicanism as that which affirmed the worthlessness of decisions made by a majority of the United States, either as a nation or a confederacy, in matters which concerned the exercise of doubtful powers. Not three years had passed since Jefferson himself penned the draft of the Kentucky Resolutions, in which he declared [1] " that in cases of an abuse of the delegated powers, the members of the general government being chosen by the people, a change by the people would be the Constitutional remedy; but where powers are assumed which have not been delegated, a nullification of the act is the rightful remedy ; that every State has a natural right, in cases not within the compact, to nullify of their own authority all assumptions of power by others within their limits ; that without this right they would be under the dominion, absolute and unlimited, of whosoever might exercise this right of

[1] Jefferson's Works, ix. 469.

judgment for them." He went so far as to advise
that every State should forbid, within its borders, the
execution of any act of the general government "not
plainly and intentionally authorized by the Constitution;" and although the legislatures of Kentucky
and Virginia softened the language, they acted on
the principle so far as to declare certain laws of the
United States unconstitutional, with the additional
understanding that whatever was unconstitutional
was void. So far from accepting with "absolute acquiescence" the decisions of the majority, Jefferson
and his followers held that freedom could be maintained only by preserving inviolate the right of every
State to judge for itself what was, and what was not,
lawful for a majority to decide.

What, too, was meant by the words which pledged
the new Administration to preserve the general government "in its whole Constitutional vigor"? The
two parties were divided by a bottomless gulf in
their theories of Constitutional powers; but until
the precedents established by the Federalists should
be expressly reversed, no one could deny that those
precedents, to be treated as acts of the majority with
absolute acquiescence, were a measure of the vigor
which the President pledged himself to preserve.
Jefferson could not have intended such a conclusion;
for how could he promise to "preserve" the powers
assumed in the Alien and Sedition laws, which then
represented the whole vigor of the general government in fact if not in theory, when he had himself

often and bitterly denounced those powers, when he had been a party to their nullification, and when he and his friends had actually prepared to resist by arms their enforcement? Undoubtedly Jefferson meant no more than to preserve the general government in such vigor as in his opinion was Constitutional, without regard to Federalist precedents; but his words were equivocal, and unless they were to be defined by legislation, they identified him with the contrary legislation of his predecessors. In history and law they did so. Neither the Alien nor the Sedition Act, nor any other Federalist precedent, was ever declared unconstitutional by any department of the general government; and Jefferson's pledge to preserve that government in its full Constitutional vigor was actually redeemed with no exception or limitation on the precedents established. His intention seemed to be different; but the sweeping language of his pledge was never afterward restricted or even more exactly defined while he remained in power.

Hence arose a sense of disappointment for future students of the Inaugural Address. A revolution had taken place; but the new President seemed anxious to prove that there had been no revolution at all. A new experiment in government was to be tried, and the philosopher at its head began by pledging himself to follow in the footsteps of his predecessors. Americans ended by taking him at his word, and by assuming that there was no break of continuity between his

ideas and those of President Washington; yet even
at the moment of these assurances he was writing privately in an opposite sense. In his eyes the past was
wrong, both in method and intention; its work must
be undone and its example forgotten. His conviction
of a radical difference between himself and his predecessors was expressed in the strongest language. His
predecessors, in his opinion, had involved the government in difficulties in order to destroy it, and to
build up a monarchy on its ruins. "The tough sides
of our Argosie," he wrote two days after his inauguration,[1] "have been thoroughly tried. Her strength
has stood the waves into which she was steered with
a view to sink her. We shall put her on her Republican tack, and she will now show by the beauty of
her motion the skill of her builders." "The Federalists," said he at one moment,[2] "wished for everything which would approach our new government to a
monarchy; the Republicans, to preserve it essentially
republican. . . . The real difference consisted in their
different degrees of inclination to monarchy or republicanism." "The revolution of 1800," he wrote many
years afterward,[3] "was as real a revolution in the
principles of our government as that of 1776 was in
its form."

Not, therefore, in the Inaugural Address, with its
amiable professions of harmony, could President Jef-

---

[1] Jefferson to J. Dickinson, March 6, 1801; Works, iv. 365.

[2] Jefferson's Works, ix. 480.

[3] Jefferson to Roane, Sept. 6, 1819 ; Works, vii. 133.

ferson's full view of his own reforms be discovered. Judged by his inaugural addresses and annual messages, Jefferson's Administration seemed a colorless continuation of Washington's; but when seen in the light of private correspondence, the difference was complete. So strong was the new President's persuasion of the monarchical bent of his predecessors, that his joy at obtaining the government was mingled with a shade of surprise that his enemies should have handed to him, without question, the power they had so long held. He shared his fears of monarchy with politicians like William B. Giles, young John Randolph, and many Southern voters; and although neither Madison nor Gallatin seemed to think monarchists formidable, they gladly encouraged the President to pursue a conservative and conciliatory path. Jefferson and his Southern friends took power as republicans opposed to monarchists, not as democrats opposed to oligarchy. Jefferson himself was not in a social sense a democrat, and was called so only as a term of opprobrium. His Northern followers were in the main democrats; but he and most of his Southern partisans claimed to be republicans, opposed by secret monarchists.

The conflict of ideas between Southern republicanism, Northern democracy, and Federal monarchism marked much of Jefferson's writing; but especially when he began his career as President his mind was filled with the conviction that he had wrung power from monarchy, and that in this sense he was the founder of a new republic. Henceforward, as he hoped, republicanism was forever safe; he had but to conciliate the misguided, and give an example to the world, for centralization was only a monarchical principle. Nearly twenty years passed before he woke to a doubt on this subject; but even then he did not admit a mistake. In the tendency to centralization he still saw no democratic instinct, but only the influence of monarchical Federalists " under the pseudo-republican mask." [1]

The republic which Jefferson believed himself to be founding or securing in 1801 was an enlarged Virginia, — a society to be kept pure and free by the absence of complicated interests, by the encouragement of agriculture and of commerce as its handmaid, but not of industry in a larger sense. " The agricultural capacities of our country," he wrote long afterward,[2] " constitute its distinguishing feature ; and the adapting our policy and pursuits to that is more likely to make us a numerous and happy people than the mimicry of an Amsterdam, a Hamburg, or a city of London." He did not love mechanics or manufactures, or the capital without which they could not exist.[3] " Banking establishments are more dangerous than standing armies," he said ; and added, " that the principle of spending money to be paid by posterity, under the name of funding, is but swindling futurity on a large

[1] Jefferson to Judge Johnson, June 12, 1823 ; Works, vii. 293.
[2] Jefferson to W. H. Crawford, June 20, 1816; Works, vii. 6.
[3] Jefferson to John Taylor, May 28, 1816; Works, vi. 608.

scale." Such theories were republican in the Virginia sense, but not democratic; they had nothing in common with the democracy of Pennsylvania and New England, except their love of freedom; and Virginia freedom was not the same conception as the democratic freedom of the North.

In 1801 this Virginia type was still the popular form of republicanism. Although the Northern democrat had already developed a tendency toward cities, manufactures, and " the mimicry of an Amsterdam, a Hamburg, or a city of London," while the republican of the South was distinguished by his dislike of every condition except that of agriculture, the two wings of the party had so much in common that they could afford to disregard for a time these divergencies of interest; and if the Virginians cared nothing for cities, banks, and manufactures, or if the Northern democrats troubled themselves little about the dangers of centralization, they could unite with one heart in overthrowing monarchy, and in effecting a social revolution.

Henceforward, as Jefferson conceived, government might act directly for the encouragement of agriculture and of commerce as its handmaid, for the diffusion of information and the arraignment of abuses; but there its positive functions stopped. Beyond that point only negative action remained, — respect for States' rights, preservation of constitutional powers, economy, and the maintenance of a pure and simple society such as already existed. With a political system which would not take from the mouth of labor the bread it had earned, and which should leave men free to follow whatever paths of industry or improvement they might find most profitable, " the circle of felicities " was closed.

The possibility of foreign war alone disturbed this dream. President Washington himself might have been glad to accept these ideas of domestic politics, had not France, England, and Spain shown an unequivocal wish to take advantage of American weakness in arms in order to withhold rights vital to national welfare. How did Jefferson propose to convert a government of judiciary and police into the strongest government on earth? His answer to this question, omitted from the Inaugural Address, was to be found in his private correspondence and in the speeches of Gallatin and Madison as leaders of the opposition. He meant to prevent war. He was convinced that governments, like human beings, were on the whole controlled by their interests, and that the interests of Europe required peace and free commerce with America. Believing a union of European Powers to be impossible, he was willing to trust their jealousies of each other to secure their good treatment of the United States. Knowing that Congress could by a single act divert a stream of wealth from one European country to another, foreign Governments would hardly challenge the use of such a weapon, or long resist their own overpowering interests. The new President found in the Constitutional power " to regulate commerce with foreign nations" the machinery for doing away with navies, armies, and wars.

During eight years of opposition the Republican party had matured its doctrines on this subject. In 1797, in the midst of difficulties with France, Jefferson wrote: [1] —

"If we weather the present storm, I hope we shall avail ourselves of the calm of peace to place our foreign connections under a new and different arrangement. We must make the interest of every nation stand surety for their justice, and their own loss to follow injury to us, as effect follows its cause. As to everything except commerce, we ought to divorce ourselves from them all."

A few months before the inauguration, he wrote in terms more general: [2] —

"The true theory of our Constitution is surely the wisest and best, that the States are independent as to everything within themselves, and united as to everything respecting foreign nations. Let the general government be reduced to foreign concerns only, and let our affairs be disentangled from those of all other nations, except as to commerce, which the merchants will manage the better the more they are left free to manage for themselves, and our general government may be reduced to a very simple organization and a very unexpensive one, — a few plain duties to be performed by a few servants."

Immediately after the inauguration the new President explained his future foreign policy to corres-

[1] Jefferson to Edward Rutledge, June 24, 1797; Works, iv. 189.
[2] Jefferson to Gideon Granger, Aug. 13, 1800; Works, iv. 330.

pondents, who, as he knew, would spread his views
widely throughout both continents. In a famous letter to Thomas Paine,[1] — a letter which was in some
respects a true inaugural address, — Jefferson told the
thought he had but hinted in public. " Determined
as we are to avoid, if possible, wasting the energies of
our people in war and destruction, we shall avoid im-
plicating ourselves with the Powers of Europe, even in
support of principles which we mean to pursue. They
have so many other interests different from ours that
we must avoid being entangled in them. We believe
we can enforce those principles as to ourselves by
peaceable means, now that we are likely to have our
public counsels detached from foreign views." A
few days later, he wrote to the well-known Pennsylvania peacemaker, Dr. Logan, and explained the process of enforcing against foreign nations " principles
as to ourselves by peaceable means." " Our commerce," said he,[2] " is so valuable to them, that they
will be glad to purchase it, when the only price we
ask is to do us justice. I believe we have in our own
hands the means of peaceable coercion ; and that the
moment they see our government so united as that
we can make use of it, they will for their own interest
be disposed to do us justice."

To Chancellor Livingston, in September, 1801,[3] the
President wrote his views of the principles which

[1] Jefferson to Thomas Paine, March 18, 1801; Works, iv. 370.
[2] Jefferson to Dr. Logan, March 22, 1801; Jefferson MSS.
[3] Jefferson to R. R. Livingston, Sept. 9, 1801; Works, iv. 408.

he meant to pursue: "Yet in the present state of things," he added, "they are not worth a war; nor do I believe war the most certain means of enforcing them. Those peaceable coercions which are in the power of every nation, if undertaken in concert and in time of peace, are more likely to produce the desired effect."

That these views were new as a system in government could not be denied. In later life Jefferson frequently asserted, and took pains to impress upon his friends, the difference between his opinions and those of his Federalist opponents. The radical distinction lay in their opposite conceptions of the national government. The Federalists wished to extend its functions; Jefferson wished to exclude its influence from domestic affairs: —

"The people," he declared in 1821,[1] "to whom all authority belongs, have divided the powers of government into two distinct departments, the leading characters of which are foreign and domestic; and they have appointed for each a distinct set of functionaries. These they have made co-ordinate, checking and balancing each other, like the three cardinal departments in the individual States, —each equally supreme as to the powers delegated to itself, and neither authorized ultimately to decide what belongs to itself or to its coparcener in government. As independent, in fact, as different nations, a spirit of forbearance and compromise, therefore, and not of encroachment and usurpation, is the healing balm of such a Constitution."

[1] Jefferson to Judge Roane, June 27, 1821; Works, vii. 212.

In the year 1824 Jefferson still maintained the same doctrine, and expressed it more concisely than ever : —

" The federal is in truth our foreign government, which department alone is taken from the sovereignty of the separate States." [1]   " I recollect no case where a question simply between citizens of the same State has been transferred to the foreign department, except that of inhibiting tenders but of metallic money, and *ex post facto* legislation." [2]

These expressions, taken together, partly explain why Jefferson thought his assumption of power to be " as real a revolution in the principles of our government as that of 1776 was in its form." His view of governmental functions was simple and clearly expressed. The national government, as he conceived it, was a foreign department as independent from the domestic department, which belonged to the States, as though they were governments of different nations. He intended that the general government should " be reduced to foreign concerns only ; " and his theory of foreign concerns was equally simple and clear. He meant to enforce against foreign nations such principles as national objects required, not by war, but by " peaceable coercion " through com-

[1] Jefferson to Robert J. Garnett, Feb. 14, 1824 ; Works, vii. 336.
[2] Jefferson to Edward Livingston, April 4, 1824 ; Works, vii. 342.

mercial restrictions. " Our commerce is so valuable to them that they will be glad to purchase it, when the only price we ask is to do us justice."

The history of his Administration will show how these principles were applied, and what success attended the experiment.

CHAPTER VIII.

In 1801, and throughout Jefferson's Administration, the Cabinet consisted of five heads of department, — the Secretaries of State, of the Treasury, of the Army, and of the Navy, with the Attorney-General. The law business of the government being light, the Attorney-General was frequently absent, and, indeed, was not required to reside permanently at Washington. Rather the official counsel of government than a head of department, he had no clerks or office-room, and his salary was lower than that of his colleagues. The true Cabinet consisted of the four secretaries; and the true government rested in still fewer hands, for it naturally fell within the control of the officers whose responsibility was greatest, — the President, the Secretary of State, and the Secretary of the Treasury.

Simple as such a system was, Jefferson found that months elapsed before his new Cabinet could be organized and set at work. Although Madison was instantly nominated and confirmed as Secretary of State, some weeks passed before he arrived in Washington and assumed his duties. Gallatin was supposed to be in danger of rejection by the Senate, and

his nomination as Secretary of the Treasury was therefore postponed till the next session. This delay was
not allowed to prevent his taking charge of the office ;
but he was obliged first to make the long journey to his
residence on the Monongahela, in southwestern Pennsylvania, in order to arrange his affairs and bring his
family to Washington. During the interval between
the inauguration and the meeting of his completed
Cabinet, Jefferson was left without means of governing. For Attorney-General he selected Levi Lincoln,
a lawyer of Worcester County in Massachusetts, who
had been recently elected to fill a vacancy in the
House of Representatives, and, being on the spot,
was useful in acting as Secretary of State, or in any
other capacity in which the services of a secretary
were required. For the War Department the President chose Henry Dearborn, a resident of the District
of Maine, then a part of Massachusetts. With such
assistance as Lincoln and Dearborn could give, and
with the aid of Samuel Dexter the Federalist Secretary of the Treasury, and Benjamin Stoddert the
Federalist Secretary of the Navy, who consented to
remain for a time, Jefferson slowly set his Administration in motion.

The Navy Department seemed likely to baffle the
President's utmost efforts. The appointment was
intended for Robert R. Livingston of New York,
who refused ; then it was offered to Samuel Smith
of Maryland, a prominent member of Congress ; but
General Smith was a merchant, and declined to aban-

don his business. Next, the place was pressed upon
John Langdon of New Hampshire, although New
England already supplied two members of the Cabi-
net.   Langdon refusing, the President wrote to
William Jones of Philadelphia, a member of the next
Congress, who declined.   Meanwhile Benjamin Stoddert became weary of waiting, and Samuel Smith
consented to perform the duties in order to give the
President time for further search.   At the end of
March, Jefferson left Washington to pass the month
of April at Monticello, and on his return, May 1, the
Navy Department was still unfilled.   Not until July
did General Smith succeed in escaping the burden of
his temporary duties.   Then the President abandoned
the attempt to place a man of public importance in
the position, and allowed Samuel Smith to substitute
in his place his brother Robert, a Baltimore lawyer,
whose fitness for naval duties was supposed to consist chiefly in the advice and aid which Samuel would
supply.

The appointment of Robert Smith, July 15, completed the Cabinet.   Of its five members, only two
— Madison and Gallatin — were much known beyond their States.   Neither Dearborn nor Lincoln
was so strong, either in political or social connections or in force of character, as greatly to affect
the course of the Cabinet, and both were too honest
to thwart it.

"General Dearborn is a man of strong sense, great
practical information on all the subjects connected with

his department, and is what is called a man of business. He is not, I believe, a scholar; but I think he will make the best Secretary of War we have as yet had. Mr. Lincoln is a good lawyer, a fine scholar, a man of great discretion and sound judgment, and of the mildest and most amiable manners. He has never, I should think from his manners, been out of his own State, or mixed much with the world, except on business. Both are men of 1776, sound and decided Republicans; both are men of the strictest integrity; and both, but Mr. Lincoln principally, have a great weight of character to the Eastward with both parties." [1]

Thus Gallatin, March 12, before his own appointment, estimated the characters of his two New England colleagues. The confidence reposed in them was justified by the result. Neither Dearborn nor Lincoln showed remarkable powers, but the work they had to do was done without complaint or objection. No charge of dishonesty, of intrigue, or of selfish ambition was made against them; and they retired from office at last with as much modesty as they showed in entering it, after serving Jefferson faithfully and well.

In some respects Robert Smith was better suited than either Dearborn or Lincoln for a seat in Jefferson's Cabinet. The Smiths were strong not only in Maryland, but also in Virginia, being connected by marriage with Wilson Cary Nicholas, one of the most influential Republican politicians of the State, whose

[1] Life of Gallatin, p. 276.

relations with Jefferson were intimate.   Robert Smith was a Baltimore gentleman, easy and cordial, glad to oblige and fond of power and show, popular in the navy, yielding in the Cabinet, but as little fitted as Jefferson himself for the task of administering with severe economy an unpopular service.   The navy was wholly Federalist in tendencies and composition. The Republican party had always denounced this Federalist creation; and that a navy caused more dangers than it prevented or corrected, was one of the deepest convictions that underlay the policy of Jefferson, Madison, and Gallatin.   In theory they had no use for a sea-going navy; at the utmost they wanted only coast and harbor defences, sloops-of-war and gunboats.   During the four years of the last Administration, of a total expenditure averaging about $11,000,000 per annum, not less than $2,500,000 had been annually spent on the navy.   The public debt itself required only about $4,500,000, and the army less than $3,000,000.   Economies in the debt were impossible; on the contrary, a mass of deferred annuities was to be met, and some provision must be made for more rapid discharge of the principal. Economies in the civil list were equally impossible; for the Federalists had there wasted little money, and salaries were low.   The army and navy could alone be cut down; and since the Western people required regular troops for their defence against the Indians, the most radical reformers hardly ventured to recommend that the army should be reduced much below an aggregate of three thousand rank-and-file. The navy, on the other hand, was believed to be wholly superfluous, and Jefferson was anxious to lay up all the larger ships, especially the frigates.

" I shall really be chagrined," he wrote from Monticello in April,[1] " if the water in the Eastern Branch will not admit our laying up the whole seven there in time of peace, because they would be under the immediate eye of the department, and would require but one set of plunderers to take care of them. As to what is to be done when everything shall be disposed of according to law, it shall be the subject of conversation when I return. It oppresses me by night and by day, for I do not see my way out of the difficulty. It is the department I understand the least, and therefore need a person whose complete competence will justify the most entire confidence and resignation."

Robert Smith was certainly not such a person as Jefferson described, and his appointment, however suitable in other respects, was not likely to attain the object which Jefferson had at heart.

Hardly was the Navy Department thus bestowed, and the new Cabinet, toward the middle of July, completely organized for the work that was still to be defined, when another annoyance distracted the President's attention from the main objects of his policy. The government had been, for eight years, in the hands of Federalist partisans. If, as Jefferson declared in his Inaugural Address, " we are all Re-

---

[1] Jefferson to S. Smith, April 17, 1801; Jefferson MSS.

publicans, we are all Federalists ; " if differences of
opinion were not differences of principle ; if he seriously wished all Americans to " restore to social intercourse that harmony and affection without which
liberty and even life itself are but dreary things," —
he could afford to make few removals for party reasons.   On the other hand, if, as he privately declared
and as was commonly believed, the actual office-holders were monarchists at heart, and could not be
trusted to carry the new Republican principles into
practice, the public welfare required great changes.
For the first time in national experience, the use of
patronage needed some definite regulation.

The most skilful politician must have failed in the
attempt to explain that a revolution had been made
which ought to satisfy every one, by methods which
no one had an excuse for opposing.   Jefferson was
embarrassed, not so much by the patronage, as by the
apparent inconsistency between his professions and
his acts concerning it.   At first he hoped to make
few removals, and these only for misconduct or other
sufficient cause.   " Of the thousands of officers in the
United States," he wrote to Dr. Rush,[1] " a very few
individuals only, probably not twenty, will be removed ; and these only for doing what they ought not
to have done."   As these removals began, the outcry of the Federalists grew loud, until the President
thought himself obliged to defend his course.   The
occasion was furnished by the State of Connecticut,

[1] Jefferson to Dr. Rush, March 24, 1801 ; Works, iv. 382.

where the necessity for a change in office-holders was proved by the temper of the office-holding class. " The spirit in that State," wrote Madison,[1] July 10, " is so perverse that it must be rectified by a peculiar mixture of energy and delicacy." The spirit of which Madison complained was illustrated, only three days before, by an oration delivered July 7, at New Haven, by Theodore Dwight. The government, said Dwight, which had been established under the auspices of Washington was the sport of popular commotion, adrift without helm or compass in a turbid and boisterous ocean.

" The great object of Jacobinism, both in its political and moral revolution, is to destroy every trace of civilization in the world, and to force mankind back into a savage state. . . . That is, in plain English, the greatest villain in the community is the fittest person to make and execute the laws. Graduated by this scale, there can be no doubt that Jacobins have the highest qualifications for rulers. . . . We have now reached the consummation of democratic blessedness. We have a country governed by blockheads and knaves; the ties of marriage with all its felicities are severed and destroyed; our wives and daughters are thrown into the stews; our children are cast into the world from the breast and forgotten; filial piety is extinguished, and our surnames, the only mark of distinction among families, are abolished. Can the imagination paint anything more dreadful on this side hell?"

[1] Madison to W. C. Nicholas, July 10, 1801; Nicholas MSS.

In the fervor of his representation, Dwight painted
what he believed was to happen as though it had
actually come to pass. He and his friends, at least,
felt no doubt of it. Madison could hardly be blamed
for thinking this spirit perverse; and the President
was as little to be censured for wishing to rectify it.
Elizur Goodrich, a person who was quite in the same
way of thinking, was Collector of New Haven. Jefferson removed him, and appointed an old man named
Bishop, whose son had made himself conspicuous by
zealous republicanism in a community where zeal in
such a cause was accounted a social crime. A keen
remonstrance was drawn up, signed by New Haven
merchants, and sent to the President. Couched, as
Madison said, "in the strongest terms that decorum
would tolerate," this vigorous paper was in effect a
challenge, for it called on the President to proclaim
whether he meant to stand by the conciliatory professions of his Inaugural Address, or on his private
convictions; and Jefferson was not slow to accept
the challenge, in order to withdraw himself from an
embarrassing position which was rapidly rousing dis-
content among his friends. He wrote a reply to the
New Haven remonstrants, in which, without going
so far as to assert that to the victors belonged the
spoils, he contented himself with claiming that to
the victors belonged half the spoils. Without abandoning his claim to establish harmony, he appealed
to the necessity under which he was placed by the
duty of doing justice to his friends.

" If a due participation of office," he said,[1] " is a matter of right, how are vacancies to be obtained? Those by death are few ; by resignation, none. Can any other mode than that of removal be proposed? This is a painful office, but it is made my duty, and I meet it as such."

The Federalists found much material for ridicule in these expressions, which were certainly open to criticism; but the chief objection was that they admitted an unwilling surrender to the demands of office-seekers.

" It would have been to me a circumstance of great relief had I found a moderate participation of office in the hands of the majority. I would gladly have left to time and accident to raise them to their just share. But their total exclusion calls for prompter corrections. I shall correct the procedure, but that done, return with joy to that state of things when the only questions concerning a candidate shall be : Is he honest? Is he capable? Is he faithful to the Constitution?"

With a degree of deference to his critics which was perhaps unnecessary, and was certainly unfortunate, Jefferson characterized the officials who were to be first removed. "I proceed in the operation," he said, " with deliberation and inquiry, that it may injure the best men least, and effect the purposes of justice and public utility with the least private distress; that it may be thrown, as much as possible, on delinquency,

---

[1] Jefferson to Elias Shipman and others, July 12, 1801; Works, iv. 402.

on oppression, on intolerance, on ante-Revolutionary adherence to our enemies." Language so mild soothed and conciliated hundreds of voters who were glad to meet Jefferson's advances, but at the cost of increasing the anger felt by the great mass of Federalists for professions which they believed to be deceptive. For this result Jefferson was probably prepared, but he could hardly have intended that his letter should, by a common accident of politics, serve to create ill-feeling in his own party.

Rules which might suit New England conveyed quite another impression elsewhere. While Jefferson professed tenderness to New England in order to undermine a Federalist majority, nothing of the sort was needed in other States of the Union. New York and Pennsylvania had grown used to the abuse of political patronage, and no sooner had the Republicans wrested these two States from Federalist hands than they rooted out all vestige of Federalist influence. Governor McKean, in Pennsylvania, was arbitrary enough; but when George Clinton, elected Governor of New York in the spring of 1801, came into power, the State government showed no disposition to imitate Jefferson's delicacy or his professions. August 8, 1801, a few weeks after the New Haven letter was written, Governor Clinton called a meeting of the Council which, under the Constitution of New York, had charge of the State patronage. Young De Witt Clinton and his friend Ambrose Spencer controlled this Council, and they were not persons who affected scruple in matters of political self-interest. They swept the Federalists out of every office even down to that of auctioneer, and without regard to appearances, even against the protests of the Governor, installed their own friends and family connections in power.

Had this been all, Jefferson might have ignored it. The difficulties he encountered in New York were caused not so much by the removal of Federalists, as by unwillingness to appoint Republicans. Jefferson did not like the Clintons, but he liked Aaron Burr still less.

The character of Burr was well understood by the party leaders on both sides long before 1800. The Virginians twice refused to vote for him as Vice-President before they were induced to do so in that year. Jefferson himself recorded that he considered Burr as for sale between 1790 and 1800; he even added that the two parties bid against each other in the latter year for the prize. " He was told by Dayton in 1800 he might be Secretary at War; but this bid was too late; his election as Vice-President was then foreseen." [1] According to this view, the Virginians bought him ; but they had no sooner done so than they prayed to be delivered from their bargain ; and De Witt Clinton undertook to deliver them, with a tacit understanding, at least on his part, that in 1808 the Virginians must reckon with him for the debt.

[1] Jefferson's Anas; Works. ix. 207.

Not, therefore, Federalists alone were victims of the scandal in New York. The exhibition of selfish intrigue which centred in New York politics was calculated to startle Jefferson from his confidence in human nature. Burr's overthrow was a matter of offices and public patronage; no principle of reform or pure motive in any person was involved in it. The New York Republicans were divided into three factions, represented by the Clinton, Livingston, and Burr interests; and among them was so little difference in principle or morals, that a politician as honest and an observer as keen as Albert Gallatin inclined to Burr as the least selfish of the three.[1] The Vice-President was popular in the city of New York, and to some extent in the country districts throughout the State. Bad as his morality was understood to be, he had at that time committed no offence that warranted ostracism; but from the moment of Governor Clinton's accession to power, he was pursued and persecuted by the whole Clinton interest.

Burr, aware of the dislike and jealousy with which the Clintons regarded him, had until then depended for a counterbalance on the Livingston interest, of which General Armstrong in the Senate and Edward Livingston in the House were the representatives at Washington; in alliance with them and in accord with Gallatin, he parcelled out the federal patronage of the State. His chief anxiety was to provide offices for his two friends, John Swartwout and Matthew L.

[1] Gallatin to Jefferson, Sept. 14, 1801; Adams's Gallatin, p. 288.

Davis ; and he succeeded in obtaining for the first the marshalship of New York, for the second a promise of the supervisorship. No sooner did the news of this arrangement reach the ears of De Witt Clinton than he remonstrated, and in a few days drew from President Jefferson a letter addressed to Governor Clinton, which in effect surrendered Burr into the hands of his enemies. " The following arrangement," wrote the President,[1] May 17, " was agreed to by Colonel Burr and some of your senators and representatives, — Daniel Gelston, collector ; Theodorus Bailey, naval officer ; and M. L. Davis, supervisor." Objections had been made. Would Governor Clinton express his opinion ?

In a short time Burr found that the President showed no alacrity for the removal of Federalist officials in New York. Neither Bailey nor Davis was appointed. Bailey, hitherto a friend of Burr, withdrew from his candidacy under a promise, as was supposed, of the postmastership ; and Davis was pressed by Burr for the post of naval officer, then held by a Federalist named Rogers, who was charged with adhesion to the British during the Revolution. Within six weeks after Jefferson's letter to Governor Clinton, Burr caught the rumor of some secret understanding, and wrote angrily to Gallatin,[2] —

" Strange reports are here in circulation respecting secret machinations against Davis. . . . This thing has,

[1] Jefferson to George Clinton, May 17, 1801 ; Jefferson MSS.
[2] Burr to Gallatin, June 28, 1801 ; Adams's Gallatin, p. 283.

in my opinion, gone too far to be now defeated. . . .
Davis is too important to be trifled with."

His remonstrances fell on deaf ears. No entreaty,
even from Gallatin himself, could thenceforward induce the President to open his mouth on the subject.
After waiting two months longer, Davis resorted to
the desperate expedient of seeking a personal interview; and early in September undertook the long
journey to Monticello, furnished with a strong letter
from Gallatin, and supported by a private letter which
was stronger still: [1] —

"I dislike much," wrote the Secretary in this remarkable paper, "the idea of supporting a section of Republicans in New York, and mistrusting the great majority
because that section is supposed to be hostile to Burr,
and he is considered as the leader of that majority. A
great reason against such policy is that the reputed
leaders of that section, — I mean the Livingstons generally, and some broken remnants of the Clintonian party
who hate Burr, — . . . are so selfish and so uninfluential
that they never can obtain their great object, the State
government, without the assistance of what is called
Burr's party, and will not hesitate a moment to bargain
for that object with him and his friends, granting in
exchange their support for anything he or they may want
out of the State. . . . I do not know that there is hardly
a man who meddles with politics in New York who does
not believe that Davis's rejection is owing to Burr's
recommendation."

[1] Gallatin to Jefferson, Sept. 14, 1801; Adams's Gallatin, p. 288.

Gallatin was not in the secret. Although he was the only Cabinet representative of the Middle States, his advice was neither asked nor followed. Jefferson had decided to let De Witt Clinton have his way, but he explained his intentions neither to Gallatin, Burr, nor to Davis. In reply to Gallatin's remonstrance, he wrote back from Monticello:[1] "Mr. Davis is now with me. He has not opened himself. When he does, I shall inform him that nothing is decided, nor can be till we get together at Washington."

That nothing had been decided was not only, as Burr called it,[2] a "commonplace" answer, but was also incorrect. Everything had been decided; and by the time Davis, amid the jeers of the press, rejoined Burr in New York, the results of the Clinton intrigue had become visible. While Jefferson withheld from Burr all sign of support, De Witt Clinton and Ambrose Spencer, acting in unison with the President, detached the Livingstons from Burr's interest. The Chancellor was already provided for. Too important to be overlooked, he was offered and had accepted the mission to France even before the inauguration.[3] Edward Livingston, Burr's friend, was made mayor of New York,—an office then in the gift of the Council, and supposed to be worth ten thousand dollars a year.[4] He also received from Jefferson the

[1] Jefferson to Gallatin ; Adams's Gallatin, p. 289.

[2] Burr to Gallatin, March 5, 1802; Adams's Gallatin, p. 289.

[3] Jefferson to Livingston, Feb. 24, 1801; Jefferson's Works, iv. 360.

[4] Hammond's Political History, i. 180.

appointment of district attorney. The chief-justice and two of the Supreme Court judges were of the Livingston connection. The secretary of state was another of the family, and General Armstrong, one of the senators in Congress, still another. In various meetings of the Council of Appointment during the summer and autumn, the State and city offices were taken from the Federalists and divided between the Clintons and Livingstons, until the Livingstons were gorged; while Burr was left to beg from Jefferson the share of national patronage which De Witt Clinton had months before taken measures to prevent his obtaining.

That Jefferson and De Witt Clinton expected and intended to drive Burr from the party was already clear to Burr and his friends as early as September, 1801, when Matthew L. Davis forced himself into Jefferson's house at Monticello, while Burr watched the tactics of De Witt Clinton's Council of Appointment. On both sides the game was selfish, and belonged rather to the intrigues of Guelfs and Ghibellines in some Italian city of the thirteenth century than to the pure atmosphere of Jefferson's republicanism. The disgust of Gallatin was deep; but he knew too well the nature of New York politics to care greatly whether Burr or Clinton were to rule, and he was anxious only to stop the use of federal patronage in the interests of party intrigue. The New Haven letter had not pleased him. Within a fortnight after that letter was written, he sent to the

President[1] the draft of a Treasury Circular which
would not only have stopped the removal of inferior
officers, but would have shut them out from active
politics. Jefferson declined to approve it. He insisted that one half the tide-waiters and other em-
ployees should be changed before he should interfere.
Gallatin replied that this had already been done.
" The number of removals is not great, but in importance they are beyond their number. The supervisors
of all the violent party States embrace all the collec-
tors. Add to that the intended change in the post-
office, and you have in fact every man in office out of
the seaports." Still Jefferson hung back, and declared
that it would be a poor manœuvre to revolt tried
friends in order to conciliate moderate Federalists.[2]
He could not follow his true instincts ; for the pressure
upon him, although trifling when compared with what
he thus helped to bring on his successors, was more
than he could bear. In New York Governor Clinton
protested in vain against the abuse of patronage, and
from Pennsylvania Governor McKean wrote:[3] " The
thirst for office is immoderate ; it has become an object of serious attention, and I wish I knew how to
check it." The scandalous proceedings of the New
York Council of Appointment sharpened the tone
of Gallatin, who declared that they disgraced the

[1] Gallatin to Jefferson, July 25, 1801 ; Gallatin's Works, i. 28.
[2] Jefferson to Gallatin, August 14, 1801 ; Gallatin's Works,
i. 36.
[3] McKean to Jefferson, August 10, 1801 ; Jefferson MSS.

Republican cause, and sank the Administration itself
to a level with its predecessor.[1] With all this, the
only removal in New York which Jefferson resolutely
resisted, was that of the supposed Revolutionary Tory
whose place was asked for Matthew L. Davis by Vice-
President Burr.

No other member of the Cabinet offered active
support to Gallatin in this struggle against the use
of federal patronage. Madison concurred with the
President in thinking the proposed Treasury Circular premature.[2] Nevertheless the Secretary of State
made no changes in the bureaus of his department,
although these were full of zealous Federalists. Not
even the chief clerk, Jacob Wagner, was removed, as
bitter a Federalist as any in the United States, whose
presence in the office was a disadvantage if not a
danger to the Government. When Duane came to
Washington, after the New York removals had begun, and urged sweeping measures of change, he
was coldly received at the State and Treasury departments,[3] which gave him contracts for supplying
paper, but declined to give him offices; and Duane
returned to Philadelphia bearing toward Madison
and Gallatin a grudge which he never forgot, and

[1] Gallatin to Jefferson, Sept. 12, 1801; Gallatin's Works,
i. 47.

[2] Jefferson to Gallatin, July 26, 1801; Gallatin's Works,
i. 29. Gallatin to Jefferson, Sept. 18, 1804; Gallatin's Works,
i. 208.

[3] Gallatin to Jefferson, August 17, 1801; Gallatin's Works,
i. 38.

which, like that of Burr, was destined in due time to envenom a party schism.

Although these disputes over patronage seemed to require more of the President's thoughts than were exacted by the study of general policy, the task of government was not severe. After passing the month of April at Monticello, Jefferson was able to rest there during the months of August and September, leaving Washington July 30. During six months, from April to October, he wrote less than was his custom, and his letters gave no clear idea of what was passing in his mind. In regard to his principles of general policy he was singularly cautious.

"I am sensible," he wrote, March 31,[1] "how far I should fall short of effecting all the reformation which reason could suggest and experience approve, were I free to do whatever I thought best; but when we reflect how difficult it is to move or inflect the great machine of society, how impossible to advance the notions of a whole people suddenly to ideal right, we see the wisdom of Solon's remark, — that no more good must be attempted than the nation can bear, and that all will be chiefly to reform the waste of public money, and thus drive away the vultures who prey upon it, and improve some little on old routines."

"Levees are done away," he wrote to Macon;[2] "the first communication to the next Congress will be, like all subsequent ones, by message, to which no answer will be expected; the diplomatic establishment in Europe will be

[1] Jefferson to Walter Jones, March 31, 1801; Works, iv. 392.
[2] Jefferson to Macon, May 14, 1801; Works, iv. 396.

reduced to three ministers; the army is undergoing a chaste reformation; the navy will be reduced to the legal establishment by the last of this month; agencies in every department will be revised; we shall push you to the utmost in economizing."

His followers were not altogether pleased with his moderation of tone. They had expected a change of system more revolutionary than was implied by a pledge to do away with the President's occasional receptions and his annual speech to Congress, to cut off three second-rate foreign missions, to chasten the army, and to execute a Federalist law about the navy, or even to revise agencies. John Randolph wrote, July 18, to his friend Joseph Nicholson, a member from Maryland:[1] "In this quarter we think that the great work is only begun, and that without a substantial reform we shall have little reason to congratulate ourselves on the mere change of men."

The task of devising what Randolph called a substantial reform fell almost wholly upon Gallatin, who arrived in Washington, May 13, and set himself to the labor of reducing to a system the theories with which he had indoctrinated his party. Through the summer and autumn he toiled upon this problem, which the President left in his hands. When October arrived, and the whole Cabinet assembled at length in Washington, under the President's eye, to prepare business for the coming session, Gallatin produced his scheme. First, he required common consent to

[1] Adams's Randolph, p. 51.

the general principle that payment of debt should take precedence of all other expenditure. This axiom of Republicanism was a party dogma too well settled to be disputed. Debt, taxes, wars, armies, and navies were all pillars of corruption; but the habit of mortgaging the future to support present waste was the most fatal to freedom and purity. Having fixed this broad principle, which was, as Gallatin afterward declared, the principal object of bringing him into office,[1] a harder task remained; for if theory required prompt payment of the debt, party interest insisted with still greater energy on reduction of taxes; and the revenue was not sufficient to satisfy both demands. The customs duties were already low. The highest *ad valorem* rate was twenty per cent; the average was but thirteen. Reduction to a lower average, except in the specific duties on salt, coffee, and sugar, was asked by no one; and Gallatin could not increase the rates even to relieve taxation elsewhere. Whatever relief the party required must come from another source.

The Secretary began by fixing the limits of his main scheme. Assuming four Administrations, or sixteen years, as a fair allowance of time for extinguishing the debt, he calculated the annual sum which would be required for the purpose, and found that $7,300,000 applied every year to the payment of interest and principal would discharge the whole within the year 1817. Setting aside $7,300,000 as

[1] Life of Gallatin, p. 270.

an annual fund to be devoted by law to this primary
object, he had to deal only with such revenue as
should remain.

The net receipts from customs he calculated at
$9,500,000 for the year, and from lands and postage
at $450,000; or $9,950,000 in all. Besides this sum
of less than ten million dollars, internal taxes, and
especially the tax on whiskey-stills, produced altogether about $650,000; thus raising the income
to $10,600,000, or $3,300,000 in excess of the fund
set apart for the debt.

If taxation were to be reduced at all, political
reasons required that the unpopular excise should
come first in order of reduction; but if the excise
were abolished, the other internal taxes were not
worth retaining. Led by the wish to relieve government and people from the whole system of internal
taxation, Gallatin consented to sacrifice the revenue
it produced. After thus parting with internal revenue to the amount of $650,000, and setting aside
$7,300,000 for the debt, he could offer to the other
heads of departments only $2,650,000 for the entire
expenses of government. Gallatin expected the army
to be supported on $930,000, while the navy was to be
satisfied with $670,000, — a charge of less than thirty-
three cents a head on the white population.

Of all standards by which the nature of Jeffersonian
principles could be gauged, none was so striking as
this. The highest expenditure of the Federalists in
1799, when preparing for war with France and con-

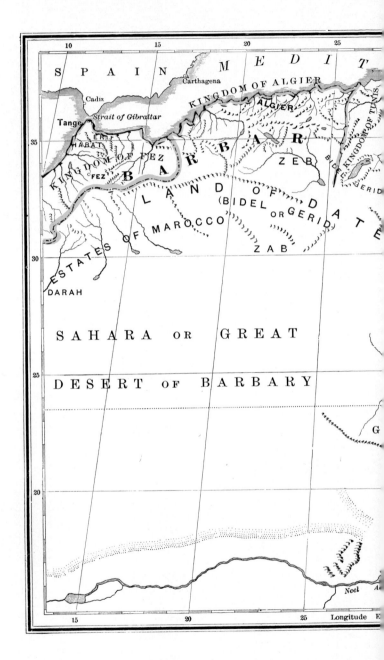

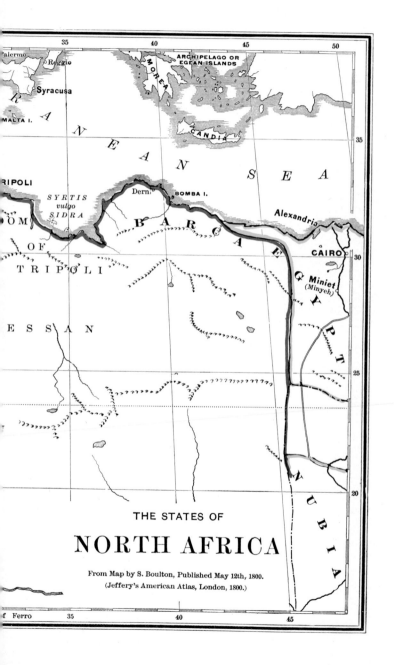

THE STATES OF

NORTH AFRICA

From Map by S. Boulton, Published May 12th, 1800.
(Jeffery's American Atlas, London, 1800.)

structing a navy and an army, was six million dollars for these two branches. Peace with France being made in 1800, the expenses of army and navy would naturally fall to a normal average of about three million dollars. At a time when the population was small, scattered, and surrounded by enemies, civilized and savage; when the Mississippi River, the Gulf region, and the Atlantic coast as far as the St. Mary's were in the hands of Spain, which was still a great power; when English frigates were impressing American seamen by scores, and Napoleon Bonaparte was suspected of having bought Louisiana ; when New York might be ransomed by any line-of-battle ship, and not a road existed by which a light field-piece could be hauled to the Lakes or to a frontier fort, — at such a moment, the people could hardly refuse to pay sixty cents apiece for providing some protection against dangers which time was to prove as serious as any one then imagined them to be. Doubtless the republican theory required the States to protect their own coasts and to enforce order within their own jurisdiction ; but the States were not competent to act in matters which concerned the nation, and the immense territory, the Lakes, and the Mississippi and Mobile rivers, belonged within the exclusive sphere of national government.

Gallatin cut down by one half the natural estimate. That he should have done this was not surprising, for he was put in office to reduce debt and taxation, not to manage the army and navy; but he could hardly have expected that all his colleagues should agree with him, — yet his estimates were accepted by the Cabinet without serious objection, and adopted as a practical scale of governmental expenditure. Encouraged by the announcement of peace in Europe, the Secretaries of War and of the Navy consented to reduce their establishments to suit Gallatin's plans, until the entire expense of both branches for the future was to be brought within $1,900,000; while Gallatin on his side made some concessions which saved his estimates from error. The army bore the brunt of these economies, and was reduced to about three thousand men. The navy was not so great a sufferer, and its calculated reductions were less certain.

Gallatin's scheme partially warranted the claim which Jefferson in his old age loved to put forward, that he had made a revolution in the principles of the government. Yet apart from the question of its success, its rigor was less extreme than it appeared to be. Doubtless, such excessive economy seemed to relieve government of duties as well as responsibilities. Congress and the Executive appeared disposed to act as a machine for recording events, without guiding or controlling them. The army was not large enough to hold the Indians in awe; the navy was not strong enough to watch the coasts; and the civil service was nearly restricted to the collection and disbursement of revenue. The country was at the mercy of any Power which might choose to rob it, and the President announced in advance that he relied for safety upon the soundness of his theory that every foreign country felt a vital interest in retaining American commerce and the use of American harbors. All this was true, and the experiment might be called revolutionary, considering the condition of the world; nevertheless there were shades of difference in the arguments on which it rested. Even Jefferson wavered in asserting the permanence of the system, while Gallatin avowedly looked forward to the time when diminished debt and increasing resources would allow wider scope of action. Viewed from this standpoint, the system was less rigid than it seemed, since a period of not more than five or six years was needed to obtain Gallatin's object.

By an unlucky chance the system never became fully established. The first step in foreign affairs taken by the new Administration plunged it into difficulties which soon forced Congress to reimpose taxation to the full amount of the internal taxes. Jefferson had not been three months in power before he found himself, by no fault of his own or of his predecessors, at war with a country against which he was forced to use in his own defence some of those frigates, the construction of which had been vehemently resisted by his party, and which he was anxious only to leave under the care of a score of marines at the Navy Yard in the Eastern Branch of the Potomac. From time immemorial the northern coast of Africa had been occupied by a swarm of pirates who played a dramatic part in the politics and literature of Europe. They figured in the story of Don Quixote as in the lies of Scapin, and enlivened with picturesque barbarism the semi-civilization of European habits and manners through centuries of slow growth. The four Barbary Powers, Morocco, Algiers, Tunis, and Tripoli, lived by blackmail. So little sense of common interest had the nations of Europe, that they submitted to the demands of these petty Mahometan despots, and paid yearly sums of money, or an equivalent in ships, arms, or warlike stores, in return for which the Barbary Powers permitted them to trade with the ports on the coast and protected their ships and men. The European consuls at Algiers, Tunis, and Tripoli intrigued to impose heavier conditions on rival commerce. Following the established custom, the United States had bought treaties with all four Powers, and had during the past ten years appropriated altogether more than two million dollars for the account of ransoms, gifts, and tribute. The treaty with Tripoli, negotiated in 1796, had been observed about three years and a half. The Pacha received under it from the United States Government $83,000 in cash and presents. He suddenly demanded more, and when his demand was refused, May 14, 1801, he ordered the consular flagstaff to be cut down, which was his formal declaration of war.

The conduct of the Dey of Algiers was almost as

threatening to peace as that of the Pacha of Tripoli; for the Dey compelled Captain Bainbridge to put his frigate, the " George Washington," under Algerine colors and carry an embassy and presents to the Grand Sultan. Rather than take the responsibility of bringing on a war, Bainbridge and Consul O'Brian submitted, under protest, to this indignity; and in October, 1800, the United States flag was first seen at Constantinople in this extraordinary company. At the same time, Algiers, Tunis, and Morocco were clamorous for money, and gave reason to fear that they would make common cause with Tripoli in the war which the Pacha was declaring.

Under these circumstances, without knowing that war had actually begun, Samuel Smith, as acting Secretary of the Navy, in May, 1801, sent out Commodore Dale in command of a squadron of three frigates and an armed schooner, the " Enterprise," with orders to meet force by force. On her way to Malta, August 1, the " Enterprise " met and destroyed a Tripolitan corsair. Commodore Dale blockaded Tripoli; and his appearance in the Mediterranean inspired Tunis and Algiers with so much respect as caused them to leave the Pacha of Tripoli to his fate, and to accept the presents which their treaties stipulated. Much injury to American commerce was prevented; but Gallatin found a war and a navy fastened on his resources.

That enlightened governments like those of England, France, and Spain should rob and plunder like

an Algerine pirate was in theory not to be admitted;
but even if they did so, a few frigates could not prevent them, and therefore Jefferson, without regard to
this partial failure of his system, prepared to meet
Congress with confidence in his reforms.

CHAPTER IX.

PRESIDENT WASHINGTON began his administration by addressing Congress in a speech, which Congress answered; and the precedent established by him in 1790 was followed by his successor. The custom was regarded by the opposition as an English habit, tending to familiarize the public with monarchical ideas, and Jefferson gave early warning that he should address Congress in a message, which would require no answer. In after times the difference between oral and written communications as signs of monarchy or republicanism became less self-evident; but the habit of writing to Congress was convenient, especially to Presidents who disliked public speaking, and Jefferson's practice remained the rule. The Federalists naturally regarded the change as a reproof, and never admitted its advantages. The Republicans also missed some of the conveniences of the old system. John Randolph, eight years afterward, seemed to regret that the speech had been abandoned: [1] —

"The answer to an Address, although that answer might finally contain the most exceptionable passages,

[1] Annals of Congress, May 26, 1809, XI. Congress, Part I. p. 92.

was in fact the greatest opportunity which the opposition
to the measures of the Administration had of canvassing
and sifting its measures. . . . This opportunity of discussion of the answer to an Address, however exceptionable the answer might be when it had received the last
seasoning for the Presidential palate, did afford the best
opportunity to take a review of the measures of the Administration, to canvass them fully and fairly, without
there being any question raised whether the gentleman
was in order or not; and I believe the time spent in
canvassing the answer to a speech was at least as well
spent as a great deal that we have expended since we
discontinued the practice."

President Jefferson did not assign political reasons
for changing the custom. "I have had a principal
regard," he said,[1] "to the convenience of the legislature, to the economy of their time, to their relief
from the embarrassment of immediate answers on
subjects not yet fully before them, and to the benefits
thence resulting to the public affairs." With this
preamble, he sent his message.

Jefferson's first Annual Message deserved study
less for what it contained than for what it omitted.
If the scope of reform was to be measured by the
President's official recommendations, party spirit was
likely to find little excuse for violence. The Message
began by announcing, in contrast with the expectations of Republicans, that while Europe had returned
to peace the United States had begun a war, and that
a hostile cruiser had been captured "after a heavy

[1] Letter to the President of the Senate, Dec. 8, 1801.

slaughter of her men." The Federalist wits made
fun of the moral which the President added to soften
the announcement of such an event: "The bravery
exhibited by our citizens on that element will, I
trust, be a testimony to the world that it is not the
want of that virtue which makes us seek their peace,
but a conscientious desire to direct the energies of
our nation to the multiplication of the human race,
and not to its destruction." The idea seemed a favorite one with the President, for he next congratulated
Congress on the results of the new census, which,
he said, " promises a duplication in little more than
twenty-two years. We contemplate this rapid growth
and the prospect it holds up to us, not with a view to
the injuries it may enable us to do to others in some
future day, but to the settlement of the extensive
country still remaining vacant within our limits, to
the multiplication of men susceptible of happiness,
educated in the love of order, habituated to self-
government, and valuing its blessings above all
price."

Just and benevolent as this sentiment might be,
Jefferson rarely invented a phrase open to more
perversion than when he thus announced his party's
" conscientious desire to direct the energies of our
nation to the multiplication of the human race."
Perhaps his want of a sense of humor prevented
his noticing this slip of the tongue which the English language had no precise word to describe; perhaps he intended the phrase rather for a European

than for an American audience ; in any case, such
an introduction to his proposed reforms, in the eyes
of opponents, injured their dignity and force. As he
approached the reforms themselves, the manner in
which he preferred to present them was characteristic. As in his Inaugural Address, he showed skill
in selecting popular ground.

"There is reasonable ground of confidence," he said,
"that we may now safely dispense with all the internal
taxes, . . . and that the remaining sources of revenue
will be sufficient to provide for the support of government, to pay the interest of the public debts, and to discharge the principals within shorter periods than the laws
or the general expectation had contemplated. War, indeed, and untoward events may change this prospect of
things, and call for expenses which the imposts could not
meet; but sound principles will not justify our taxing
the industry of our fellow-citizens to accumulate treasure
for wars to happen we know not when, and which might
not perhaps happen but for the temptations offered by
that treasure."

Assuming that "the States themselves have principal care of our persons, our property, and our reputation, constituting the great field of human concerns,"
the Message maintained that the general government
was unnecessarily complicated and expensive, and
that its work could be better performed at a smaller
cost.

"Considering the general tendency," it said, "to mul-
tiply offices and dependencies, and to increase expense to

the ultimate term of burden which the citizen can bear, it behooves us to avail ourselves of every occasion which presents itself for taking off the surcharge, that it never may be seen here that, after leaving to labor the smallest portion of its earnings on which it can subsist, government shall itself consume the residue of what it was instituted to guard."

No one could deny that these sentiments were likely to please a majority of citizens, and that they announced principles of government which, if not new, were seldom or never put into practice on a great scale. As usual in such cases, the objections came from the two classes who stood at the extremes of the political movement. The Federalists denied that they had ever asked " to accumulate treasures for wars." They asked for cannon and muskets in the armories ; for timber and ship-stores in the navy-yards; for fortifications to defend New York, and for readiness to resist attack. Gallatin's economies turned on the question whether the national debt or the risk of foreign aggression were most dangerous to America. Freedom from debt and the taxation which debt entailed was his object, not in order to save money, but to prevent corruption. He was ready to risk every other danger for the short time required. " Eight years hence," he afterward wrote,[1] " we shall, I trust, be able to assume a different tone ; but our exertions at present consume the seeds of our greatness, and retard to an indefinite time the epoch

[1] Gallatin to Jefferson, Aug. 16, 1802 ; Works, i. 88.

of our strength." The epoch of strength once reached, Gallatin had no objection to tax, and tax freely, for any good purpose, even including ships-of-the-line. "Although I have been desirous," he wrote some four years later,[1] "that the measure might at least be postponed, I have had no doubt for a long time that the United States would ultimately have a navy." Nothing in his political theories prevented his spending money on defensive armaments or internal improvements or any other honest object, provided he had the money to spend.

The Federalists disagreed with Gallatin rather on a question of fact than of principle. They asserted that the country could not safely disarm ; Gallatin, on the other hand, thought that for a few years military helplessness might be risked without too much danger. Time could alone decide which opinion was correct; but in this issue the Federalists could see no suggestion such as Jefferson made, that " sound principles will not justify our taxing the industry of our fellow-citizens to accumulate treasures for wars to happen we know not when." If this was the true principle of government, and if the hands of Congress were to be tied so fast that no provision could ever be made for national defence except in actual presence of war, this " sound principle " should have been announced, according to Federalist theories, not as a detail of administration but as a constitutional amendment.

[1] Gallatin to Jefferson, Sept. 12, 1805; Works, i. 253.

In this opinion the true Virginia school probably concurred. Economy for its own sake was not the chief object of that class of men, and any reform on such narrow ground was not wholly to their taste. Even they were well aware at the moments when they complained most of extravagance that the United States, compared with any powerful European government, had always been a model of economy,— and indeed the most obvious criticism of the system was that economy had been its only extravagance. In the year 1800, when expenses were swollen to their highest point, in consequence of a *quasi* war with France, the disbursements reached about $11,-500,000, of which the sum of $4,578,000 was on account of public debt. The running expenses of the government, including the creation of an army and a navy, did not then exceed $7,000,000, or about $1.30 a head to each inhabitant. The average annual expenditure for the past ten years had been about $9,000,000,— a smaller sum than Jefferson ever succeeded in spending. This example of economy was enough to strike the imagination of any observer; and still greater parsimony, even though it should reduce the running expenses by one half, could do no more than strengthen the same impression, or at most create an idea that republican government was too economical for its own safety. This was no revolution such as the Virginians wished to effect. They aimed at restricting power even more than at relieving taxation.

The Message put economy in the place of principle in dealing with patronage, while in regard to constitutional powers it ignored the existence of a problem. In this silence, which for the first time since 1787 fell on the lips of those who had hitherto shown only jealousy of government; in this alacrity with which Republicans grasped the powers which had, as they affirmed, made " monocrats " of their old opponents,— a European would have seen the cynicism of conscious selfishness. Certain phrases in the Constitution had been shown by experience to be full of perils, and were so well established by precedent in their dangerous meaning as to be susceptible only of excision. The clause which gave Congress sweeping power to make all laws which a majority might think " necessary and proper " for carrying the Constitution into effect, was, as settled by precedents, fatal not only to the theory of State-rights, but to the doctrine of strict construction on which American liberties were supposed to rest. The war and treaty making powers, with their undefined and therefore unlimited consequences, were well understood. These loopholes for the admission of European sovereignty into the citadel of American liberty were seen in 1800 as clearly as when the children and grandchildren of the Southern statesmen broke up the Union because they feared the consequences of centralization. Yet Jefferson called no man's attention to the danger, took no step toward averting it, but stretched out his hand to seize the powers he had denounced.

Even in regard to the Judiciary, the most dangerous part of the system, he recommended no legislation but for the apparent purpose of saving money.

"The judiciary system of the United States," continued the Message, "and especially that portion of it recently erected, will of course present itself to the contemplation of Congress; and that they may be able to judge of the proportion which the institution bears to the business it has to perform, I have caused to be procured from the several States, and now lay before Congress, an exact statement of all the causes decided since the first establishment of the Courts, and of those which were depending when additional Courts and Judges were brought in to their aid."

That he should have shown no anxiety to limit the vague powers of Legislature and Executive was less surprising, because these powers were henceforward to remain in the hands of his own party; but the Judiciary was in the hands of Federalists, whose constitutional theories were centralization itself.   The essence of Virginia republicanism lay in a single maxim: THE GOVERNMENT SHALL NOT BE THE FINAL JUDGE OF ITS OWN POWERS.   The liberties of America, as the Republican party believed, rested in this nutshell; for if the Government, either in its legislative, executive, or judicial departments, or in any combination of them, could define its own powers in the last resort, then its will, and not the letter of the Constitution, was law.   To this axiom of republicanism the Federalist Judiciary opposed what amounted to a flat

negative. Chief-Justice Marshall and his colleagues
meant to interpret the Constitution as seemed to
them right, and they admitted no appeal from their
decision.

The question how to deal with the Judiciary was,
therefore, the only revolutionary issue before the
people to be met or abandoned ; and if abandoned then,
it must be forever. No party could claim the right
to ignore its principles at will, or imagine that theories
once dropped could be resumed with equal chance of
success. If the revolution of 1800 was to endure,
it must control the Supreme Court. The object
might be reached by constitutional amendment, by
impeachment, or by increasing the number of judges.
Every necessary power could be gained by inserting
into the United States Constitution the words of the
Constitution of Massachusetts, borrowed from English
constitutional practice, that judges might be removed
by the President on address by both Houses of the
Legislature. Federalists were certain to denounce
both object and means as revolutionary and dangerous to public repose ; but such an objection could
carry little weight with men who believed themselves to have gained power for no other purpose
than to alter, as Jefferson claimed, the principles
of government. Serious statesmen could hardly
expect to make a revolution that should not be
revolutionary.

Had Jefferson overlooked the danger, costly as the
oversight was, it might cause no surprise ; but he

perceived it clearly, and in private denounced it with
as much keenness as though he already knew what
was to be judged "necessary and proper" for the
purposes of a government which, as Virginians foresaw, would in the end interpret its own powers.
"They have retired into the Judiciary as a stronghold," cried he in the same breath with which he
talked to Congress only of economy.[1] "There the
re mains of federalism are to be preserved and fed
ron. n the Treasury; and from that battery all the
orks of republicanism are to be beaten down and
estroyed." Some twenty years afterward Jefferson
woke to s ee his prophecy come true, and he then
rew respons ibility on the Constitution.

"The nation de clared its will," he said,[2] "by dismiss-
g functionaries of one principle and electing those of
other in the two br nches, executive and legislative,
bmitted to their electio n. Over the judiciary depart-
nt the Constitution had d prived them of their control.
at, therefore, has continued the reprobated system;
l although new matter has oc asionally been incorpo-
ed into the old, yet the leaven f the old mass seems
assimilate to itself the new; and fter twenty years'
firmation of the federated system b the voice of the
ion, declared through the medium of ele tions, we find
Judiciary, on every occasion, still drivi g us into
solidation."

of
uch was the fact; and when Jefferson spoke
e leaven of the old mass," he meant Chief-Justice

Jefferson to J. Dickinson, Dec. 19, 1801; W orks, iv. 424.
Jefferson to Roane, Sept. 6, 1819; Works, vii. 133.

Marshall, who had won a slow, certain victory over
State-rights, and had thrust powers on the national
government which, if Jefferson were right, must end
in corrupting and destroying it. Whose was the
fault? Was it true that the Constitution deprived
the people of their control over the Judiciary? Even
if it were so, did not Jefferson for years control with
autocratic power the strength necessary for altering
the Constitution? When at last, four years before his
death, the impending certainty of defeat forced itself
on Jefferson's mind, he made what amounted to a
confession of his oversight, and withdrew the apology
which threw blame on the Constitution: "Before the
canker is become inveterate,—before its venom has
reached so much of the body politic as to get beyond
control,—remedy should be applied. Let the future
appointments of judges be for four or six years, and
renewable by the President and Senate."[1] If this
could be done, as his words implied, in 1822 under
the Presidency of James Monroe, when J. Q. Adams,
Calhoun, Clay, and Andrew Jackson were each in his
own way laboring to consolidate a nation still hot
with the enthusiasm of foreign war, why was it not
attempted in 1801, when a word from Jefferson would
have decided the action of his party?

If this were all, some explanation of the President's
silence might be offered; for in 1801–1802 his majority in the Senate was small, and only a political
leader as bold as Andrew Jackson would have dared

[1] Jefferson to W. T. Barry, July 2, 1822; Works, vii. 257.

to risk his popularity on such a venture. The judges held office for life; the Constitution required for amendment two thirds of the Senate and three fourths of the States; any violent shock might have thrown Connecticut and Massachusetts into open secession; but these objections to a revolution in constitutional law did not apply to partisan Federalist legislation. Why did not Jefferson officially invite Congress to confirm the action of Virginia and Kentucky by declaring the Alien and Sedition Laws to be unconstitutional and null as legislative precedents? In the absence of such a declaratory act, the Republican party left on the statute book the precedent established by those laws, which had expired only by limitation. Had the Alien and Sedition Laws been alone in dispute, the negligence might have seemed accidental; but the statute-book contained another Federalist law, aimed against State-rights, which had roused alarm on that account. The Judiciary Act of 1789, the triumph of Federalist centralization, had conferred on the Supreme Court jurisdiction over the final judgment of State courts in cases where the powers of the general government had been "drawn in question" and the decision was unfavorable to them. This concession of power to the Supreme Court, — a concession often alleged to be more dangerous to the States than the "necessary and proper" clause itself, — was believed to be dictated by a wish to make the State judiciaries inferior courts of the central government, because the

powers of the general government might be " drawn
in question" in many ways and on many occasions,
and thus the authority of the State courts made contemptible.   Chief-Justice Marshall achieved one of
his greatest triumphs by causing Judge Story, a republican raised to the bench in 1811 for the purpose of contesting his authority, to pronounce in
1816 the opinion of the court in the case of Martin
vs. Hunter's Lessee, by which the Virginia Court of
Appeals was overruled upon the question of constitu-
tionality raised by the State court in regard to Section 25 of the Judiciary Act.   Such a result would
hardly have happened had the Republicans in 1801
revised the laws which they considered unconstitutional ; but with what propriety could Virginia in
1816 assert the unconstitutionality of a law which
she had for fifteen years possessed the power to repeal, without making an attempt or expressing a wish
to exercise it ?

Whatever was the true cause of the inaction, it was
certainly intentional.   President Jefferson wished to
overthrow the Federalists and annihilate the last
opposition before attempting radical reforms.   Confident that State-rights were safe in his hands, he
saw no occasion to alarm the people with legislation directed against past rather than future dangers.   His party acquiesced, but not without mis-
givings.   John Taylor of Caroline, most consistent
of the State-rights school, thought that reforms
should have been made.   John Randolph, eight years

afterward, expressed his opinion with characteristic frankness : —

" You know very well," he said,[1] addressing Speaker Varnum, " that there were many of us, and I was one, who thought that at the commencement of Mr. Jefferson's administration it would be proper for us to pass a sort of declaratory Act on the subject of the Sedition Law ; . . . but on this subject, as well as the reduction of the army below its then standard, as on some others, I had the honor, or dishonor as some might esteem it, to be in the minority. I had thought that we ought to have returned the fines of all those who suffered under the law ; . . . but you know that it was said that we came in as reformers ; that we should not do too much ; that we should go on little by little ; that we should fire minute-guns, I think was the expression, — which produced no other effect, that I ever found, than the keeping up a spirit of irritation."

Speaker Macon, Joseph Nicholson, and William B. Giles were probably among those who held the same opinion, and were overruled by the Northern democrats. They never quite forgave Madison, to whose semi-Federalist influence they ascribed all Jefferson's sins. Distrust of Madison was natural, for neither Virginian nor New Englander understood how Madison framed the Constitution and wrote the " Federalist " with the same hand which drafted the Virginia Resolutions of 1798; but Jefferson himself would have been last to admit the correctness of such an explanation. He could point to the sentence of his

[1] Annals of Congress, May 25, 1809. XI. Congress, Part I. 87.

Inaugural Address which pledged him to " the preservation of the general government in its whole constitutional vigor." If in redeeming the pledge he
preserved vigor that his friends deemed unconstitutional, his own habits of mind, not Madison's semi-
Federalist tendencies, explained the error.

Another reason partly accounted for the President's
silence. In theory the Executive received its instructions from the Legislature. Upon no point had the
Republican party, when in opposition, laid more stress
than on the necessity of reducing Executive influence.
President Washington's personal authority, even more
than the supposed monarchical tendencies of his
successor, inspired anger, if not terror, in the minds
of his opponents. Jefferson wished to avoid this
error, and to restore the true constitutional theory to
its place in practice. His recommendations were
studiously restrained, and the Federalists were so far
silenced that they could only say with Chief-Justice
Marshall, " By weakening the office of President,
he will increase his personal power." The concluding
sentences of the Message expressed in a few words
the two leading ideas which Jefferson wished most to
impress on the people, — his abnegation of power and
his wish for harmony : —

" Nothing shall be wanting on my part to inform, as
far as in my power, the legislative judgment, nor to
carry that judgment into faithful execution. The prudence and temperance of your discussions will promote,
within your own walls, that conciliation which so much

befriends rational conclusion, and by its example will encourage among our constituents that progress of opinion. which is tending to unite them in object and will. That all should be satisfied with any one order of things is not to be expected, but I indulge the pleasing persuasion that the great body of our citizens will cordially concur in honest and disinterested efforts, which have for their object to preserve the General and State governments in their constitutional form and equilibrium; to maintain peace abroad, and order and obedience to the laws at home; to establish principles and practices of administration favorable to the security of liberty and property, and to reduce expenses to what is necessary for the useful purposes of government."

CHAPTER X.

Honest as Jefferson undoubtedly was in his wish to diminish executive influence, the task was beyond his powers. In ability and in energy the Executive overshadowed Congress, where the Republican party, though strong in numbers and discipline, was so weak in leadership, especially among the Northern democrats, that the weakness almost amounted to helplessness. Of one hundred and five members, thirty-six were Federalists; of the sixty-nine Republicans, some thirty were Northern men, from whom the Administration could expect little more than votes. Boston sent Dr. Eustis; from New York came Dr. Samuel L. Mitchill, — new members both; but two physicians, or even two professors, were hardly competent to take the place of leaders in the House, or to wield much influence outside. The older Northern members were for the most part men of that respectable mediocrity which followed where others led. The typical Northern democrat of that day was a man disqualified for great distinction by his want of the habits of leadership; he was obliged, in spite of his principles, to accept the guidance of aristocrats like the Livingstons, Clintons, and Burrs, or like

Gallatin, Jefferson, John Randolph, and the Smiths, because he had never been used to command, and could not write or speak with perfect confidence in his spelling and grammar, or enter a room without awkwardness. He found himself ill at ease at the President's dinner-table; he could talk only upon subjects connected with his district, and he could not readily accustom himself to the scale of national affairs. Such men were thrust aside with more or less civility by their leaders, partly because they were timid, but chiefly because they were unable to combine under the lead of one among themselves. The moment true democrats produced a leader of their own, they gave him the power inherent in leadership, and by virtue of this power he became an aristocrat, was admitted into the circle of Randolphs and Clintons, and soon retired to an executive office, a custom-house or a marshalship; while the never-failing succession of democratic Congressmen from the North continued to act as before at the command of some aristocratic Virginian or educated gentleman from the city of New York.

Owing to this peculiarity, the Northern democrats were and always remained, in their organization as a party, better disciplined than their opponents. Controlling the political power of New York, New Jersey, and Pennsylvania, they wielded it as they were bid. Their influence was not that of individuality, but of mass; they affected government strongly and permanently, but not consciously; their steady attraction

served to deflect the Virginia compass several degrees
from its supposed bearings; but this attraction was
commonly mechanical. Jefferson might honestly strip
himself of patronage, and abandon the receptions of
other Presidents; he might ride every day on horseback to the Capitol in " overalls of corduroy, faded,
by frequent immersions in soapsuds, from yellow to
a dull white," and hitch his horse in the shed, — he
alone wielded power. The only counterpoise to his
authority was to be found among his Southern equals
and aristocratic Northern allies, whose vantage-ground
was in the United States Senate or at the head of
State governments; but the machinery of faction was
not yet well understood. In the three former Administrations, the House had been the most powerful part
of the body politic, and the House was ill-suited for
factious purposes. The Senate was not yet a favorite
place for party leaders to fortify themselves in power;
its debates were rarely reported, and a public man
who quitted the House for the Senate was thrown
into the background rather than into prominence.
In 1803 De Witt Clinton resigned a seat there in
order to become mayor of New York. In the same
year Theodorus Bailey resigned the other seat, in order to become postmaster of New York, leaving the
State unrepresented. While senators had not yet
learned their power, representatives were restrained
by party discipline, which could be defied only by
men so strong as to resist unpopularity. As long
as this situation lasted, Jefferson could not escape

the exercise of executive influence even greater than
that which he had blamed in his predecessors.

The House chose for Speaker Nathaniel Macon, a
typical, homespun planter, honest and simple, erring
more often in his grammar and spelling than in his
moral principles, but knowing little of the world beyond the borders of Carolina.   No man in American
history left a better name than Macon; but the name
was all he left.   An ideal Southern republican, independent, unambitious, free from intrigue, true to his
convictions, a kindly and honorable man, his influence
with President Jefferson was not so great as that of
some less respectable and more busy politicians.

The oldest members of much authority were William B. Giles of Virginia, and Samuel Smith of
Maryland.   In the characters of both these men was
something which, in spite of long service and fair
abilities, kept them subordinate.   Whether on account
of indolence or temper, restlessness or intrigue, they
seldom commanded the full weight to which their
service entitled them.   Speaker Macon, in appointing
his standing committees, passed over both in order to
bring forward a young favorite of his own, — a Virginian barely twenty-eight years old, whose natural
quickness of mind and faculty for ready speaking
gave him prominence in a body of men so little
marked by ability as was the Seventh Congress.
During several years the Federalist newspapers never
wearied of gibing at the long lean figure, the shrill
voice and beardless face of the boyish Republican

leader, among whose peculiarities of mind and person common shrewishness seemed often to get the
better of intense masculine pride.   Besides his natural abilities and his superior education, the young man
had the advantage of belonging to the most widely-
connected of all Virginia families ; and this social
distinction counted for everything in a party which,
although reviled as democratic, would be led by no
man without birth and training.   Incomprehensible
to New England Federalists, who looked on him as a
freak of Nature ; obnoxious to Northern democrats,
who groaned in secret under his insane spur and
curb ; especially exasperating to those Southern Republicans whose political morality or whose manners
did not suit him, — Randolph, by his independence,
courage, wit, sarcasm, and extreme political orthodoxy, commanded strong influence among the best
Virginians of the State-rights school.   More than
half the Virginia delegation belonged to the same
social and political caste ; but none of them could
express so well as Randolph the mixture of contradictory theories, the breadth and narrowness, the aspirations and ignorance, the genius and prejudices
of Virginia.

The experiment of placing Randolph at the head
of the Ways and Means Committee was hazardous ;
and to support him the Speaker put as second member their friend Joseph Nicholson of Maryland, while
General Smith retained his old place at the head
of the Committee on Commerce, and Giles was quite

neglected.   The Federalists even in their reduced
condition, numbering barely one third of the House,
still overmatched the majority in debate.   Randolph,
Nicholson, Samuel Smith, and Giles were hardly
equal to Bayard, Griswold, Dana, John Cotton Smith,
and John Rutledge.

No member of the House wielded serious influence
over the President, or represented with authority the
intentions of the party; and although in the Senate
the Republicans were stronger in ability, they were
weaker in numbers, and therefore more inclined to
timidity.   The ablest of the Republican senators was
a new man, John Breckinridge of Kentucky, another
Virginia aristocrat, chiefly known as the putative
father of the Kentucky Resolutions of 1798.   Breckinridge was bold enough to support any policy that the
Adminstration would consent to impose; but he was
new to the Senate, and, like Randolph, had yet to
win the authority of a leader against a strong Federalist opposition.

The business of the first session of the Seventh
Congress quickly took shape in two party struggles
on the lines marked out by the Message; and the
same caution which made the Message disappointing
as a declaration of principles, affected the debates
and laws.   Although the Federalists offered challenge
after challenge, charging the majority with revolutionary schemes which no honest democrat needed
to deny, the Republicans, abiding carefully for the
most part within the defences selected by the Presi-

dent, seemed unwilling to avow the legitimate objects of their acts. The two measures over which
the struggle took place were not so important as to
touch the foundations of government, unless they
were parts of more sweeping changes to come. They
required the overthrow of two Federalist creations,
but not expressly of any Federalist principle. They
abolished the internal taxes and the circuit courts,
but touched no vital power of government.

Resistance to the abolition of taxes was impossible
after the promise which the President's Message held
out. The Federalists themselves had made peace
with France, and hostilities between France and
England had ceased. For the first time in ten years
no danger of foreign war was apparent, and if the
Administration offered to effect economies in the
public service, Congress could hardly deny that economies were possible. The opposition preferred not
to question the estimates, but to rival the Government in zeal for reduction of taxes; and on this
point they argued with some force that although the
ad valorem duties were low, — averaging about thirteen per cent, — the specific duties on necessaries
of life like salt and sugar, tea and coffee, amounted
to fifty and a hundred per cent; and reduction of
these would surely give more relief than would be
afforded by repealing the tax on whiskey, — a proper
object of taxation, — or the stamp-duty, which was
one of the best and cheapest taxes on the list. The
majority replied that to abolish the internal revenue

system was to diminish by one half the Executive patronage. Forcible as this reasoning was, it did not convince the Federalist leaders in the House, who insisted upon moving amendments. The majority became irritated; a Kentucky member advised that the Federalists should be left unanswered, and their motions voted down. A Republican caucus decided to adopt for a time this course; and the next day, Jan. 25, 1802, when a New York Federalist called for returns in regard to the stamp-tax, the House by a vote of fifty-four to thirty-four bluntly refused the information. Such motions were usually adopted by courtesy, and the Federalists, in their twelve years of rule, were rarely accused of a course so high-handed as that of the new majority. James A. Bayard, of Delaware, who led the Federalists, instantly called up another motion of the same class. After he had spoken in its favor, John Randolph rose and ordered the clerk to read an extract from Gallatin's report. No other reply was offered. One Federalist member after another remonstrated against this tyranny of silence; but not a member of the majority spoke, and the returns were refused by a vote of fifty-seven to thirty-seven. Immediately John Rutledge called up a third resolution of the same nature, and Samuel Dana of Connecticut made a sensation long remembered, by quoting to the majority the remark, then quite new, of Bonaparte to Sieyès: "That dumb legislature will immortalize your name."

Neither in the Senate nor in the House did Gallatin's financial schemes meet with serious question; they were accepted without change, and embodied in legislation evidently the work of the secretary's own hand. So cautious was Gallatin, that notwithstanding the assertions of the President's Message, he would not make himself responsible for the repeal of internal taxes, but left his colleagues of the War and Navy to pledge themselves to John Randolph for economies to the amount of $600,000, which the event proved to be not wholly practicable. Dearborn and Robert Smith in good faith gave to Randolph the required pledges, and Congress gladly acted upon them. The internal taxes were swept away, and with them one half the government patronage; while a sinking fund was organized, by means of which the public debt, amounting to a nominal capital of about $80,000,000, was to be paid off in sixteen years.

This financial legislation was the sum of what was accomplished by Congress toward positive reform. The whole of Jefferson's theory of internal politics, so far as it was embodied in law, rested in the Act making an annual appropriation of $7,300,000 for paying interest and capital of the public debt; and in the Act for repealing the internal taxes. In these two measures must be sought the foundation for his system of politics abroad and at home, as this system has been described; for his policy flowed in a necessary channel as soon as these measures were adopted.

Great as the change was which under the guise of economy Congress thus quietly effected, — a change which in Jefferson's intention was to substitute commercial restrictions in the place of armaments, for purposes of national defence, — so skilfully was it done that the Federalists could muster only twenty-four votes against it. Jefferson succeeded in carrying his preliminary measures through Congress without meeting, or even raising, the question of their ultimate objects and practical scope; but this manner of dealing with a free people had disadvantages, for it caused them to adopt a system which they did not wholly understand, and were not fully prepared to carry out. A few Virginians knew what Jefferson meant; a clique of members in the House and Senate might have foretold every step in the movement of Government: but the Northern and Western democrats thought only of economy, and accepted the President's partial reasoning as sufficient; while the Federalists, although they saw the truth more clearly, could not oblige the Administration to enter into a full and candid discussion, which, without affecting the result, would have educated the public and saved much misunderstanding in the future.

The Federalists, left to an issue involving mere details of taxation, wasted their strength on a subordinate point. Perhaps their exertions were not wholly wasted, for their outcries may have had some effect in persuading the majority that the new reforms were extreme; but in reality the opposition resisted

feebly the vital financial scheme, and exerted all its
energies against the second and less serious Administration measure, — the repeal of the Judiciary Act
of 1801.

The previous history of the Judiciary Act belonged
to the administration of Jefferson's predecessor and to
the records of the Federalist party.   Before 1801 the
Supreme Court consisted of six justices, who held two
terms a year at Washington, and twice a year rode
their circuits, each justice then sitting in association
with a district judge.   The system pleased no one.
The justices, men of age and dignity, complained that
they were forced twice a year, in the most trying
seasons and through the roughest country, to ride
hundreds of miles on horseback " with the agility of
post-boys ; " the lawyers found fault because the
errors of the inferior court were corrected by the
judges who had made them; the suitors were annoyed by the delays and accidents inevitable to such
journeys and such judges.   In the last year of Federalist power a new arrangement was made, and the
Judiciary Act of 1801 reduced the Supreme Court to
five judges, who were fixed at Washington, while
their circuit duties were transferred to a new class of
circuit judges, eighteen in number.   Twenty-three
districts were divided into six circuits, and the circuit
judges sat independently of the district judges, as
well as of the Supreme Bench.   This separation of
the machinery of the District, Circuit, and Supreme
Courts caused a multiplication of judicial offices and

an increased annual expense of some thirty thousand dollars.

No sooner did this Bill become law, Feb. 13, 1801, than the Federalists used their last moments of power to establish themselves in the posts it created. In Jefferson's words, they retreated into the Judiciary as a stronghold. They filled the new courts as well as the vacancies on the old bench with safe men, at whose head, as Chief-Justice of the Supreme Court, was placed the Secretary of State, John Marshall. That Jefferson should have been angry at this manœuvre was natural ; but, apart from greed for patronage, the Federalists felt bound to exclude Republicans from the bench, to prevent the overthrow of those legal principles in which, as they believed, national safety dwelt. Jefferson understood the challenge, and was obliged to accept or decline it.

On one ground alone could the President and his party fully meet the issue thus offered. They had sought and won popularity on the principle of State-rights. The Judiciary Act of 1789, even more than its supplement of 1801, was notoriously intended to work against the object they had most at heart. The effect of both these Acts was, in their belief, to weaken the State judiciaries and to elevate the national judiciary at their expense, until the national courts should draw to themselves all litigation of importance, leaving the State courts without character or credit. From their point of view, the whole judiciary system should be remodelled, with the purpose

of reversing this centralizing movement; and that
such a reform must begin with the Supreme Court
was too evident for discussion. The true question
for Congress to consider was not so much the repeal of the Judiciary Act of 1801, as the revision of
that which had set in motion the whole centripetal
machine in 1789.

Jefferson's Message, as has been shown, offered
to Congress an issue quite different, at least in
appearance.

" The judiciary system of the United States," — so his
words ran, — " and especially that portion of it recently
erected, will of course present itself to the contemplation
of Congress; and that they may be able to judge of the
proportion which the institution bears to the business it
has to perform, I have caused to be procured from the
several States, and now lay before Congress, an exact
statement of all the causes decided since the first establishment of the courts, and of those which were depending
when additional courts and judges were brought in to
their aid."

From the true Virginia standpoint, the fewer the
causes the less danger. What the Virginians feared
most was the flow of business to the national courts;
and Jefferson's statistics tended only to show that as
yet the new courts had done no harm, inasmuch as
they had little to do. Their abolition on the ground
of economy would still leave the Judiciary establishment of 1789 untouched, merely in order to lop off
an excrescence which might be restored whenever

increase of business should require it, — and which Jefferson's argument in a manner pledged him in such an event to re-establish.

The contradictions in Jefferson's character have always rendered it a fascinating study. Excepting his rival Alexander Hamilton, no American has been the object of estimates so widely differing and so difficult to reconcile. Almost every other American statesman might be described in a parenthesis. A few broad strokes of the brush would paint the portraits of all the early Presidents with this exception, and a few more strokes would answer for any member of their many cabinets; but Jefferson could be painted only touch by touch, with a fine pencil, and the perfection of the likeness depended upon the shifting and uncertain flicker of its semi-transparent shadows. Of all the politicians and writers of that day, none could draw portraits with a sharper outline than Hamilton, whose clear-cut characterizations never failed to fix themselves in the memory as distinctly as his own penetrating features were fixed in Ceracchi's marble or on Trumbull's canvas; and Hamilton's contrasted portraits of Jefferson and Burr, drawn in an often-quoted letter written to Bayard in January, 1801, painted what he believed to be the shifting phase of Jefferson's nature.

" Nor is it true," he said,[1] " that Jefferson is zealot enough to do anything in pursuance of his principles

[1] Hamilton to Bayard, Jan. 15, 1801; Hamilton's Works, vi. 419.

which will contravene his popularity or his interest.   He
is as likely as any man I know to temporize, to calculate
what will be likely to promote his own reputation and
advantage; and the probable result of such a temper is
the preservation of systems, though originally opposed,
which, being once established, could not be overturned
without danger to the person who did it.   To my mind,
a true estimate of Mr. Jefferson's character warrants
the expectation of a temporizing rather than a violent
system."

Never was a prophecy more quickly realized.   Jefferson's suggestion that the new Judiciary was unnecessary because it had not enough business to keep
it fully employed, although by implication admitting
that more business would justify its creation, became
at once the doctrine of his party.   Jan. 8, 1802,
Breckenridge undertook the task of moving in the
Senate the repeal of the Act; and his argument
closely followed the President's suggestion, that the
new courts, being unnecessary and therefore improper, might and should be abolished.   The Federalists took the ground that the Constitution secured to
the judges their office during good behavior, and that
to destroy the office was as distinct a violation of the
compact as to remove the judge.   Thus from the
beginning the debate was narrowed to a technical
issue.   On the one side was seen an incessant effort
to avoid the broader issues which the Federalists
tried to force; on the other side, a certain dramatic
folding of robes, a theatrical declamation over the

lay-figure which Federalists chose to declare a mangled and bleeding Constitution. Gouverneur Morris of New York, whose oratory was apt to verge on the domain of melodrama, exceeded himself in lamentations over the grave of the Constitution: —

" Cast not away this only anchor of our safety. I have seen its progress. I know the difficulties through which it was obtained. I stand in the presence of Almighty God and of the world, and I declare to you that if you lose this charter, never, no, never will you get another! We are now, perhaps, arrived at the parting point. Here, even here, we stand on the brink of fate. Pause! pause! For Heaven's sake, pause!"

If ever a party had paused, it was the Republicans. The progress of what Gouverneur Morris, with characteristic rhetoric, called the " anchor," was thus far arrested only in appearance; and there were already symptoms that the Virginians had reached not only the limit of their supposed revolutionary projects, but also of their influence, and that they were themselves anxious to go no farther. Signs of trouble appeared among the Northern democrats, and sharp hints were given that the Virginians might expect revolt, not so much against their principles as against their patronage. Vice-President Burr did not appear in Washington until six weeks of the session had passed; and when he took the chair of the Senate, Jan. 15, 1802, the Virginians had every reason to expect that he would show them no kindness. Under the affected polish and quiet of his manner, he nursed as

bitter a hatred as his superficial temper could feel
against the whole Virginia oligarchy. Any suggestion
that Burr held scruples of conscience in regard to
the Federalist judiciary would border on satire, for
Burr's conscience was as elastic as his temper; but
he made grave inquiries as to the law, and hinted
doubts calculated to alarm the Virginians. Had he
been content to affect statesmanship, Breckinridge
could have afforded to ignore his demonstrations;
but the behavior of General Armstrong, the democratic senator from New York, and the accidental
absence of Senator Bradley of Vermont unexpect-
edly threw into Burr's hands the power to do mischief. Armstrong failed to appear at Washington,
and his vote was lost. Breckinridge's motion for a
committee of inquiry was carried, January 19, only
by fifteen against thirteen votes; and no sooner had
his committee, with all practicable speed, reported a
Bill for the repeal of the Judiciary Act of 1801, than
it appeared that the Senate was tied, fifteen to fifteen,
with Armstrong and Bradley absent, and the Vice-
President controlling the fate of the Bill. Burr lost
no time in giving a first warning to the Virginians.
Dayton of New Jersey, a Federalist, but an intimate
friend of the Vice-President, moved January 27 to
recommit the Bill to a select committee, and Burr's
casting vote carried the motion.

That Breckinridge and his friends were angry at
this check need not be said; but they were forced
to wait several days for Bradley's return, before

Breckinridge could move and obtain, February 2,
the discharge of the special committee, and recover
control of the Bill. Burr was never given another
opportunity to annoy his party by using his casting
vote; but meanwhile symptoms of hesitation appeared
among the Northern democrats, even more significant
than the open insubordination of Burr. On the day
when Breckinridge succeeded in discharging the
special committee, Senator Ross of Pennsylvania
presented a memorial from the Philadelphia Bar,
declaring their conviction that the actual Circuit
Court was a valuable institution, which could not
be abolished without great public inconvenience; and
this memorial was enforced by a letter in strong
terms, signed by A. J. Dallas, Jefferson's own district
attorney, and by the Republican Attorney-General of
Pennsylvania, Governor McKean's son. The behavior
of Senator Armstrong raised a fear that the Livingstons were not to be depended upon; and hardly
had the Bill passed the Senate, February 3, by a vote
of sixteen to fifteen, than Armstrong resigned his
post in order to let De Witt Clinton take it. In the
House, Dr. Eustis of Boston, alone among the Republicans, opposed the repeal; but the tone of the
debate and of the press showed that few Northern
democrats cared to risk the odium of a genuine
assault on the authority of the Supreme Court.

Another and still sharper hint was soon given to
the Virginians. At the moment when the Bill coming before the House roused there an acrimonious

debate, in which the Federalists assumed a tone that exasperated and alarmed their opponents, the anniversary of Washington's birthday occurred.   The Federalist Congressmen were accustomed to give, February 22, what was called a banquet, — a practice which verged so closely on monarchism that Jefferson made a secret of his own birthday, for fear that his followers should be misled by the example into making him a monocrat against his will.   Either at Burr's secret instigation, or in a spirit of mischief, the Federalists this year, on the pretence that they had voted for Burr as President only a year before, invited him to their banquet.

"We knew," wrote Bayard to Hamilton,[1] "the impression which the coincidence of circumstances would make upon a certain great personage; how readily that impression would be communicated to the proud and aspiring lords of the Ancient Dominion; and we have not been mistaken as to the jealousy we expected it would excite through the party."

In the middle of the feast the door opened, and the Vice-President, courteous and calm as though he were taking the chair of the Senate, entered and took a seat of honor at the table.   His appearance was expected, and roused no surprise; but to the startled amusement of the Federalists he presently rose and pronounced a toast: "The union of all honest men!"

[1] Bayard to Hamilton, April 12, 1802; Hamilton's Works, vi. 539.

This dramatic insult, thus flung in the face of the President and his Virginia friends, was the more significant to them because they alone understood what it meant. To the world at large the toast might seem innocent; but the Virginians had reason to know that Burr believed himself to have been twice betrayed by them, and that his union of honest men was meant to gibbet them as scoundrels. They had no choice but to resent it. Henceforward the party could not contain both him and them. Within a few days De Witt Clinton's newspaper, the "American Citizen," began the attack, and its editor Cheetham henceforward pursued Burr with a vindictiveness which perplexed and divided the Northern democrats, who had no great confidence in Clinton. What was of far more consequence, Duane and the Philadelphia "Aurora," after a moment's hesitation, joined in the hue-and-cry.

CHAPTER XI.

THE Bill repealing the new Judiciary Act, having passed the Senate, February 3, was taken into consideration by the House, in Committee of the Whole, February 4, and caused the chief debate of the session. By common consent Giles and Bayard were accepted as the champions of the two parties, and their speeches were taken as the official arguments on either side. The men were equal to their tasks. For ten years William Branch Giles had been the most active leader of the extreme Republicans. A Virginian, born in 1762, he began his career as a Member of Congress in 1791, by opposing the creation of a national bank. In 1793 he distinguished himself by an attack on Secretary Hamilton, charging him with peculation. In 1796 he led the opposition to Jay's Treaty. After opposing Washington's administration with consistency and severity during six years, he retired from Congress in 1798 in order to oppose Washington's successor with more effect in the legislature of Virginia. With James Madison, John Taylor of Caroline, and Wilson Cary Nicholas, he had taken an active part in the Resolutions of 1798, and his remarks in the debate of December, 1798, showed that he carried the extreme conclusions of the Virginia school to their extreme practical consequences.[1] He "said that the measures of our present government tended to the establishment of monarchy, limited or absolute. . . . If . . . the government were a social compact, he pronounced monarchy to be near at hand, the symptoms and causes of which he particularly pointed out; and concluded that the State legislatures alone, at this time, prevented monarchy." In language perfectly intelligible to his friends he hinted that his party "had no arms, but they would find arms." Even men naturally benevolent, like Jefferson, could rarely resist the conviction that the objects of political opponents were criminal, but Giles exceeded every prominent partisan on either side by the severity of his imputations. As late as June, 1801, he wrote from Richmond to President Jefferson:[2] "The ejected party is now almost universally considered as having been employed, in conjunction with Great Britain, in a scheme for the total destruction of the liberties of the people." No man in the Union was more cordially detested by the Federalists; and even between parties that held each other in little or no respect, few men of so much eminence were so little respected as Giles. The dislike and distrust were mutual. Giles's nature was capable of no pleasure greater than that of exasper-

---

[1] The Virginia Report of 1799-1800, etc.   Richmond, 1850, pp. 143–148.

[2] Giles to Jefferson, June 1, 1801.   Hamilton's History, vii. 585 n.

ating his Federalist opponents; and he rarely enjoyed
a better opportunity for irritation than on Feb. 18,
1802, when, with a great majority behind him, and
with the consciousness of triumph attained, he broke
into the dull debate on the Judiciary Bill.

Both sides were weary of the narrow question
whether Congress had the power to remove Judges
by legislation. Whether such a power existed or
not, every one knew that the Republican majority
meant to use it, and the Federalists were chiefly
anxious to profit by the odium they could attach
to its abuse. The Federalists, in a character new
to them, posed as the defenders of the Constitution
against sacrilegious attacks; while the Republicans,
for the first time in their history as a party, made
light of constitutional objections, and closed their
ears to warnings in which they had themselves hitherto found their chief rhetorical success. With Giles's
appearance on the floor the tedious debate started
into virulence. He began by insinuating motives,
as though he were still discussing the Alien and
Sedition Laws in the Virginia legislature of 1798:
" A great portion of the human mind," he began,
" has been at all times directed toward monarchy
as the best form of government to enforce obedience
and insure the general happiness; whereas another
portion of the human mind has given a preference
to the republican form as best calculated to produce
the same end." On this difference of opinion the
two parties had been founded, the one wishing " to

place in executive hands all the patronage it was possible to create for the purpose of protecting the President against the full force of his constitutional responsibility to the people;" the other contending "that the doctrine of patronage was repugnant to the opinions and feelings of the people; that it was unnecessary, expensive, and oppressive; and that the highest energy the government could possess would flow from the confidence of the mass of the people, founded upon their own sense of their common interest." Thus patronage, or in other words the creation of partial interests for the protection and support of government, had become the guiding principle of the Federalists. For this purpose the debt was funded; under cover of an Indian war, an army was created; under cover of an Algerine war, a navy was built; to support this system, taxation was extended; and finally, by availing itself of French depredations on commerce, the Administration succeeded in pushing all the forms of patronage to an extreme. When the people at last rebelled, and the Federalists saw themselves in danger, " it was natural for them to look out for some department of the government in which they could intrench themselves in the event of an unsuccessful issue in the election, and continue to support those favorite principles of irresponsibility which they could never consent to abandon."

Whatever amount of truth was contained in these charges against the Federalists, they had the merit of consistency ; they reaffirmed what had been the doctrine of the party when in opposition ; what Jefferson was saying in private, and what was a sufficient argument not so much against the circuit judges as against the Federalist Judiciary altogether ; but the position seemed needlessly broad for the support of the technical argument by which Giles proved the power of Congress in regard to the measure under discussion : —

" On one side it is contended that the office is the vested property of the judge, conferred on him by his appointment, and that his good behavior is the consideration of his compensation ; so long, therefore, as his good behavior exists, so long his office must continue in consequence of his good behavior ; and that his compensation is his property in virtue of his office, and therefore cannot be taken away by any authority whatever, although there may be no service for him to perform. On the other it is contended that the good behavior is not the consideration upon which the compensation accrues, but services rendered for the public good ; and that if the office is to be considered as a property, it is a property held in trust for the benefit of the people, and must therefore be held subject to that condition of which Congress is the constitutional judge."

Assuming that the latter view was correct, Giles gave his reasons for holding that the new Judiciary should be abolished ; and the subject led him into a history of the circumstances under which the Act passed, at the moment when the House of Representatives was in permanent session, " in the highest paroxysm of party rage," disputing over the choice between Jefferson and Burr as President. He charged that members of the legislature who voted for the law " were appointed to offices, not indeed created by the law, the Constitution having wisely guarded against an effect of that sort, but to judicial offices previously created by the removal, or what was called the promotion, of judges from the offices they then held to the offices newly created, and supplying their places by members of the legislature who voted for the creation of the new offices." He showed that the business of the courts " is now very much declined, and probably will decline still more."

" Under the view of the subject thus presented, he considered the late courts as useless and unnecessary, and the expense therefore was to him highly objectionable. He did not consider it in the nature of a compensation, for there was no equivalent rendition of service. He could not help considering it as a tribute for past services ; as a tribute for the zeal displayed by these gentlemen in supporting principles which the people had denounced."

Such arguments, if good for the new circuit courts, were still stronger in their application to the Supreme Court itself. Giles affirmed that the " principles advanced in opposition . . . go to the establishment of a permanent corporation of individuals invested with ultimate censorial and controlling power over all the

departments of the government, over legislation, execution, and decision, and irresponsible to the people."
He believed that these principles were "in direct
hostility with the great principle of representative
government." Undoubtedly these principles, if they
existed anywhere, were strongest, not in the circuit,
but in the Supreme Court; and if any judge was to
be set aside because his appointment might be considered as a reward for zeal displayed in supporting
" principles which the people had denounced," Chief-
Justice Marshall, the person most likely to exercise
" ultimate censorial and controlling power over all
the departments of government," was peculiarly subject to suspicion and removal. To no man had the
last President been more indebted, and to no one
had he been more grateful.

Only incidentally, at the close of his speech, Giles
advanced a final, and in his mind fatal, objection to
the new courts, " because of their tendency to produce a gradual demolition of State Courts." Of all
arguments this seemed to be the most legitimate,
for it depended least on the imputation of evil motives to the Congress which passed the Act. No
one need be supposed criminal for wishing, as was
often admitted, to bring justice to every man's door;
and as little need any one be blamed for wishing to
maintain or to elevate the character of his State
Judiciary. Parties might honestly and wisely differ,
and local interests might widely diverge in a matter
so much depending upon circumstances; but no

argument seemed to satisfy Giles unless it carried
an implication of criminality against his opponents.

Giles's speech was such as an orator would select
to answer, and James Asheton Bayard could fairly
claim the right to call himself an orator. Born in
Philadelphia, in 1767, Bayard was five years younger
than Giles, and had followed the opposite path in
politics. Without being an extreme Federalist, he
had been since 1796 a distinguished member of the
Federalist party in Congress, and had greatly contri-
buted to moderate the extravagances of his friends.
In the style of personality which Giles affected, Bayard
was easily a master. Virulence against virulence,
aristocracy had always the advantage over democracy; for the aristocratic orator united distinct styles
of acrimony, and the style of social superiority was
the most galling. Giles affected democratic humility
to the last, and partly for that reason never became
a master even of invective; while John Randolph,
finding the attitude of a democrat unsuited for his
rhetoric, abandoned it, and seemed to lose his mental
balance in the intoxication of his recovered social
superiority. Giles's charges, by an opposite illusion,
seemed to crawl; his contempt resembled fear; his
democratic virtues crouched before the aristocratic
insolence they reproved. Bayard appeared to carry
with him the sympathy of all that was noble in
human character when, taking the floor as Giles sat
down, he turned on the Virginian with a dignity of
retort which, whatever might be its value as argu-

ment, cut the deeper because its justice could not be denied.

Jefferson's administration was not yet a year old ; the Federalists had twelve long years abounding in mistakes and misfortunes to defend, and Giles's arraignment embraced the whole. Bayard accepted the challenge, and his speech, too historical for compression, varied between long periods of defence and brief intervals of attack. The defence belonged to past history ; the attack concerned the actual moment, and need alone be noticed here. He began by refusing belief that Giles ever seriously felt the fear of monarchy he expressed ; he was led by other motives : —

" I pray to God I may be mistaken in the opinions I entertain as to the designs of gentlemen to whom I am opposed. Those designs I believe hostile to the powers of this government. State pride extinguishes a national sentiment. Whatever power is taken from this government is given to the States. The ruins of this government aggrandize the States. There are States which are too proud to be controlled, whose sense of greatness and resource renders them indifferent to our protection, and induces a belief that if no general government existed, their influence would be more extensive and their importance more conspicuous. There are gentlemen who make no secret of an extreme point of depression to which the government is to be sunk. To that point we are rapidly progressing."

The charge was certainly emphatic, and deserved as clear an answer from Giles as Bayard gave to the charge of monarchical tendencies. On the constitutional point involved in the Bill before the House, Bayard was equally distinct: —

" The point on which I rely is that you can do no act which impairs the independence of a judge. When gentlemen assert that the office may be vacated notwithstanding the incumbency of a judge, do they consider that they beg the very point which is in controversy? The office cannot be vacated without violating the express provision of the Constitution in relation to the tenure. . . . The second plain, unequivocal provision on this subject is that the compensation of the judge shall not be diminished during the term he continues in office. This provision is directly levelled at the power of the legislature: they alone could reduce the salary. Could this provision have any other design than to place the judge out of the power of Congress? You cannot reduce a part of the compensation, but you may extinguish the whole. What is the sum of this notable reasoning? You cannot remove the judge from the office, but you may take the office from the judge; you cannot take the compensation from the judge, but you may separate the judge from the compensation. If your Constitution cannot resist reasoning like this, then indeed is it waste paper."

When Bayard reached Giles's favorite doctrine that patronage was a Federalist system, and the charge that two senators who voted for the Judiciary Act of 1801 were rewarded by the offices vacated in consequence of promotions to circuit judgeships, he produced a true oratorical sensation by a retort that sank deep into the public memory: —

" The case to which I refer carries me once more to
the scene of the Presidential election. I should not have
introduced it into this debate, had it not been called up
by the honorable member from Virginia. In that scene I
had my part; it was a part not barren of incident, and
which has left an impression which cannot easily depart
from my recollection. I know who were rendered important characters, either from the possession of personal
means or from the accident of political situation. And
now, Sir, let me ask the honorable member what his
reflections and belief will be when he observes that every
man on whose vote the event of the election hung has
since been distinguished by presidential favor. I fear,
Sir, I shall violate the decorum of parliamentary proceeding in the mentioning of names, but I hope the example which has been set me will be admitted as an
excuse. Mr. Charles Pinckney of South Carolina was
not a member of the House, but he was one of the most
active, efficient, and successful promoters of the election
of the present chief magistrate. It was well ascertained
that the votes of South Carolina were to turn the equal
balance of the scales. The zeal and industry of Mr.
Pinckney had no bounds; the doubtful politics of South
Carolina were decided, and her votes cast in the scale of
Mr. Jefferson. Mr. Pinckney has since been appointed
Minister Plenipotentiary to the Court of Madrid, — an
appointment as high and honorable as any within the
gift of the Executive. I will not deny that this preferment is the reward of talents and services, although, Sir,
I have never yet heard of the talents or services of Mr.
Charles Pinckney. In the House of Representatives I
know what was the value of the vote of Mr. Claiborne
of Tennessee; the vote of a State was in his hands.

Mr. Claiborne has since been raised to the high dignity
of Governor of the Mississippi Territory. I know how
great, and how greatly felt, was the importance of the
vote of Mr. Linn of New Jersey. The delegation of the
State consists of five members; two of the delegation
were decidedly for Mr. Jefferson, two were decidedly
for Mr. Burr. Mr. Linn was considered as inclining to
one side, but still doubtful; both parties looked up to
him for the vote of New Jersey. He gave it to Mr.
Jefferson; and Mr. Linn has since had the profitable
office of supervisor of his district conferred upon him.
Mr. Lion of Vermont was in this instance an important
man; he neutralized the vote of Vermont; his absence
alone would have given the vote of a State to Mr. Burr.
It was too much to give an office to Mr. Lion, — his character was low; but Mr. Lion's son has been handsomely
provided for in one of the Executive offices. I shall add
to the catalogue but the name of one more gentleman,
Mr. Edward Livingston of New York. I knew well —
full well I knew — the consequence of this gentleman.
His means were not limited to his own vote; nay, I always considered more than the vote of New York within
his power. Mr. Livingston has been made the Attorney
for the District of New York; the road of preferment
has been opened to him, and his brother has been raised
to the distinguished place of Minister Plenipotentiary to
the French Republic."

Such charges would have caused little feeling at
any subsequent period, but the Republican party was
the first opposition that gained power in the United
States, and hitherto it had believed in its own virtue.
Such a state of things could never occur again, for

only a new country could be inexperienced in politics; but the cynical indifference with which Europe looked on while patriots were bought, was as yet unknown to Jefferson's friends. They were honest; they supposed themselves to have crushed a corrupt system, and to have overthrown in especial the influence of Executive patronage upon Congress. Men like Gallatin, Giles, Randolph, Macon, Nicholson, Stanford, and John Taylor of Caroline listened to Bayard's catalogue of Executive favors as though it were a criminal indictment. They knew that he might have said more, had he been deeper in Executive secrets. Not only had he failed to include all the rewards given to Jefferson's friends, but he omitted the punishments inflicted on those who were believed to be Jefferson's enemies. He did not know that Theodorus Bailey, another of Burr's friends who had voted for Jefferson, was soon to be made postmaster of New York, while Burr himself was not only refused the appointment of Matthew L. Davis, but was to be condemned without a trial.

The acrimony which Giles's tongue thus threw into the debate continued to the end of the session, but had no deeper effect than to make the majority cautious. They were content to show that the Constitution did not expressly forbid the act they meant to perform. In truth the legality of the act depended on the legitimacy of the motive. Of all the root-and-branch Virginians, John Randolph was perhaps the most extreme; and his speech of February 20 laid down an honest principle of action. "It is not on account of the paltry expense of the establishment that I want to put it down," he protested ; and with still more energy he said, " I am free to declare that if the intent of this Bill is to get rid of the judges, it is a perversion of your power to a base purpose ; it is an unconstitutional act."

As a matter of expediency and public convenience, no one seriously denied that the Federalists were altogether in the right. The introduction of railways and steamboats greatly altered the problem of judicial organization ; but no system could have been better adapted to its time and purposes than that of 1801. The only solid argument brought against it was that it attained its object too completely, bringing Federal justice to every man's door, and removing every difficulty or objection to suing in Federal courts. There was truth in the complaint that it thus placed the State judiciaries at a disadvantage. Beyond and above this, the controversy involved another question of far-reaching consequences which the Republicans were too timid to avow. A true democrat might have said openly that he wanted an elective judiciary, or would have insisted that the whole judiciary must be made subject to removal by the legislature. In neither of these opinions was anything disgraceful or improper ; yet such was the dread of Federalist and conservative outcry, that although many of the Republican speakers went to the verge of the avowal, none dared make the issue.

Their timidity cost the Virginians dear. They knew, and never ceased to complain, that power grew mechanically; and only their want of experience excused them for over-confidence in the strength of their own virtue. They saw that the only part of Federalist centralization still remaining beyond their control was the judiciary; and they knew that if the judiciary were allowed to escape them in their first fervor of Republican virtue, they never could grapple with it after their own hands had learned the use of centralized power and felt the charm of office. In-stead of acting, they temporized, threatened without daring to strike, and were made to appear like secret conspirators, planning what they feared to avow.

The repeal of the Judiciary Act passed the House, March 3, by a party vote of fifty-nine to thirty-two; but the Federalists were far from feeling themselves beaten. They had measured the strength of the majority, and felt that the revolutionary impulse was exhausted. As the Federalists grew bolder, the Re-publicans grew more timid. They passed a supple-mentary Judiciary Act, to quiet complaint and to pre-vent the Supreme Court from holding its customary autumn term, lest Marshall should declare the abolition of the circuit courts unconstitutional. The evidences of timidity were not confined to judiciary measures. On no subject had the Republicans expressed stronger convictions than against the navy; yet when Michael Leib of Pennsylvania, in the heat of the judiciary debate, moved for a committee to consider the ques-

tion of abolishing the navy, his motion was allowed
to lie on the table until Roger Griswold, an extreme
Connecticut Federalist, called it up, March 5, in a
spirit of defiance. The House sustained Griswold,
and took up the Resolution; whereat Leib withdrew
his own motion, and evaded the issue he had chal-
lenged. In regard to another Federalist creation
which had been the subject of Republican attacks,
a similar failure occurred. The mint cost nearly as
much as the circuit courts, and accomplished less.
Since its foundation it had coined, in gold, silver, and
copper, only $3,000,000, at a cost of nearly $300,000;
while a gold or silver coin of the United States was
still a rare sight. The Republican party when in opposition had opposed the mint as a monarchical institution, — unnecessary, expensive, and symbolic of
centralized power. Giles accordingly moved, January 29, that the Act under which it existed should be
repealed. In a speech, February 8, he avowed his
hostility to the establishment from the beginning;
he thought none but self-supporting establishments
should exist. "There is a difference," said he, "between this and other countries. Other nations need
to coin their own money; it is not with them the
general but the partial good; it is aggrandizement
of individuals, the trappings of royalty. Here, it is
true, you established a mint, you have raised armies
and fleets, to create an Executive influence; but what
do the people say now? They send men here now to
govern, who shall not govern for themselves but for

the people." This was party doctrine. John Randolph adopted it in principle, asserting that nineteen-
twentieths of the silver in circulation was Spanish-
milled dollars or their parts, and that sovereignty
was no more affected by using foreign coin than by
using foreign cordage or cannon. The House accepted
these views ; Giles brought in his Bill for abolishing the mint; and after a short debate the House
passed it, April 26, without a division. On the same
day the Senate, quietly, without discussion or a call
of yeas and nays, rejected it.

Perhaps the limit of Virginian influence was shown
with most emphasis in the fate of a fugitive-slave
Bill reported Dec. 18, 1801, by a committee of
which Joseph Nicholson was chairman. The Bill
imposed a fine of five hundred dollars on any one
who should employ a strange negro without adver-
tising in two newspapers a description of the man.
Every free negro in the North must under this law
carry about him a certificate of his freedom. To this
sweeping exercise of a " centralized despotism " the
Northern democrats objected, and, with only half-a-
dozen exceptions, voted against it, although Bayard
and several Southern Federalists joined Giles, Michael
Leib, and John Randolph in its support. The Bill
was rejected, January 18, by a vote of forty-six to
forty-three.

Before the session closed, sensible Federalists were
reassured, and the Administration was glad to repose
on such triumphs as had been won.

"The President's party in Congress," wrote Bayard to Hamilton,[1] "is much weaker than you would be led to judge from the printed state of the votes. Here we plainly discern that there is no confidence, nor the smallest attachment prevails among them. The spirit which existed at the beginning of the session is entirely dissipated; a more rapid and radical change could not have been anticipated. An occasion is only wanting for Virginia to find herself abandoned by all her auxiliaries, and she would be abandoned upon the ground of her inimical principles to an efficient federal government."

The general legislation of the year showed no partisan character. A naturalization law was adopted, re-establishing the term of five years' residence as a condition of citizenship, — a measure recommended by the annual Message. A new apportionment Act was passed, fixing the ratio of Congressional representation at one member for 33,000 citizens. During the next ten years the House was to consist of one hundred and forty-one members. The military peace establishment was fixed at three regiments, one of artillery and two of infantry, comprising in all about three thousand men, under one brigadier-general. By Sections 26 and 27 of the Act, approved March 16, 1802, the President was authorized to establish a corps of engineers, to be stationed at West Point in the State of New York, which should constitute a military academy; and the Secretary of War was

[1] Bayard to Hamilton, April 25, 1802; Hamilton's Works, vi. 534.

authorized to procure the necessary apparatus for the institution. Great as the influence of this new establishment was upon the army, its bearing on the general education of the people was still greater, for the government thus assumed the charge of introducing the first systematic study of science in the United States.

Perhaps the most important legislation of the year was an Act approved April 30, which authorized the people of Ohio to form a Constitution and enter the Union; for not only was the admission of Ohio a formidable increase of power to the Northern democracy, but Gallatin inserted into the law a contract, which bound the State and nation to set aside the proceeds of a certain portion of the public lands for the use of schools and for the construction of roads between the new State and the seaboard. This principle, by which education and internal improvements were taken under the protection of Congress, was a violation of State-rights theories, against which, in after years, the strict constructionists protested; but in this first year of their sway Gallatin and the Northern democrats were allowed to manage their own affairs without interference. John Randolph would not vote for the admission of a new State, but Giles and Nicholson gave their votes for the bill, which passed without a murmur.

Gallatin's influence carried another point, more annoying to the Southern Republicans, although less serious. After years of wrangling, Georgia surren-

dered to the United States government all right
and title to the territory which was afterward to become the States of Alabama and Mississippi. This
immense region, shut from the Gulf of Mexico by the
Spaniards, who owned every river-mouth, was inhabited by powerful Indian tribes, of whom the Geor-
gians stood in terror. The Creeks and Cherokees,
Choctaws and Chickasaws, owned the land, and were
wards of the United States government. No one
could say what was the value of Georgia's title, for
it depended on her power to dispossess the Indians;
but however good the title might be, the State would
have been fortunate to make it a free gift to any
authority strong enough to deal with the Creeks and
Cherokees alone. In the year 1795, ignoring the
claims of the national government, the Georgia Legislature sold its rights over twenty million acres of
Indian land to four land-companies for the gross sum
of five hundred thousand dollars. With one exception, every member of the Legislature appeared to
have a pecuniary interest in the transaction; yet
no one could say with certainty that the title was
worth more than half a million dollars, or indeed was
worth anything to the purchasers, unless backed by
the power of the United States government, which
was not yet the case. Nevertheless, the people of
Georgia, like the people of Massachusetts and Pennsylvania, being at the moment in the fever of land-
speculation, partly because they thought the land too
cheap, partly because they believed their representa-

tives to have been bribed, rose in anger against their
Legislature and elected a new one, which declared
the sales " null and void," burned the Yazoo Act, as
it was called, in the public square of Louisville, and
called a State Convention which made the repealing
Act a part of the Constitution.

This series of measures completed the imbroglio.
No man could say to whom the lands belonged.
President Washington interposed on the part of the
central government; the Indians quietly kept posses
sion; hundreds of individuals in the Eastern States
who had bought land-warrants from the Yazoo com-
panies, claimed their land; while Georgia ignored
President Washington, the Indians, the claimants,
and the law, insisting that as a sovereign State she
had the right to sell her own land, and to repudiate
that sale for proper cause. In this case the State
maintained that the sale was vitiated by fraud.

Doubtless the argument had force. If a sovereign
State had not the power to protect itself from its own
agents, it had, in joining the Union, entered into a
relation different from anything hitherto supposed.
Georgia put the utmost weight on the Rescinding
Act as a measure of State-rights, and the true
Virginia school made common cause with Georgia.
Republicans who believed in the principles of 1798
considered the maintenance of the Rescinding Act
a vital issue.

At length Congress took the matter in hand. Madison, Gallatin, and Levi Lincoln were appointed com-

missioners to make a settlement; and Senator James Jackson, the anti-Yazoo leader, supported by his colleague Senator Baldwin and by Governor Milledge, met them on behalf of Georgia, — a formidable array of high officials, whose whole authority was needed to give their decision weight. April 24, 1802, they reached a settlement so liberal to Georgia that Jackson and his associates took the risk of yielding more than they liked to concede. The western boundary was fixed to please the State; an immediate cession of land was obtained from the Indians, and the United States undertook to extinguish at their own expense, as early as they could reasonably do it, the Indian title to all lands within the limits of Georgia; the sum of $1,250,000 was to be paid to the State from the first net proceeds of land-sales; the ceded territory was to be admitted as a State, with slavery, whenever its population should reach sixty thousand; and in consideration for these advantages the Georgians unwillingly agreed that five million acres should be set aside for the purpose of compromising claims. The commissioners did not venture to affirm the legality of the Yazoo sale, but, while expressing the opinion that " the title of the claimants cannot be supported," declared that " the interest of the United States, the tranquillity of those who may hereafter inhabit that territory, and various equitable considerations which may be urged in favor of most of the present claimants, render it expedient to enter into a compromise on reasonable terms."   With this concession to the principle of State-rights, the Georgians were appeased, and the commissioners hoped that all parties would be satisfied. The brunt of the negotiation fell upon Gallatin; but Madison found no difficulty in giving his support to the compromise.

These two measures greatly affected the Government and increased its power. The admission of Ohio into the Union gave two more senators to the Administration, and the acquisition of the southwestern territory relieved it from an annoying conflict of authority. Jefferson was henceforward better able to carry out his humane policy toward the Indians, — a policy which won him praise from some of his bitterest enemies; while Gallatin turned his energies toward developing the public-land system, in which he had, when in opposition, taken active interest. The machinery of government worked more easily every day.

CHAPTER XII.

WHEN the session of Congress closed, May 3, the Administration was left to administer a system greatly reduced in proportions. In Jefferson's own words, he had " put the ship on her republican tack," where she was to show by the beauty of her motion the skill of her builders. Nothing remained, with respect to internal politics, but to restore harmony by winning recalcitrant New England, a task which he confidently hoped to accomplish within the course of the year. "If we are permitted," he wrote,[1] in October, 1801, " to go on so gradually in the removals called for by the Republicans, as not to shock or revolt our well-meaning citizens who are coming over to us in a steady stream, we shall completely consolidate the nation in a short time, — excepting always the royalists and priests." So hopeful was he of immediate success, that he wrote to his French correspondent, Dupont de Nemours,[2] in January, 1802: "I am satisfied that within one year from this time, were an election to take place between two candidates, merely Republican and Federal, where no personal opposition existed against either, the Federal candidate would

[1] Jefferson to Peter Carr, Oct. 25, 1801 ; Jefferson MSS.
[2] Jefferson to M. Dupont, Jan. 18, 1802 ; Jefferson MSS.

not get the vote of a single elector in the United States." To revolutionize New England, he concentrated Executive influence, and checked party spirit. He began by placing two Massachusetts men in his Cabinet; before long he appointed as Postmaster-General an active Connecticut politician, Gideon Granger. The Postmaster-General was not then a member of the Cabinet, but his patronage was not the less important. Granger and Lincoln carried on a sapper's duty of undermining and weakening the Federalists' defences, while the Republican party refrained from acts that could rouse alarm.

Although in cooler moments Jefferson was less sanguine, he still so far miscalculated the division between himself and New England, that when the spring elections showed less increase than he expected in the Republican vote, he could not explain the cause of his error. "I had hoped," he wrote,[1] in April, 1802, " that the proceedings of this session of Congress would have rallied the great body of citizens at once to one opinion; but the inveteracy of their quondam leaders has been able, by intermingling the grossest lies and misrepresentations, to check the effect in some small degree until they shall be exposed." Nevertheless, he flattered himself that the work was practically done.[2] " In Rhode Island the late election gives us two to one through the whole

[1] Jefferson to Cæsar A. Rodney, April 24, 1802 ; Jefferson MSS.

[2] Jefferson to Joel Barlow, May 3, 1802 ; Works, iv. 437.

State. Vermont is decidedly with us. It is said and believed that New Hampshire has got a majority of Republicans now in its Legislature, and wanted a few hundreds only of turning out their Federal governor. He goes assuredly the next trial. Connecticut is supposed to have gained for us about fifteen or twenty per cent since the last election; but the exact issue is not yet known here, nor is it certainly known how we shall stand in the House of Representatives of Massachusetts; in the Senate there we have lost ground. The candid Federalists acknowledge that their party can never more raise its head." This was all true; he had won also in national politics a triumph that warranted confidence. "Our majority in the House of Representatives has been about two to one; in the Senate, eighteen to fifteen. After another election it will be of two to one in the Senate, and it would not be for the public good to have it greater. A respectable minority is useful as censors; the present one is not respectable, being the bitterest remains of the cup of Federalism rendered desperate and furious by despair."

Jefferson resembled all rulers in one peculiarity of mind. Even Bonaparte thought that a respectable minority might be useful as censors; but neither Bonaparte nor Jefferson was willing to agree that any particular minority was respectable. Jefferson could not persuade himself to treat with justice the remnants of that great party which he himself, by opposition not more "respectable" than theirs, had driven from power and " rendered desperate and furious by despair." Jefferson prided himself on his services to free-thought even more than on those he had rendered to political freedom: in the political field he had many rivals, but in the scientific arena he stood, or thought he stood, alone. His relations with European philosophers afforded him deep enjoyment; and in his Virginian remoteness he imagined his own influence on thought, abroad and at home, to be greater than others supposed it. His knowledge of New England was so slight that he readily adopted a belief in the intolerance of Puritan society toward every form of learning; he loved to contrast himself with his predecessor in the encouragement of science, and he held that to break down the theory and practice of a state-church in New England was necessary not only to his own complete triumph, but to the introduction of scientific thought. Had he known the people of New England better, he would have let them alone; but believing that Massachusetts and Connecticut were ruled by an oligarchy like the old Virginia tobacco-planters, with no deep hold on the people, he was bent upon attacking and overthrowing it. At the moment when he was thus preparing to introduce science into New England by political methods, President Dwight, the head of New England Calvinism, was persuading Benjamin Silliman to devote his life to the teaching of chemistry in Yale College.[1] Not long afterward, the Corpora-

---

[1] Life of Benjamin Silliman, i. 90–96.

tion of Harvard College scandalized the orthodox by
electing as Professor of Theology, Henry Ware, whose
Unitarian sympathies were notorious.   All three
authorities were working in their own way for the
same result ; but Jefferson preferred to work through
political revolution, — a path which the people of New
England chose only when they could annoy their rulers.
To effect this revolution from above, to seduce the hesitating, harass the obstinate, and combine the champions of free-thought against the priests, was Jefferson's ardent wish.   Soon after his inauguration he
wrote to Dr. Priestley,[1] —

" Yours is one of the few lives precious to mankind,
and for the continuance of which every thinking man is
solicitous.   Bigots may be an exception.   What an effort,
my dear sir, of bigotry, in politics and religion, have we
gone through !   The barbarians really flattered themselves
they should be able to bring back the times of Vandalism,
when ignorance put everything into the hands of power
and priestcraft.   All advances in science were proscribed
as innovations.   They pretended to praise and encourage
education, but it was to be the education of our ances-
tors.   We were to look backwards, not forwards, for
improvement, — the President himself declaring, in one
of his Answers to Addresses, that we were never to expect to go beyond them in real science.   This was the
real ground of all the attacks on you.   Those who live
by mystery and *charlatanerie*, fearing you would render
them useless by simplifying the Christian philosophy, —

[1] Jefferson to Priestley, March 21, 1801 ; Works, iv. 373.

the most sublime and benevolent, but most perverted, system that ever shone on man, — endeavored to crush your well-earned and well-deserved fame."

Who was it that lived " by mystery and *charlatanerie ?* " Some three years before, in the excitement of 1798, Jefferson wrote to his friend John Taylor of Caroline his opinion of the New Englanders, with the serious air which sometimes gave to his occasional exaggerations the more effect of humor because no humor was intended :[1] —

" Seeing that we must have somebody to quarrel with, I had rather keep our New England associates for that purpose than to see our bickerings transferred to others. They are circumscribed within such narrow limits, and their population so full, that their numbers will ever be the minority ; and they are marked, like the Jews, with such a perversity of character as to constitute, from that circumstance, the natural division of our parties. A little patience, and we shall see the reign of witches pass over, their spells dissolved, and the people recovering their true sight, restoring their government to its true principles."

The letters to Priestley and Taylor gave comparatively mild expression of this dislike for New Englanders and Jews. Another letter, written at the same time with that to Priestley, spoke more plainly :[2] —

[1] Jefferson to John Taylor, June 1, 1798 ; Works, iv. 247.

[2] Jefferson to Moses Robinson, March 23, 1801; Works, iv. 379.

"The Eastern States will be the last to come over, on account of the dominion of the clergy, who had got a smell of union between Church and State, and began to indulge reveries which can never be realized in the present state of science. If, indeed, they could have prevailed on us to view all advances in science as dangerous innovations, and to look back to the opinions and practices of our forefathers instead of looking forward for improvement, a promising groundwork would have been laid; but I am in hopes their good sense will dictate to them that since the mountain will not come to them, they had better go to the mountain; that they will find their interest in acquiescing in the liberty and science of their country; and that the Christian religion, when divested of the rags in which they have enveloped it, and brought to the original purity and simplicity of its benevolent institutor, is a religion of all others most friendly to liberty, science, and the freest expansion of the human mind."

If the New England Calvinists ever laughed, one might suppose that they could have found in this letter, had it been published, material for laughter as sardonic as the letter itself. Their good sense was not likely then to dictate, their interest certainly would not induce them to believe, that they had best adopt Jefferson's views of the "benevolent institutor" of Christianity; and Jefferson, aware of the impossibility, regarded his quarrel with them as irreconcilable. "The clergy," he wrote again, a few weeks later,[1] "who have missed their union with the

[1] Jefferson to Gideon Granger, May 3, 1801; Works, iv. 395.

State, the Anglo-men who have missed their union with England, and the political adventurers who have lost the chance of swindling and plunder in the waste of public money, will never cease to bawl on the breaking up of their sanctuary." Of all these classes the clergy alone were mortal enemies. " Of the monarchical Federalists," he wrote to his attorney-general,[1] " I have no expectations ; they are incurables, to be taken care of in a mad-house if necessary, and on motives of charity." The monarchical Federalists, as he chose to call them, were the Essex Junto, — George Cabot, Theophilus Parsons, Fisher Ames, Timothy Pickering, Stephen Higginson, and their followers ; but it was not with them or their opinions that Jefferson was angriest. " The ' Palladium,' " he went on, " is understood to be the clerical paper, and from the clergy I expect no mercy. They crucified their Saviour, who preached that their kingdom was not of this world ; and all who practise on that precept must expect the extreme of their wrath. The laws of the present day withhold their hands from blood, but lies and slander still remain to them."

This was strong language. When Jefferson cried that law alone withheld the hands of the New England clergy from taking his blood, his words were not wholly figures of speech. He had fought a similar battle in Virginia, and still felt its virulence. What was more to the purpose, every politician could see that his strategy was correct. The New England church was

[1] Jefferson to Levi Lincoln, Aug. 26, 1801 ; Works, iv. 406.

the chief obstacle to democratic success, and New-England society, as then constituted, was dangerous to the safety of the Union. Whether a reform could be best accomplished by external attack, or whether Massachusetts and Connecticut had best be left in peace to work out their own problems, was a matter of judgment only. If Jefferson thought he had the power to effect his object by political influence, he could hardly refuse to make the attempt, although he admitted that his chance of success in Connecticut was desperate. " I consider Rhode Island, Vermont, Massachusetts, and New Hampshire," he wrote to Pierpoint Edwards, of Connecticut,[1] " as coming about in the course of this year, . . . but the nature of your government being a subordination of the civil to the ecclesiastical power, I consider it as desperate for long years to come. Their steady habits exclude the advances of information, and they seem exactly where they were when they separated from the Saints of Oliver Cromwell ; and there your clergy will always keep them if they can. You will follow the bark of Liberty only by the help of a tow-rope."

Expecting no mercy from the clergy, Jefferson took pains to show that they were to look for no mercy from him. At the moment he began the attempt to " completely consolidate the nation," he gave what amounted to a formal notice that with the clergy he would neither make peace nor accept truce. A few

[1] Jefferson to Pierpoint Edwards, July 21, 1801 ; Jefferson MSS.

days after announcing in his Inaugural Address, " We are all Republicans — we are all Federalists," and appealing for harmony and affection in social intercourse, Jefferson wrote a letter to the famous Thomas Paine, then at Paris waiting for means of conveyance to America. A sloop-of-war, the " Maryland," was under orders for Havre to carry the ratification of the new treaty with France, and the President made his first use of the navy to pay a public compliment to Paine.

" You expressed a wish," he wrote,[1] " to get a passage to this country in a public vessel. Mr. Dawson is charged with orders to the captain of the ' Maryland' to receive and accommodate you with a passage back, if you can be ready to depart at such short warning. . . . I am in hopes you will find us returned generally to sentiments worthy of former times. In these it will be your glory steadily to have labored, and with as much effect as any man living. That you may long live to continue your useful labors, and to reap their reward in the thankfulness of nations, is my sincere prayer. Accept assurances of my high esteem and affectionate attachment."

The sentiments in which Paine gloried " steadily to have labored," so far as they were recent, chiefly consisted in applause of the French Revolution, in libels on President Washington and his successor, and in assaults on the Christian religion. Whether he was right or wrong need not be discussed. Even though he were correct in them all, and was entitled to

[1] Jefferson to Thomas Paine, March 18, 1801 ; Works, iv. 370.

higher respect than any which Jefferson could show
him, he was at that time regarded by respectable society, both Federalist and Republican, as a person to be
avoided, a character to be feared. Among the New
England churches the prejudice against him amounted
to loathing, which epithets could hardly express. Had
Jefferson written a letter to Bonaparte applauding his
"useful labors" on the 18th Brumaire, and praying
that he might live long to continue them, he would
not have excited in the minds of the New England
Calvinists so deep a sense of disgust as by thus seeming to identify himself with Paine. All this was
known to him when he wrote his letter; he knew too
that Paine would be likely to make no secret of such
a compliment; and even if Paine held his tongue, the
fact of his return in a national vessel must tell the
story.

Jefferson's friends took a tone of apology about the
letter to Paine, implying that he acted without reflection. They treated the letter as a formal civility,
such as might without complaint have been extended
to Gates or Conway or Charles Lee,[1] — a reminiscence
of Revolutionary services which implied no personal
feeling. Had Jefferson meant no more than this, he
would have said only what he meant. He was not
obliged to offer Paine a passage in a ship-of-war; or
if he felt himself called upon to do so, he need not
have written a letter; or if a letter must be written,
he might have used very cordial language without

[1] Randall's Jefferson, ii. 643.

risking the charge of applauding Paine's assaults on Christianity, and without seeming to invite him to continue such "useful labors" in America. No man could express more delicate shades of sympathy than Jefferson when he chose. He had smarted for years under the lashing caused by his Mazzei letter, and knew that a nest of hornets would rise about him the moment the "Maryland" should arrive; yet he wrote an assurance of his "high esteem and affectionate attachment" to Paine, with a "sincere prayer" that he might "long live to continue" his "useful labors." These expressions were either deceptive, or they proved the President's earnestness and courage. The letter to Paine was not, like the letter to Mazzei, a matter of apology or explanation. Jefferson never withdrew or qualified its language, or tried to soften its effect. "With respect to the letter," he wrote [1] to Paine in 1805, "I never hesitated to avow and to justify it in conversation. In no other way do I trouble myself to contradict anything which is said." Believing that the clergy would have taken his blood if the law had not restrained them, he meant to destroy their church if he could; and he gave them fair notice of his intention.

Although the letter to Paine was never explained away, other expressions of the President seemed to contradict the spirit of this letter, and these the President took trouble to explain. What had he meant by his famous appeal in behalf of harmony

[1] Jefferson to Paine, June 5, 1805 ; Works, iv. 582.

and affection in social intercourse, " without which liberty and even life itself are but dreary things " ? What was to become of the still more famous declaration, " We are all Republicans — we are all Federalists " ? Hardly had he uttered these words than he hastened to explain them to his friends. " It was a conviction," he wrote to Giles,[1] " that these people did not differ from us in principle which induced me to define the principles which I deemed orthodox, and to urge a reunion on those principles; and I am induced to hope it has conciliated many. I do not speak of the desperadoes of the quondam faction in and out of Congress. These I consider as incurables, on whom all attentions would be lost, and therefore will not be wasted; but my wish is to keep their flock from returning to them." He intended to entice the flock with one hand and to belabor the shepherds with the other. In equally clear language he wrote to Governor McKean of Pennsylvania:[2] —

" My idea is that the mass of our countrymen, even of those who call themselves Federalist, are Republican. They differ from us but in a shade of more or less power to be given to the Executive or Executive organs. . . . To restore that harmony which our predecessors so wickedly made it their object to break up, to render us again one people acting as one nation, — should be the object of every man really a patriot. I am satisfied

[1] Jefferson to W. B. Giles, March 23, 1801; Works, iv. 382.

[2] Jefferson to Governor McKean, July 24, 1801; Jefferson MSS.

it can be done, and I own that the day which should
convince me to the contrary would be the bitterest of
my life."

This motive, he said, had dictated his answer to
the New Haven remonstrants, — a paper, he added,
which "will furnish new texts for the monarchists;
but from them I ask nothing: I wish nothing but
their eternal hatred."

The interest of Jefferson's character consisted, to
no small extent, in these outbursts of temper, which
gave so lively a tone to his official, and still more to
his private, language. The avowal in one sentence of
his duty as a patriot to restore the harmony which
his predecessors (one of whom was President Washington) had " so wickedly made it their object to
break up," and the admission that the day of his
final failure would be the bitterest of his life, contrasted strangely with his wish, in the next sentence, for the eternal hatred of a class which embraced most of the bench and bar, the merchants
and farmers, the colleges and the churches of New
England! In any other man such contradictions
would have argued dishonesty. In Jefferson they
proved only that he took New England to be like Virginia, — ruled by a petty oligarchy which had no sympathies with the people, and whose artificial power,
once broken, would vanish like that of the Virginia church. He persuaded himself that if his system were politically successful, the New England
hierarchy could be safely ignored. When he said

that all were Republicans and all Federalists, he meant that the churches and prejudices of New England were, in his opinion, already so much weakened as not to be taken into his account.

At first the New Englanders were half inclined to believe his assurances. The idea of drawing a line between the people on one side and the bulk of their clergy, magistrates, political leaders, learned professions, colleges, and land-owners on the other did not occur to them, and so thoroughly Virginian was this idea that it never came to be understood; but when they found Jefferson ejecting Federalists from office and threatening the clergy with Paine, they assumed, without refined analysis, that the President had deliberately deceived them. This view agreed with their previous prejudices against Jefferson's character, and with their understanding of the Mazzei letter. Their wrath soon became hot with the dry white heat peculiar to their character. The clergy had always hated Jefferson, and believed him not only to be untruthful, but to be also a demagogue, a backbiter, and a sensualist. When they found him, as they imagined, actually at work stripping not only the rags from their religion, but the very coats from their backs, and setting Paine to bait them, they were beside themselves with rage and contempt.

Thus the summer of 1802, which Jefferson's hopes had painted as the term of his complete success, was marked by an outburst of reciprocal invective and slander such as could not be matched in American

history.　The floodgates of calumny were opened.
By a stroke of evil fortune Jefferson further roused
against himself the hatred of a man whose vileness
made him more formidable than the respectability of
New England could ever be.　James Thompson Callender, a Scotch adventurer compared with whom
the Cobbetts, Duanes, Cheethams, and Woods who
infested the press were men of moral and pure life,
had been an ally of Jefferson during the stormy days
of 1798, and had published at Richmond a volume
called "The Prospect before us," which was sufficiently libellous to draw upon him a State prose-
cution, and a fine and some months' imprisonment
at the rough hands of Judge Chase.　A few years
later the Republicans would have applauded the sentence, and regretted only its lightness.　In 1800 they
were bound to make common cause with the victim.
When Jefferson became President, he pardoned Callender, and by a stretch of authority returned to
him the amount of his fine.　Naturally Callender
expected reward.　He hastened to Washington, and
was referred to Madison.　He said that he was in
love, and hinted that to win the object of his affection nothing less than the post-office at Richmond
was necessary for his social standing.[1]　Meeting with
a positive refusal, he returned to Richmond in extreme anger, and became editor of a newspaper called
"The Recorder," in which he began to wage against
Jefferson a war of slander that Cobbett and Cheet-

[1] Madison to Monroe, June 1, 1801 ; Madison's Works, ii. 173.

ham would have shrunk from. He collected every story he could gather, among overseers and scandal-mongers, about Jefferson's past life, — charged him with having a family of negro children by a slave named Sally; with having been turned out of the house of a certain Major Walker for writing a secret love-letter to his wife; with having swindled his creditors by paying debts in worthless currency, and with having privately paid Callender himself to write " The Prospect before us," besides furnishing materials for the book. Disproof of these charges was impossible. That which concerned Black Sally, as she was called, seems to have rested on a confusion of persons which could not be cleared up; that relating to Mrs. Walker had a foundation of truth, although the parties were afterward reconciled;[1] that regarding the payment of debt was true in one sense, and false only in the sense which Callender gave it; while that which referred to " The Prospect before us " was true enough to be serious. All these charges were welcomed by the Federalist press, reprinted even in the New York " Evening Post," and scattered broadcast over New England. There men's minds were ready to welcome any tale of villany that bore out their theory of Jefferson's character; and, at the most critical moment, a mistake made by himself went far to confirm their prejudice.

Jefferson's nature was feminine; he was more re-

[1] Madison to Monroe, April 20, 1803; Madison's Writings, ii. 181.

fined than many women in the delicacy of his private
relations, and even men as shameless as Callender
himself winced under attacks of such a sort. He was
sensitive, affectionate, and, in his own eyes, heroic.
He yearned for love and praise as no other great
American ever did. He hated the clergy chiefly because he knew that from them he could expect neither love nor praise, perhaps not even forbearance.
He had befriended Callender against his own better
judgment, as every party leader befriended party
hacks, not because the leaders approved them, but
because they were necessary for the press. So far as
license was concerned, "The Prospect before us" was
a mild libel compared with Cobbett's, Coleman's, and
Dennie's cataracts of abuse; and at the time it was
written, Callender's character was not known and his
habits were still decent. In return for kindness and
encouragement, Callender attempted an act of das-
tardly assassination, which the whole Federalist press
cheered. That a large part of the community, and
the part socially uppermost, should believe this drunken
ruffian, and should laugh while he bespattered their
President with his filth, was a mortification which
cut deep into Jefferson's heart. Hurt and angry,
he felt that at bottom it was the old theological hatred
in Virginia and New England which sustained this
mode of warfare; that as he had flung Paine at
them, they were flinging Callender at him. "With
the aid of a lying renegade from Republicanism, the
Federalists have opened all their sluices of calumny,"

he wrote;[1] and he would have done wisely to say no more. Unluckily for him, he undertook to contradict Callender's assertions.

James Monroe was Governor of Virginia. Some weakness in Monroe's character caused him more than once to mix in scandals which he might better have left untouched. July 7, 1802, he wrote to the President, asking for the facts in regard to Jefferson's relations with Callender. The President's reply confessed the smart of his wound:[2] —

" I am really mortified at the base ingratitude of Callender. It presents human nature in a hideous form. It gives me concern because I perceive that relief which was afforded him on mere motives of charity, may be viewed under the aspect of employing him as a writer."

He explained how he had pitied Callender, and repeatedly given him money.

" As to myself," he continued, " no man wished more to see his pen stopped ; but I considered him still as a proper object of benevolence. The succeeding year [1800] he again wanted money to buy paper for another volume. I made his letter, as before, the occasion of giving him another fifty dollars. He considers these as proofs of my approbation of his writings, when they were mere charities, yielded under a strong conviction that he was injuring us by his writings."

[1] Jefferson to R. R. Livingston, Oct. 10, 1802; Works, iv. 448.
[2] Jefferson to Monroe, July 15 and 17, 1802; Works, iv. 444–447.

Unfortunately, Jefferson could not find the press-copies of his letters to Callender, and let Monroe send out these apologies without stopping to compare them with his written words. No sooner had the Republican newspapers taken their tone from Monroe, and committed themselves to these assertions of fact, than Callender printed the two letters which Jefferson had written to him,[1] which proved that not only had Jefferson given him at different times some two hundred dollars, but had also supplied information, of a harmless nature, for "The Prospect before us," and under an injunction of secrecy had encouraged Callender to write. His words were not to be explained away: "I thank you for the proof-sheets you enclosed me; such papers cannot fail to produce the best effect."[2]

No man who stood within the circle of the President's intimates could be perplexed to understand how this apparent self-contradiction might have occurred. Callender was neither the first nor the last to take advantage of what John Randolph called the "easy credulity" of Jefferson's temper. The nearest approach Jefferson could make toward checking an over-zealous friend was by shades of difference in the strength of his encouragement. To tell Callender that his book could not fail to produce the best effect was a way of hinting that it might do harm; and, however specious such an excuse might seem, this

[1] The Recorder, September–October, 1802.
[2] Jefferson to Callender, Oct. 6, 1799; Jefferson MSS.

language was in his mind consistent with a secret wish that Callender should not write. More than one such instance of this kindly prevarication, this dislike for whatever might seem harsh or disobliging, could be found in Jefferson's correspondence.

A man's enemies rarely invent specious theories of human nature in order to excuse what they prefer to look upon as falsehood and treason. July 17, 1803, Callender was drowned in some drunken debauch; but the Federalists never forgot his calumnies, or ceased ringing the changes on the President's self-contradictions, — and throughout New England the trio of Jefferson, Paine, and Callender were henceforward held in equal abhorrence. That this prejudice did not affect Jefferson's popular vote was true, but it seriously affected his social relations; and it annoyed and mortified him more than coarser men could understand, to feel in the midst of his utmost popularity that large numbers of his worthiest fellow-citizens, whose respect he knew himself to deserve, despised him as they did the vermin they trod upon.

In the ferment of the Callender scandal, October 29, Paine arrived from Europe. Unable to come by the " Maryland," he had waited a year, and then appeared at Baltimore. The Republican newspapers made the same blunder in regard to Paine which they had made in regard to Callender, — they denied at first that he had been invited to return in a Government ship, or that Jefferson had written him any such letter as was rumored ; and they were altogether perplexed to

know how to deal with so dangerous an ally, until
the President invited Paine to the White House and
gave him all the support that political and social influence could command. In a few days the " National
Intelligencer," Jefferson's more than semi-official organ, published the first of a series of letters addressed
by Paine to the American people ; and no one could
longer doubt what kind of " useful labors " Jefferson
had invited him to continue. Fourteen years of absence had not abated the vigor of that homely style
which once roused the spirits of Washington's soldiers ; and age lent increased virulence to powers of invective which had always been great. His new series
of letters overflowed with abuse of the Federalists,
and bristled with sarcasms on the Federalist Presidents. Unfortunately for Jefferson's object Paine had
exhausted the effect of such weapons, which resem-
ble the sting of a bee lost in the wound it makes.
The bee dies of her own mutilation. Paine, too, was
dying from the loss of his sting. Only once in any
man's career could he enjoy the full pleasure of saying, as Paine said to President Washington: " You
are treacherous in private friendship, and a hypocrite
in public life." To repeat it in other forms, to fum-
ble and buzz about a wound meant to be deadly, was
to be tiresome and ridiculous. Paine, too, was no
longer one of a weak minority struggling for freedom of speech or act ; he represented power, and was
the mouthpiece of a centralized Government striking at the last remnants of Puritan independence.

The glory of wounding Cæsar on his throne was one thing; that of adding one more stab to his prostrate body was another. Paine's weapon no longer caused alarm. The Federalist newspapers were delighted to reprint his letters, and to hold the President responsible for them. The clergy thundered from their pulpits. The storm of recrimination raged with noisy violence amid incessant recurrence to the trio of godless ruffians, — Jefferson, Paine, and Callender; but the only permanent result was to leave a fixed prejudice in the New England mind, — an ineradicable hatred for President Jefferson, in due time to bear poisonous fruit.

The summer of 1802 was a disappointment to Jefferson. He had hoped for better things. The time-servers and those voters whose love of nationality was stronger than their local interests or personal prejudices were for the most part drawn over to the Administration, — even Boston and Salem chose Republican Congressmen; yet Massachusetts as a whole was still Federalist, and of course, as the Federalists became fewer, the extreme wing became more influential in the party. The Essex Junto were still far from control, but they succeeded better than the moderate Federalists in holding their own. Thus these three influences in Massachusetts had nearly reached an equilibrium, and Jefferson was at a loss to understand why the growth of his popularity had been checked. He saw that provincial jealousies were strengthened, and this consequence of isolation he

chose to look upon as its cause. Even an odc of
the Massachusetts poet Thomas Paine, whose better-
known name of Robert Treat Paine recorded the political passions which caused him to petition for the
change, served to console Jefferson for the partial
defeat of his consolidating schemes. Paine's refrain
ran, —

"Rule, New England! New England rules and saves!"

and this echo of Virginia sentiments in 1798, this
shadowy suggestion of a New England Confederacy,
jarred on the President's ear. Toward autumn he
wrote to his friend Langdon, of New Hampshire:[1]—

"Although we have not yet got a majority into the
fold of Republicanism in your State, yet one long pull
more will effect it. We can hardly doubt that one twelve-
month more will give an executive and legislature in that
State whose opinions may harmonize with their sister
States, — unless it be true, as is sometimes said, that New
Hampshire is but a satellite of Massachusetts. In this
last State the public sentiment seems to be under some
influence additional to that of the clergy and lawyers. I
suspect there must be a leaven of State pride at seeing
itself deserted by the public opinion, and that their late
popular song of 'Rule, New England,' betrays one principle of their present variance from the Union. But I am
in hopes they will in time discover that the shortest road
to rule is to join the majority."

The struggle was full of interest; for if Jefferson
had never yet failed to break down every opponent,

[1] Jefferson to John Langdon; Jefferson MSS.

from King George III. to Aaron Burr, the New England oligarchy for near two hundred years were a fatal enemy to every ruler not of their own choice, from King Charles I. to Thomas Jefferson.

Had the clergy and lawyers, the poets and magistrates of Massachusetts been the only troublesome element with which Jefferson had to deal, the task of the Republican party would have been simple ; but virulent as party feeling was in New England during the summer of 1802, a feud broke out in New York which took a darker hue. Vice-President Burr, by his birthday toast to the " Union of honest men " and by his vote on the Judiciary Bill, flung down a challenge to the Virginians which De Witt Clinton, on their behalf, hastened to take up. With a violence that startled uninitiated bystanders, Cheetham in his " American Citizen " flung one charge after another at Burr: first his Judiciary vote ; then his birthday toast; then the suppression of a worthless history of the last Administration written by John Wood, another foreign adventurer, whose book Burr bought in order, as Cheetham believed, to curry favor with the New England Federalists ; finally, with the rhetorical flourish of an American Junius, Cheetham charged that Burr had tried to steal the Presidency from Jefferson in February, 1801, when the House of Representatives was divided. All the world knew that not Cheetham, but De Witt Clinton thus dragged the Vice-President from his chair, and that not Burr's vices but his influence made his crimes heinous ;

that behind De Witt Clinton stood the Virginia
dynasty, dangling Burr's office in the eyes of the
Clinton family, and lavishing honors and money on
the Livingstons.   All this was as clear to Burr and
his friends as though it were embodied in an Act of
Congress.   No one ever explained why Burr did not
drag De Witt Clinton from his ambush and shoot
him, as two years later he shot Alexander Hamilton
with less provocation.   At midsummer the city was
startled by the report that John Swartwout the marshal, one of Burr's intimates, had charged Clinton
with attacking the Vice-President from personal and
selfish motives ; that Clinton had branded Swartwout
as a liar, a scoundrel, and a villain ; that they had
met at Weehawken, where, after lodging two bullets
in his opponent, Clinton had flung down his pistol at
the sixth shot, swearing that he would have no more
to do with the bloody business.   Among the stories
current was one that Clinton had expressed regret at
not having Swartwout's *principal* before his pistol.
Swartwout, wounded as he was, returned directly to
Burr's house.   In the face of all this provocation, the
Vice-President behaved with studied caution and reserve.   Never in the history of the United States did
so powerful a combination of rival politicians unite to
break down a single man as that which arrayed itself
against Burr ; for as the hostile circle gathered about
him, he could plainly see not only Jefferson, Madison,
and the whole Virginia legion, with Duane and his
" Aurora " at their heels : not only De Witt Clinton

and his whole family interest, with Cheetham and his " Watchtower " by their side; but — strangest of companions — Alexander Hamilton himself joining hands with his own bitterest enemies to complete the ring.

Under the influence of these personal hatreds, which raged from the Penobscot to the Potomac, American politics bade fair to become a faction-fight. The President proposed no new legislation; he had come to the end of his economies, and was even beginning to renew expenditures; he had no idea of amending the Constitution or reconstructing the Supreme Court; he thought only of revolutionizing the State governments of New England.[1] "The path we have to pursue is so quiet, that we have nothing scarcely to propose to our Legislature," — so he wrote a few days before Congress was to meet. " If we can prevent the government from wasting the labors of the people under the pretence of taking care of them, they must become happy." The energy of reform was exhausted, the point of departure no longer in sight; the ever-increasing momentum of a governmental system required constant care; and with all this, complications of a new and unexpected kind began, which henceforward caused the chief interest of politics to centre in foreign affairs.

[1] Jefferson to Dr. Cooper, Nov. 29, 1802 ; Works, iv. 453.

CHAPTER XIII.

Most picturesque of all figures in modern history, Napoleon Bonaparte, like Milton's Satan on his throne of state, although surrounded by a group of figures little less striking than himself, sat unapproachable on his bad eminence; or, when he moved, the dusky air felt an unusual weight. His conduct was often mysterious, and sometimes so arbitrary as to seem insane; but later years have thrown on it a lurid illumination. Without the mass of correspondence and of fragmentary writings collected under the Second Empire in not less than thirty-two volumes of printed works, the greatness of Napoleon's energies or the quality of his mind would be impossible to comprehend. Ambition that ground its heel into every obstacle; restlessness that often defied common-sense; selfishness that eat like a cancer into his reasoning faculties; energy such as had never before been combined with equal genius and resources; ignorance that would have amused a school-boy; and a moral sense which regarded truth and falsehood as equally useful modes of expression, — an unprovoked war or secret assassination as equally natural forms of activity, — such a combination of qualities as Europe had forgotten since the Middle Ages, and could realize only by reviving the Eccelinos and Alberics of the thirteenth century, had to be faced and overawed by the gentle optimism of President Jefferson and his Secretary of State.

As if one such character were not riddle enough for any single epoch, a figure even more sinister and almost as enigmatical stood at its side. On the famous 18th Brumaire, the 9th November, 1799, when Bonaparte turned pale before the Five Hundred, and retired in terror from the hall at St. Cloud, not so much his brother Lucien, or the facile Sieyès, or Barras, pushed him forward to destroy the republic, but rather Talleyrand, the ex-Bishop of Autun, the Foreign Secretary of the Directory. Talleyrand was most active in directing the *coup d'état*, and was chiefly responsible for the ruin of France.[1] Had he profited by his exile in America, he would have turned to Moreau rather than to Bonaparte; and some millions of men would have gone more quietly to their graves. Certainly he did not foresee the effects of his act; he had not meant to set a mere soldier on the throne of Saint Louis. He betrayed the republic only because he believed the republic to be an absurdity and a nuisance, not because he wanted a military despotism. He wished to stop the reign of violence and scandal, restore the glories of Louis XIV., and maintain France in her place at the head of civilization. To carry out these views was the work of a lifetime. Every successive government

[1] M. de Talleyrand, par Sainte-Beuve, p. 70.

was created or accepted by him as an instrument for
his purposes ; and all were thrown aside or broke in
his hands. Superior to Bonaparte in the breadth and
steadiness of his purpose, Talleyrand was a theorist
in his political principles ; his statecraft was that
of the old *régime*, and he never forgave himself for
having once believed in a popular revolution.

This was the man with whom Madison must deal,
in order to reach the ear of the First Consul. In
diplomacy, a more perplexing task could scarcely be
presented than to fathom the policy which might result from the contact of a mind like Talleyrand's
with a mind like Bonaparte's. If Talleyrand was an
enigma to be understood only by those who lived in
his confidence, Bonaparte was a freak of nature such
as the world had seen too rarely to comprehend.
His character was misconceived even by Talleyrand
at this early period ; and where the keenest of observers failed to see through a mind he had helped
to form, how were men like Jefferson and Madison,
three thousand miles away, and receiving at best only
such information as Chancellor Livingston could collect and send them every month or six weeks, —
how were they, in their isolation and ignorance, to
solve a riddle that depended on the influence which
Talleyrand could maintain over Bonaparte, and the
despotism which Bonaparte could establish over
Talleyrand ?

Difficult as this riddle was, it made but a part of
the problem. France had no direct means of con-

trolling American policy. Within the last four years she had tried to dictate, and received severe discipline. If France was a political factor of the first class in Jefferson's mind, it was not because of her armies or fleets, or her almost extinguished republican character, or her supposed friendship for Jefferson's party in its struggle with Anglican federalism. The 18th Brumaire severed most of these sentimental ties. The power which France wielded over American destinies sprang not from any direct French interest or fear of French arms, but from the control which Napoleon exercised over the Spanish government at Madrid. France alone could not greatly disturb the repose of Jefferson; but France, acting through Spain on the hopes and fears of the Southern States, exercised prodigious influence on the Union.

Don Carlos IV. reigned at Madrid, — a Bourbon, but an ally of the French republic, and since the 18th Brumaire a devoted admirer of the young Corsican who had betrayed the republic. So far as Don Carlos was king of Spain only, his name meant little to Americans; but as an American ruler his empire dwarfed that of the United States. From the sources of the Missouri and Mississippi to the borders of Patagonia, two American continents acknowledged his rule. From the mouth of the St. Mary's, southward and westward, the shores of Florida, Louisiana, Texas, and Mexico were Spanish; Pensacola, Mobile, and New Orleans closed all the rivers by which the United States could reach the gulf.

The valley of the Ohio itself, as far as Pittsburg, was at the mercy of the King of Spain; the flour and tobacco that floated down the Mississippi, or any of the rivers that fell into the Gulf, passed under the Spanish flag, and could reach a market only by permission of Don Carlos IV. Along an imaginary line from Fernandina to Natchez, some six hundred miles, and thence northward on the western bank of the Mississippi River to the Lake of the Woods, some fourteen hundred miles farther, Spanish authority barred the path of American ambition. Of all foreign Powers Spain alone stood in such a position as to make violence seem sooner or later inevitable even to the pacific Jefferson; and every Southern or Western State looked to the military occupation of Mobile, Pensacola, and New Orleans as a future political necessity.

By a sort of tacit agreement, the ordinary rules of American politics were admitted not to apply to this case. To obtain Pensacola, Mobile, and New Orleans, the warmest State-rights champions in the South, even John Taylor of Caroline and John Randolph of Roanoke, were ready to employ every instrument of centralization. On the Southern and Western States this eagerness to expel Spain from their neighborhood acted like a magnet, affecting all, without regard to theories or parties. The people of Kentucky, Tennessee, and Georgia could not easily admit restrictions of any sort; they were the freest of the free; they felt keenly their subjection to the arbi-

trary authority of a king, — and a king of Spain.
They could not endure that their wheat, tobacco,
and timber should have value only by sufferance of
a Spanish official and a corporal's guard of Spanish
soldiers at New Orleans and Mobile. Hatred of a
Spaniard was to the Tennesseean as natural as hatred
of an Indian, and contempt for the rights of the
Spanish government was no more singular than for
those of an Indian tribe. Against Indians and Spaniards the Western settler held loose notions of law;
his settled purpose was to drive both races from the
country, and to take their land.

Between the Americans and the Spaniards no permanent friendship could exist. Their systems were
at war, even when the nations were at peace. Spain,
France, and England combined in maintaining the
old colonial system; and Spain, as the greatest owner
of American territory, was more deeply interested
than any other Power in upholding the rule that
colonies belonged exclusively to the mother country,
and might trade only with her. Against this exclusive system, although it was one with which no foreign Power had the legal right to meddle, Americans
always rebelled. Their interests required them to
maintain the principles of free-trade; and they persuaded themselves that they had a natural right to
sell their produce and buy their home cargoes in the
best market, without regard to protective principles.
Americans were the professional smugglers of an age
when smuggling was tolerated by custom. Occasion-

ally the laws were suddenly enforced, and the American trader was ruined; but in war times the business was comparatively safe and the profits were large. Naturally Americans wanted the right to do always what they did by sufferance as neutrals; and they were bent not only upon gaining foothold on the Gulf of Mexico, but on forcing Spain and England to admit them freely to their colonial ports. To do these two things they needed to do more. That the vast and inert mass of Spanish possessions in America must ultimately be broken up, became the cardinal point of their foreign policy. If the Southern and Western people, who saw the Spanish flag flaunted every day in their faces, learned to hate the Spaniard as their natural enemy, the Government at Washington, which saw a wider field, never missed an opportunity to thrust its knife into the joints of its unwieldy prey. In the end, far more than half the territory of the United States was the spoil of Spanish empire, rarely acquired with perfect propriety. To sum up the story in a single word, Spain had immense influence over the United States; but it was the influence of the whale over its captors, — the charm of a huge, helpless, and profitable victim.

Throughout the period of Spain's slow decomposition, Americans took toward her the tone of high morality. They were ostensibly struggling for liberty of commerce; and they avowed more or less openly their wish to establish political independence and popular rights throughout both continents. To them

Spain represented despotism, bigotry, and corruption; and they were apt to let this impression appear openly in their language and acts. They were persistent aggressors, while Spain, even when striking back, as she sometimes timidly did, invariably acted in self-defence. That the Spaniards should dread and hate the Americans was natural; for the American character was one which no Spaniard could like, as the Spanish character had qualities which few Americans could understand. Each party accused the other of insincerity and falsehood; but the Spaniards also charged the Americans with rapacity and shamelessness. In their eyes, United States citizens proclaimed ideas of free-trade and self-government with no other object than to create confusion, in order that they might profit by it.

With the characters of English and French rulers — of George III. and Bonaparte, Pitt, Canning, Castlereagh, and Talleyrand — Americans were more or less familiar. The face and mind of King George III. were almost as well known to them as those of George Washington. Of Spaniards and Spanish rulers Americans knew almost nothing; yet Spanish weaknesses were to enrich the Union with more than half a continent from the ruin of an empire which would hardly have felt the privation had it been the chief loss the Spanish Crown was forced to suffer.

Europe could show no two men more virtuous in their private lives than King George III. of England

and King Charles IV. of Spain. If personal purity
was a test of political merit, these two rulers were the
best of kings. Had George III. been born a Spanish
prince, he might perhaps have grown into another
Charles IV.; and Don Carlos was a kind of Spanish
George. Every morning throughout the whole year
King Charles rose at precisely five o'clock and heard
Mass.[1] Occasionally he read a few minutes in some
book of devotion, then breakfasted and went to his
workrooms, where the most skilful gunsmiths in his
kingdom were always busy on his hunting weapons.
His armory was a part of his court; the gunsmiths,
joiners, turners, and cabinet-makers went with him
from Madrid to Aranjuez, and from Aranjuez to La
Granja. Among them he was at his ease; taking
off his coat, and rolling his shirt-sleeves up to the
shoulder, he worked at a dozen different trades
within the hour, in manner and speech as simple
and easy as the workmen themselves. He was skilful with his tools, and withal a dilettante in his
way, capable of enjoying not only the workmanship
of a gunlock, but the beauties of his glorious pic-
ture-gallery, — the " Fecondità " of Titian, and the
" Hilanderas " of Velasquez.

From his workshops he went to his stables, chatted
familiarly with the grooms, and sometimes roughly
found fault with them. After this daily duty was
done, he received the Queen and the rest of his fam-

[1] Alquier to Talleyrand, 26 Vendémiaire, An ix. (Oct. 18,
1800); Archives des Aff. Etr. MSS.

ily, who came to kiss his hand, — a ceremony which took some ten minutes ; after which, precisely at noon, he sat down to dinner. He dined alone, eat enormously, and drank only water. " Find if you can," said the Spaniards, " another king who never got out of his bed later than five o'clock; never drank wine, coffee, or liqueur; and in his whole life never so much as looked at any woman but his wife! " After dinner, every day at one o'clock, except when court etiquette interfered, King Charles set out, no matter what might be the weather, and drove post with guards and six coaches of companions to the ground where he was to shoot. Three hundred men drove the game toward him ; seven hundred men and five hundred horses were daily occupied in this task of amusing him. The expenses were enormous ; but the King was one of the best shots in Europe, and his subjects had reason to be grateful that his ambition took so harmless a path as the destruction of vast swarms of game.

From this sport he returned toward evening, and always found the Queen and the Court waiting his arrival. For some fifteen minutes he chatted with them; then his ministers were admitted, each separately presenting his business, while the Queen was present ; and about half an hour was thus devoted to the welfare of many million subjects scattered in several continents. Cabinet councils were rare at this court, and no other council or assembly for legislative or executive purposes was imagined. Business disposed of, Don Carlos took his violin, which was as dear to him as his gun, — although in playing he gave himself no trouble to keep time with the other musicians, but played faster or slower, without apparent consciousness. After music he sat down to cards, and played ombre with two old courtiers, who for fifteen years had been required to perform this daily service; and he regularly went to sleep with the cards in his hand. Almost as regularly the other players, as well as the lookers-on, went to sleep also, and aroused themselves only when the major-domo came to announce supper. This meal at an end, the King gave his orders for the next day, and at eleven o'clock went to bed.

Such, word for word, was the official account of the Spanish court given by the French minister at Madrid to his Government in the year 1800; but it told only half the story. Charles was a religious man, and strictly observed all the fasts of the Church. To rouse in his mind an invincible repugnance against any individual, one had only to say that such a person had no religion. He held the priesthood in deep respect; his own character was open and frank; he possessed the rare quality of being true at any cost to his given word; he was even shrewd in his way. with a certain amount of common-sense; but with all this he was a nullity, and his career was that of a victim. Far above all distinctions of rank or class, the King was alone in Spain, as isolated as an Eastern idol; even the great nobles who in the feudal theory stood next him, and should have been his confidential advisers, appeared to have no more influence than ploughboys. So extreme was this isolation, even for the traditions of Spanish etiquette, that the Court believed it to be intentionally encouraged by the Queen, Doña Maria Luisa de Parma, who was supposed to have many reasons for keeping her husband under watch. The society of Madrid was never delicate in such matters, nor was there a court in Europe which claimed to be free from scandal; but hardened as Europe was to royal license, Queen Luisa became notorious from Madrid to Petersburg. Her conduct was the common talk of Spain, and every groom and chambermaid about the royal palaces had the list of the Queen's lovers at their tongue's end; yet Don Carlos shut his eyes and ears. Those who knew him best were first to reject the idea that this conduct was the mere blindness of a weak mind. Charles's religion, honor, personal purity, and the self-respect of a king of Spain made it impossible for him to believe ill of one who stood toward him in such a relation. Never for a moment was he known to swerve in his loyalty.

Of all supposed facts in history, scandal about women was the commonest and least to be trusted. Queen Luisa's character may have been good, notwithstanding the gossip of diplomats and courtiers; but her real or supposed vices, and her influence over the King had much to do with the fate of Louisiana. Sooner or later, no doubt, Louisiana must have be-

come a part of the American Union; but if court
intrigues had little to do with actual results, they
had, at least in Spain, everything to do with the
way in which results were reached. At the court
of Madrid the Queen was, in some respects, more
influential than the King, and a man who was supposed to be one of the Queen's old lovers exercised
the real authority of both.

In the year 1792 King Charles, then in his forty-
fifth year, suddenly raised to the post of his prime
minister a simple gentleman of his guard, Don Manuel Godoy, barely twenty-five years old. The scandalous chronicle of the court averred that two of the
Queen's children bore on their faces incontrovertible
evidence of their relation to Godoy. From 1792 until
1798 he was prime minister; he conducted a war
with France, and made a treaty which procured for
him the remarkable title of the Principe de la Paz, —
the Prince of Peace. In 1798 he retired from office,
but retained his personal favor. In 1800 he was not
a minister, nor did even the scandal-mongers then
charge him with improper relations with the Queen,
for all were agreed that the Queen had found another
lover. The stories of the palace were worthy of
Saint-Simon. The King himself was far from refined
in manners or conversation, and gave even to his
favors some of the roughness of insults. If a servant suffered from any personal infirmity, he was
forced to hear cruel derision from the King's lips;
while the commonest of royal jokes was to slap cour-

tiers and grooms on the back with a violence that
brought tears into their eyes, followed by shouts of
royal laughter and by forced smiles from the victim.
This roughness of manner was not confined to the
King.   Most of the stories told about the Queen
would not bear repeating, and, whether true or false,
reflected the rottenness of a society which could invent or believe them ; but among the many tales
echoed by the gentlemen and ladies who were nearest her chamber was one worthy of Gil Blas, and as
such was officially reported to Talleyrand and Bonaparte.   The Queen's favorite in the year 1800 was a
certain Mallo, whom she was said to have enriched,
and who, according to the women of the bed-chamber,
beat her Majesty in return as though she were any
common Maritornes.   One day in that year, when the
Prince of Peace had come to San Ildefonso to pay
his respects to the King, and as usual was having his
interview in the Queen's presence, Charles asked him
a question : " Manuel," said the King, " what is this
Mallo ?   I see him with new horses and carriages
every day.   Where does he get so much money ? "
" Sire," replied Godoy, " Mallo has nothing in the
world ; but he is kept by an ugly old woman who
robs her husband to pay her lover."   The King
shouted with laughter, and turning to his wife, said :
" Luisa, what think you of that ? "   " Ah, Charles ! "
she replied ; " do you not know that Manuel is always
joking ? "

Europe rang with such stories, which were proba-

bly as old as the tales of folk-lore, but none the less
characterized the moral condition of Spain. Whatever had been Godoy's relations with the Queen
they had long ceased, yet the honors, the wealth,
and the semi-royal position of the Prince of Peace
still scandalized the world. According to the common talk of Madrid, his riches and profligacy had no
limits ; his name was a by-word for everything that
was shameless and corrupt. A young man, barely
thirty-three years old, on whose head fortune rained
favors, in an atmosphere of corruption, was certainly
no saint ; yet this creature, Manuel Godoy, reeking
with vice, epitome of the decrepitude and incompe-
tence of Spanish royalty, was a mild, enlightened,
and intelligent minister so far as the United States
were concerned, capable of generosity and of courage, quite the equal of Pitt or Talleyrand in diplomacy, and their superior in resource. In the eyes
of Spain, Godoy may have been the most contemptible of mortals ; but American history cannot estimate
his character so low.

Godoy negotiated the treaty of 1795 with the United
States, and did it in order to redress the balance
which Jay's treaty with England disturbed.[1] The
Spanish treaty of 1795 never received the credit it
deserved ; its large concessions were taken as a
matter of course by the American people, who assumed that Spain could not afford to refuse anything that America asked, and who resented the

[1] Mémoires du Prince de la Paix, iii. 36–38.

idea that America asked more than she had a right
to expect. Fearing that the effect of Jay's treaty
would throw the United States into the arms of
England at a moment when Spain was about to declare war, Godoy conceded everything the Americans wanted. His treaty provided for a settlement
of the boundary between Natchez and New Orleans ;
accepted the principle of "free ships, free goods," so
obnoxious to England ; gave a liberal definition of
contraband such as Jay had in vain attempted to get
from Lord Grenville ; created a commission to settle
the claims of American citizens against Spain on account of illegal captures in the late war ; granted to
citizens of the United States for three years the right
to deposit their merchandise at New Orleans without
paying duty ; and pledged the King of Spain to continue this so-called *entrepôt*, or "right of deposit,"
at the same place if he found it not injurious to
his interests, or if it were so, to assign some similar
place of deposit on another part of the banks of the
Mississippi.

This treaty came before the Senate at the same
time with that which Jay negotiated with Lord Grenville ; and in the midst of the bitter attacks made
upon the British instrument, not a voice was raised
against the Spanish. Every one knew that it was the
most satisfactory treaty the United States had yet
negotiated with any foreign Power ; and if Frederick
the Great of Prussia deserved praise for the liberality of his treaty of 1785, — a liberality which implied

no concessions and led to no consequences, — King
Charles IV. had right to tenfold credit for the settlement of 1795.

If the Americans said but little on the subject,
they felt the full value of their gain. Doubtless they
grumbled because the Spanish authorities were slow
to carry out the provisions of the treaty ; but they
had reason to know that this was not the fault
of Godoy. Had France been as wisely directed as
Spain, no delay would have occurred ; but the French
Directory resented the course taken by the United
States in accepting Jay's treaty, and being angry
with America, they turned a part of their wrath
against Godoy. Before his American treaty was
known to the world, Spain was driven to declare
war against England, and thenceforth became an
almost helpless appendage to France. The French
government not only tried to prevent the delivery of
the Spanish forts on the Mississippi, but, in defiance
of law, French privateers made use of Spanish ports
to carry on their depredations against American commerce ; and scores of American vessels were brought
into these ports and condemned by French consuls
without right to exercise such a jurisdiction, while
the Spanish government was powerless to interfere.
In the end, Godoy's want of devotion to the interests of France became so evident that he could no
longer remain prime minister. In March, 1798, he
announced to King Charles that one of two measures
must be chosen, — either Spain must prepare for a

rupture with France, or must be guided by a new ministry. His resignation was accepted, and he re tired from office. Fortunately for the United States, the last days of his power were marked by an act of friendship toward them which greatly irritated Talleyrand. March 29, 1798, the Spanish posts on the eastern bank of the Mississippi were at last delivered to the United States government; and thus Godoy's treaty of 1795 was faithfully carried out.

CHAPTER XIV.

In July, 1797, eight months before Godoy's retirement from power at Madrid, Talleyrand became Minister for Foreign Affairs to the French Directory. If the Prince of Peace was a man of no morals, the ex-Bishop of Autun was one of no morality. Colder than Pitt, and hardly less corrupt than Godoy, he held theories in regard to the United States which differed from those of other European statesmen only in being more aggressive. Chateaubriand once said, "When M. Talleyrand is not conspiring, he traffics." The epigram was not an unfair description of Talleyrand's behavior toward the United States. He had wandered through America in the year 1794, and found there but one congenial spirit. "Hamilton avait deviné l'Europe," was his phrase : Hamilton had felt by instinct the problem of European conservatives. After returning from America and obtaining readmission to France, Talleyrand made almost his only appearance as an author by reading to the Institute, in April, 1797, a memoir upon America and the Colonial System.[1] This paper was the clew to his

[1] Mémoire, etc., lu à l'Institut National le 15 Germinal, An v. (April 4, 1797).

ambition, preparing his return to power by laying the foundation for a future policy. The United States, it said, were wholly English, both by tastes and by commercial necessity; from them France could expect nothing; she must build up a new colonial system of her own, — but "to announce too much of what one means to do, is the way not to do it at all."

In Talleyrand's new colonial scheme lay the germ of the ideas and measures which were to occupy his life. From first to last, he had the great purpose of restoring France to a career of sound and conservative development. France had never ceased to regret the loss of Louisiana. The creation of Louis XIV., whose name it bore, this province was always French at heart, although in 1763 France ceded it to Spain in order to reconcile the Spanish government to sacrifices in the treaty of Paris. By the same treaty Florida was given by Spain to England, and remained twenty years in English hands, until the close of the Revolutionary War, when the treaty of 1783 restored it to Spain. The Spanish government of 1783, in thus gaining possession of Florida and Louisiana together, aimed at excluding the United States, not France, from the Gulf. Indeed, when the Count de Vergennes wished to recover Louisiana for France, Spain was willing to return it, but asked a price which, although the mere reimbursement of expenses, exceeded the means of the French treasury, and only for that reason Louisiana remained a Spanish province. After Godoy's war with France, at the

Peace of Bâle the French Republic again tried to obtain the retrocession of Louisiana, but in vain. Nevertheless some progress was made, for by that treaty, July 22, 1795, Spain consented to cede to France the Spanish, or eastern, part of St. Domingo, — the cradle of her Transatlantic power, and the cause of yearly deficits to the Spanish treasury. Owing to the naval superiority of England, the French republic did not ask for immediate possession. Fearing Toussaint Louverture, whose personal authority in the French part of the island already required forbearance, France retained the title, and waited for peace. Again, in 1797, Carnot and Barthelemy caused the Directory to offer the King of Spain a magnificent bribe for Louisiana.[1] They proposed to take the three legations just wrung from the Pope, and joining them with the Duchy of Parma, make a principality for the son of the Duke of Parma, who had married a daughter of Don Carlos IV. Although this offer would have given his daughter a splendid position, Charles refused it, because he was too honest a churchman to share in the spoils of the Church.

These repeated efforts proved that France, and especially the Foreign Office, looked to the recovery of French power in America. A strong party in the Government aimed at restoring peace in Europe and extending French empire abroad. Of this party Talleyrand was, or aspired to be, the head; and his memoir, read to the Institute in April and July, 1797,

---

[1] Mémoires du Prince de la Paix, iii. 23.

was a cautious announcement of the principles to be pursued in the administration of foreign affairs which he immediately afterward assumed.

July 24, 1797 , commissioners arrived from the United States to treat for a settlement of the difficulties then existing between the two countries ; but Talleyrand refused to negotiate without a gift of twelve hundred thousand francs,— amounting to about two hundred and fifty thousand dollars. Two of the American commissioners, in the middle of April, 1798, returned home, and war seemed inevitable.

Thus the month of April, 1798, was a moment of crisis in American affairs. Talleyrand had succeeded in driving Godoy from office, and in securing greater subservience from his successor, Don Mariano Luis de Urquijo, who had been chief clerk in the Foreign Department, and who acted as Minister for Foreign Affairs. Simultaneously Talleyrand carried his quarrel with the United States to the verge of a rupture ; and at the same time Godoy's orders compelled Governor Gayoso of Louisiana to deliver Natchez to the United States. The actual delivery of Natchez was hardly yet known in Europe ; and the President of the United States at Philadelphia had but lately heard that the Spaniards were fairly gone, when Talleyrand drafted instructions for the Citizen Guillemardet, whom he was sending as minister to Madrid. These instructions offered a glimpse into the heart of Talleyrand's policy.[1]

[1] Instructions données au Citoyen Guillemardet, Prairial, An vi. (May 20–June 19, 1798); Archives des Aff. Étr. MSS.

"The Court of Madrid," said he, "ever blind to its own interests, and never docile to the lessons of experience, has again quite recently adopted a measure which cannot fail to produce the worst effects upon its political existence and on the preservation of its colonies. The United States have been put in possession of the forts situated along the Mississippi which the Spaniards had occupied as posts essential to arrest the progress of the Americans in those countries."

The Americans, he continued, meant at any cost to rule alone in America, and to exercise a preponderating influence in the political system of Europe, although twelve hundred leagues of ocean rolled between.

"Moreover, their conduct ever since the moment of their independence is enough to prove this truth: the Americans are devoured by pride, ambition, and cupidity; the mercantile spirit of the city of London ferments from Charleston to Boston, and the Cabinet of St. James directs the Cabinet of the Federal Union."

Chateaubriand's epigram came here into pointed application. Down to the moment of writing this despatch, Talleyrand had for some months been engaged in trafficking with these Americans, who were devoured by cupidity, and whom he had required to pay him two hundred and fifty thousand dollars for peace. He next conspired.

"There are," he continued, "no other means of putting an end to the ambition of the Americans than that of shutting them up within the limits which Nature seems to have traced for them; but Spain is not in a condition to do this great work alone. She cannot, therefore, hasten too quickly to engage the aid of a preponderating Power, yielding to it a small part of her immense domains in order to preserve the rest."

This small gratuity consisted of the Floridas and Louisiana.

" Let the Court of Madrid cede these districts to France, and from that moment the power of America is bounded by the limit which it may suit the interests and the tranquillity of France and Spain to assign her. The French Republic, mistress of these two provinces, will be a wall of brass forever impenetrable to the combined efforts of England and America. The Court of Madrid has nothing to fear from France."

This scheme was destined to immediate failure, chiefly through the mistakes of its author; for not only had Talleyrand, a few weeks before, driven the United States to reprisals, and thus sacrificed what was left of the French colonies in the West Indies, but at the same moment he aided and encouraged young Bonaparte to carry a large army to Egypt, with the idea, suggested by the Duc de Choiseul many years before, that France might find there compensation for the loss of her colonies in America. Two years were consumed in retrieving these mistakes. Talleyrand first discovered that he could not afford a war with the United States; and even at the moment of writing these instructions to his minister at Madrid, he was engaged in conciliating

the American commissioner who still remained un-
willingly at Paris.   The unexpected revelation by the
United States government of his demands for money
roused him, May 30, to consciousness of his danger.
He made an effort to recover his lost ground.[1]   " I
do not see what delay I could have prevented.   I
am mortified that circumstances have not rendered
our progress more rapid."   When Gerry coldly
refused to hear these entreaties, and insisted upon
receiving his passport, Talleyrand was in genuine
despair.   " You have not even given me an opportunity of proving what liberality the executive Directory would use on the occasion." [2]   He pursued Gerry
with entreaties to use his influence on the President for peace ; he pledged himself that no obstacle
should be put in the path of negotiation if the American government would consent to renew it.   At first
the Americans were inclined to think his humility
some new form of insult ; but it was not only real,
it was unexampled.   Talleyrand foresaw that his
blunder would cost France her colonies, and this
he could bear ; but it would also cost himself his office, and this was more than he could endure.   His
fears proved true.   A year later, July 20, 1799, he
was forced to retire, with little hope of soon recovering his character and influence, except through subservience to some coming adventurer.

[1] Talleyrand to E. Gerry, June 27, 1798 ; State Papers, ii.
215.

[2] Talleyrand to E. Gerry, July 12, 1798; Ibid. 219.

Thus occurred a delay in French plans. By a sort of common agreement among the discontented factions at Paris, Bonaparte was recalled from Egypt. Landing at Fréjus early in October, 1799, a month afterward, November 9, he effected the *coup d'état* of the 18th Brumaire. He feared to disgust the public by replacing Talleyrand immediately in the office of foreign minister, and therefore delayed the appointment. " The place was naturally due to Talleyrand," said Napoleon in his memoirs,[1] " but in order not too much to shock public opinion, which was very antagonistic to him, especially on account of American affairs, Reinhard was kept in office for a short time." The delay was of little consequence, for internal reorganization preceded the establishment of a new foreign policy; and Talleyrand was in no haste to recall the blunders of his first experiment.

Although Talleyrand had mismanaged the execution of his plan, the policy itself was a great one. The man who could pacify Europe and turn the energies of France toward the creation of an empire in the New World was the more sure of success because, in the reactionary spirit of the time, he commanded the sympathies of all Europe in checking the power of republicanism in its last refuge. Even England would see with pleasure France perform this duty, and Talleyrand might safely count upon a tacit alliance to support him in curbing American democ-

[1] Correspondance de Napoléon Premier, xxx. 330.

racy. This scheme of uniting legitimate governments in peaceful combination to crush the spirit of license ran through the rest of Talleyrand's political life, and wherever met, whether in France, Austria, or England, was the mark of the school which found its ablest chief in him.

The first object of the new policy was to restore the peace of Europe; and the energy of Bonaparte completed this great undertaking within two years after the 18th Brumaire. France was at variance with the United States, Great Britain, and Austria. Peace with Austria could be obtained only by conquering it; and after passing a winter in organizing his government, Bonaparte sent Moreau to attack the Austrians on the line of the Danube, while he himself was to take command in Italy. As yet diplomacy could not act with effect; but early in the spring, March 1, 1800, before campaigning began, new American commissioners reached Paris, rather as dictators than as suppliants, and informed Talleyrand that the President of the United States was still ready to take him at his word. They were received with marked respect, and were instantly met by French commissioners, at whose head was Joseph Bonaparte, the First Consul's brother. While their negotiations were beginning, Bonaparte left Paris, May 20, crossed the Alps, and wrung from the Austrians, June 14, a victory at Marengo, while Moreau on the Danube pressed from one brilliant success to another. Hurrying back to Paris, July 2, Bonaparte instantly be-

gan the negotiations for peace with Austria; and thus
two problems were solved.

Yet Talleyrand's precipitation in pledging France
to prompt negotiation with the United States became a source of annoyance to the First Consul,
whose shrewder calculation favored making peace
first with Europe, in order to deal with America
alone, and dictate his own terms. His brother Joseph, who was but an instrument in Napoleon's
hands, but who felt a natural anxiety that his first
diplomatic effort should succeed, became alarmed
at the First Consul's coldness toward the American
treaty, and at the crisis of negotiation, when failure was imminent, tried to persuade him that peace
with the United States was made necessary by the
situation in Europe. Napoleon met this argument by
one of his characteristic rebuffs. "You understand
nothing of the matter," he said;[1] "within two years
we shall be the masters of the world." Within two
years, in fact, the United States were isolated. Nevertheless Joseph was allowed to have his way. The
First Consul obstinately refused to admit in the
treaty any claim of indemnity for French spoliations on American commerce; and the American
commissioners as resolutely refused to abandon the
claim. They in their turn insisted that the new
treaty should abrogate the guaranties and obligations
imposed on the United States government by the
old French treaty of alliance in 1778; and although

[1] Mémoires de Miot de Melito, i. 288.

Bonaparte cared nothing for the guaranty of the United States, he retained this advantage in order that he might set it off against the claims. Thus the negotiators were at last obliged to agree, by the second article of the treaty, that these two subjects should be reserved for future negotiation; and Sept. 30, 1800, the Treaty of Morfontaine, as Joseph Bonaparte wished to call it, was signed. It reached America in the confusion of a presidential election which threatened to overthrow the government; but the Senate voted, Feb. 3, 1801, to ratify it, with the omission of the second article. The instrument, with this change, was then sent back to Paris, where Bonaparte in his turn set terms upon his ratification. He agreed to omit the second article, as the Senate wished, "provided that by this retrenchment the two States renounced the respective pretensions which are the object of the said article." The treaty returned to America with this condition imposed upon it, and Jefferson submitted it to the Senate, which gave its final approval Dec. 19, 1801.

Thus Bonaparte gained his object, and won his first diplomatic success. He followed an invariable rule to repudiate debts and claims wherever repudiation was possible. For such demands he had one formula:[1] "Give them a very civil answer, — that I will examine the claim, etc.; but of course one never pays that sort of thing." In this case he meant to extinguish the spoliation claims; and nothing could

[1] Gallatin's Writings, ii. 490.

be more certain than that he would thenceforward peremptorily challenge and resist any claim, direct or indirect, founded on French spoliations before 1800, and would allege the renunciation of Article II. in the treaty of Morfontaine as his justification. Equally certain was it that he had offered, and the Senate had approved his offer, to set off the guaranties of the treaty of alliance against the spoliation claims, — which gave him additional reason for rejecting such claims in future. The United States had received fair consideration from him for whatever losses American citizens had suffered.

Meanwhile the First Consul took action which concerned America more closely than any of the disputes with which Joseph Bonaparte was busied. However little admiration a bystander might feel for Napoleon's judgment or morals, no one could deny the quickness of his execution. Within six weeks after the battle of Marengo, without waiting for peace with the United States, England, or Austria, convinced that he held these countries in the hollow of his hand, he ordered [1] Talleyrand to send a special courier to the Citizen Alquier, French minister at Madrid, with powers for concluding a treaty by which Spain should retrocede Louisiana to France, in return for an equivalent aggrandizement of the Duchy of Parma. The courier was at once despatched, and returned with a promptitude and suc-

[1] Correspondance, vi. 415 ; Bonaparte to Talleyrand, July 22, 1800.

cess which ought to have satisfied even the restlessness of Bonaparte. The Citizen Alquier no sooner received his orders than he went to Señor Urquijo, the Spanish Secretary for Foreign Relations, and passing abruptly over the well-worn arguments in favor of retrocession, he bluntly told Urquijo to oppose it if he dared.

" ' France expects from you,' I said to him,[1] ' what she asked in vain from the Prince of Peace. I have dispersed the prejudice which had been raised against you in the mind of the French government. You are to-day distinguished by its esteem and its consideration. Do not destroy my work; do not deprive yourself of the only counterpoise which you can oppose to the force of your enemies. The Queen, as you know, holds by affection as much as by vanity to the aggrandizement of her house; she will never forgive you if you oppose an exchange which can alone realize the projects of her ambition, — for I declare to you formally that your action will decide the fate of the Duke of Parma, and should you refuse to cede Louisiana you may count on getting nothing for that Prince. You must bear in mind, too, that your refusal will necessarily change my relations with you. Obliged to serve the interests of my country and to obey the orders of the First Consul, who attaches the highest value to this retrocession, I shall be forced to receive for the first time the offers of service that will inevitably be made to me; for you may be sure that your enemies will not hesitate to profit by that occasion to increase their strength — already a very real force —

[1] Alquier to Talleyrand, 19 Thermidor, An viii. (Aug. 7, 1800) ; Archives des Aff. Étr. MSS.

by the weight of the French influence ; they will do what you will not do, and you will be abandoned at once by the Queen and by us. "

Urquijo's reply measured the degradation of Spain :

" ' Eh ! who told you that I would not give you Louisiana? But we must first have an understanding, and you must help me to convince the King.' "

At this reply, which sounded like Beaumarchais' comedies, Alquier saw that his game was safe. " Make yourself easy on that score," he replied ; " the Queen will take that on herself." So the conference ended.

Alquier was right. The Queen took the task on herself, and Urquijo soon found that both King and Queen were anxious to part with Louisiana for their daughter's sake. They received the offer with enthusiasm, and lavished praises upon Bonaparte. The only conditions suggested by Urquijo were that the new Italian principality should be clearly defined, and that Spain should be guaranteed against the objections that might be made by other Governments.

Meanwhile Bonaparte reiterated his offer on a more definite scale. August 3, immediately after the interview with Urquijo, Alquier put the first demand on record in a note important chiefly because it laid incidental stress on Talleyrand's policy of restraining the United States : [1] —

[1] Note adressée par l'Ambassadeur da la République, etc., 15 Thermidor, An viii. (Aug. 3, 1800) ; Archives des Aff. Étr. MSS.

" The progress of the power and population of America, and her relations of interest always maintained with England, may and must some day bring these two powers to concert together the conquest of the Spanish colonies. If national interest is the surest foundation for political calculations, this conjecture must appear incontestable. The Court of Spain will do, then, at once a wise and great act if it calls the French to the defence of its colonies by ceding Louisiana to them, and by replacing in their hands this outpost of its richest possessions in the New World."

Before this note was written, the First Consul had already decided to supersede Alquier by a special agent who should take entire charge of this negotiation. July 28 he notified Talleyrand[1] that General Berthier, Bonaparte's right hand in matters of secrecy and importance, was to go upon the mission. Talleyrand drafted the necessary instructions,[2] which were framed to meet the fears of Spain lest the new arrangement should cause complications with other Powers ; and toward the end of August Berthier started for Madrid, carrying a personal letter of introduction from the First Consul to King Charles[3] and the *projet* of a treaty of retrocession drawn by Talleyrand. This *projet* differed in one point from the scheme hitherto put forward, and,

[1] Correspondance, vi. 426; Bonaparte to Talleyrand, 9 Thermidor, An viii. (July 28, 1800).

[2] Rapport au Premier Consul, 6 Fructidor, An viii. (Aug. 24, 1800) ; Archives des Aff. Étr. MSS.

[3] Correspondance, vi. 445.

if possible, was still more alarming to the United States.[1]

" The French Republic," it ran, " pledges itself to procure for the Duke of Parma in Italy an aggrandizement of territory to contain at least one million inhabitants; the Republic charges itself with procuring the consent of Austria and the other States interested, so that the Duke may be put in possession of his new territory at the coming peace between France and Austria. Spain on her side pledges herself to retrocede to the French Republic the colony of Louisiana, with the same extent it actually has in the hands of Spain, and such as it should be according to the treaties subsequently passed between Spain and other States. Spain shall further join to this cession that of the two Floridas, eastern and western, with their actual limits."

Besides Louisiana and the two Floridas, Spain was to give France six ships of war, and was to deliver the provinces to France whenever the promised territory for the Duke of Parma should be delivered by France to Spain. The two Powers were further to make common cause against any person or persons who should attack or threaten them in consequence of executing their engagement.

In the history of the United States hardly any document, domestic or foreign, to be found in their archives has greater interest than this *projet;* for from it the United States must trace whatever legal

[1] Instructions au Général Berthier, 8 Fructidor, An viii. (Aug. 26, 1800) ; Projet de Traité préliminaire et secret, 10 Fructidor, An viii. (Aug. 28, 1800); Archives des Aff. Ètr. MSS.

title they obtained to the vast region west of the
Mississippi. The treaties which followed were made
merely in pursuance of this engagement, with such
variations as seemed good for the purpose of carrying out the central idea of restoring Louisiana to
France.

That the recovery of colonial power was the first of
all Bonaparte's objects was proved not only by its being
the motive of his earliest and most secret diplomatic
step, but by the additional evidence that every other
decisive event in the next three years of his career
was subordinated to it. Berthier hastened to Madrid,
and consumed the month of September, 1800, in
negotiations. Eager as both parties were to con-
clude their bargain, difficulties soon appeared. So
far as these concerned America, they rose in part
from the indiscretion of the French Foreign Office,
which announced the object of Berthier's mission in
a Paris newspaper, and thus brought on Urquijo a
demand from the American minister at Madrid for
a categorical denial. Urquijo and Alquier could silence the attack only by denials not well calculated
to carry conviction. This was not all. Alquier had
been told to ask for Louisiana; Berthier was instructed to demand the Floridas and six ships of
war in addition. The demand for the Floridas should
have been made at first, if Bonaparte expected it to
be successful. King Charles was willing to give back
to France a territory which was French in character,
and had come as the gift of France to his father; but

he was unwilling to alienate Florida, which was a part of the national domain. Urquijo told Berthier[1] that "for the moment the King had pronounced himself so strongly against the cession of any portion whatever of Florida as to make it both useless and impolitic to talk with him about it;" but he added that, "after the general peace, the King might decide to cede a part of the Floridas between the Mississippi and the Mobile, on the special demand which the First Consul might make for it." Berthier was embarrassed, and yielded.

Thus at last the bargain was put in shape. The French government held out the hope of giving Tuscany as the equivalent for Louisiana and six seventy-fours. If not Tuscany, the three legations, or their equivalent, were stipulated. The suggestion of Tuscany delighted the King and Queen. Thus far the secret was confined to the parties directly interested; but after the principle had been fixed, another person was intrusted with it. The Prince of Peace was suddenly called to the Palace by a message marked "luego, luego, luego!"— the sign of triple haste.[2] He found Don Carlos in a paroxysm of excitement; joy sparkled in his eyes. "Congratulate me," he cried, "on this brilliant beginning of Bonaparte's relations with Spain! The Prince-presumptive of Parma, my son-in-law and nephew, a Bourbon, is

[1] Rapport à l'Empereur, 28 Brumaire, An xiii. (Nov. 19, 1804); Archives des Aff. Étr. MSS.

[2] Mémoires, iii. 20, 55.

invited by France to reign, on the delightful banks of the Arno, over a people who once spread their commerce through the known world, and who were the controlling power of Italy, — a people mild, civilized, full of humanity; the classical land of science and art!" The Prince of Peace could only offer congratulations; his opinion was asked without being followed, and a few days later the treaty was signed.[1]

On the last day of September, 1800, Joseph Bonaparte signed the so-called Treaty of Morfontaine, which restored relations between France and the United States. The next day, October 1, Berthier signed at San Ildefonso the treaty of retrocession, which was equivalent to a rupture of the relations established four-and-twenty hours earlier. Talleyrand was aware that one of these treaties undid the work of the other. The secrecy in which he enveloped the treaty of retrocession, and the pertinacity with which he denied its existence showed his belief that Bonaparte had won a double diplomatic triumph over the United States.

Moreau's great victory at Hohenlinden, December 3, next brought Austria to her knees. Joseph Bonaparte was sent to Lunéville in Lorraine, and in a few weeks negotiated the treaty which advanced another step the cession of Louisiana. The fifth article of this treaty, signed Feb. 9, 1801, deprived the actual Grand Duke of his Grand Duchy, and established

[1] Traité préliminaire et secret, Oct. 1, 1800; Recueil de Traités de la France, par De Clercq, i. 411.

the young Duke of Parma in Tuscany. To complete the transaction, Lucien Bonaparte was sent as ambassador to Madrid.

Lucien had the qualities of his race. Intelligent, vivacious, vain, he had been a Jacobin of the deepest dye; and yet his hands were as red with the crime of the 18th Brumaire as those of his brother Napoleon. Too troublesome at Paris to suit the First Consul's arbitrary views, he was sent to Spain, partly to remove him, partly to flatter Don Carlos IV. The choice was not wise; for Lucien neither could nor would execute in good faith the wishes of his dictatorial brother, and had no idea of subordinating his own interests to those of the man whose blunders on the 18th Brumaire, in his opinion, nearly cost the lives of both, and whose conduct since had turned every democrat in France into a conspirator. To make the selection still more dangerous, Lucien had scarcely reached Madrid before Urquijo was sent into retirement and Godoy restored to power in some anomalous position of general superintendence, supporting the burden, but leaving to Don Pedro Cevallos the title of Foreign Secretary. The secret of this restoration was told by Godoy himself with every appearance of truth.[1] The King insisted on his return, because Godoy was the only man who could hold his own against Bonaparte; and at that moment Bonaparte was threatening to garrison Spain with a French army, under pretence of a war with Portu-

[1] Mémoires, iii. 76–78.

gal. The measure showed that Charles IV. was not wanting in shrewdness, for Godoy was well suited to deal with Lucien. He was more subtle, and not less corrupt.

Lucien's first act was to negotiate a new treaty closing the bargain in regard to Parma and Tuscany. Here Godoy offered no resistance. The Prince of Parma was created King of Tuscany, and the sixth article provided that the retrocession of Louisiana should at once be carried out. This treaty was signed at Madrid, March 21, 1801. The young King and Queen of Tuscany — or, according to their title, of Etruria — were despatched to Paris. Lucien remained to overlook the affair of Portugal. To the extreme irritation of Napoleon, news soon came that the Prince of Peace had signed at Badajos, June 5, 1801, a treaty with Portugal, to which Lucien had put his name as ambassador of France, and which baffled Napoleon's military designs in the Peninsula.

Lucien, with inimitable effrontery, wrote to his brother two days later:[1] "For the treaty of Tuscany I have received twenty good pictures out of the Gallery of the Retiro for my gallery, and diamonds to the value of one hundred thousand crowns have been set for me. I shall receive as much more for the Peace of Portugal." Two hundred thousand crowns and twenty pictures from the Retiro, besides flattery that would have turned the head of Talleyrand himself, were what Lucien acknowledged receiv-

[1] Lucien Bonaparte et ses Mémoires, Th. Jung, ii. 104.

ing; but there was reason to believe that this was not all, and that the Prince of Peace gorged him with spoil, until he carried back to France wealth which made him the richest member of his family, and gave him an income of sixty or eighty thousand dollars a year. Godoy paid this price to save Spain for seven years.

The treaty of Badajos into which Godoy thus drew Lucien not only checked Napoleon's schemes, but came on the heels of other reverses which threatened to place the First Consul in an awkward position, unless he should hasten the general pacification to which he was tending. The assassination of his ally, the Czar Paul I. March 23, 1801, cost him the aid of Russia, as Godoy's return to power cost him the control of Spain. A few days after Paul's murder, April 9, 1801, Nelson crushed the Danish fleet at Copenhagen, and tore Denmark from his grasp. More serious than all, the fate of the French army which Bonaparte had left in Egypt could not be long delayed, and its capitulation would give a grave shock to his credit. All these reasons forced the First Consul to accept the check he had received from Godoy and Lucien, and to hasten peace with England; but he yielded with a bad grace. He was furious with Godoy.[1] "If this prince, bought by England, draws the King and Queen into measures contrary to the honor and interests of the republic, the last hour

[1] Correspondance, vii. 190; Bonaparte to Talleyrand, 21 Messidor, An ix. (July 10, 1801).

of the Spanish monarchy will have sounded." So
he wrote to Talleyrand in anger at finding himself
checked, and Talleyrand instructed Lucien accordingly.[1] Within a fortnight Bonaparte sent orders to
London which rendered peace with England certain;[2]
and without waiting to hear further, acting at length
on the conviction that nothing could be gained by delay, he ordered Talleyrand to demand of the Court of
Spain the authority to take possession of Louisiana.[3]

Supple and tenacious as any Corsican, Godoy's
temper was perfect and his manners charming; he
eluded Bonaparte with the skill and coolness of a
picador. After causing the First Consul to stumble
and fall on the very threshold of Portugal, Godoy
kept Louisiana out of his control. As the affair then
stood, surrender of Louisiana except at the sword's
point would have been inexcusable. The young King
of Etruria had been entertained at Paris by the First
Consul with a patronizing hospitality that roused
more suspicion than gratitude; he had been sent to
Italy, and had there been told that he possessed a
kingdom and wore a crown, — but French armies occupied the territory; French generals administered
the government; no foreign Power recognized the
new kingdom, and no vestige of royal authority went

[1] Lucien Bonaparte, Jung, ii. 466.

[2] Correspondance, vii. 200; Note à remettre à Lord Hawkesbury, 4 Thermidor, An ix. (July 23, 1801).

[3] Ibid.; Bonaparte to Talleyrand, 8 Thermidor, An ix. (July
27, 1801).

with the royal title. Godoy and Cevallos gave it to be understood that they did not consider the First Consul to have carried out his part of the bargain in such a sense as to warrant Charles IV. in delivering Louisiana. They were in the right; but Bonaparte was angrier than ever at their audacity, and drafted with his own hand the note which Talleyrand was to send in reply.[1]

"It is at the moment when the First Consul gives such strong proofs of his consideration for the King of Spain, and places a prince of his house on a throne which is fruit of the victories of French arms, that a tone is taken toward the French Republic such as might be taken with impunity toward the Republic of San Marino. The First Consul, full of confidence in the personal character of his Catholic Majesty, hopes that from the moment he is made aware of the bad conduct of some of his ministers, he will look to it, and will recall them to the sentiments of esteem and consideration which France does not cease to entertain for Spain. The First Consul will never persuade himself that his Catholic Majesty wishes to insult the French people and their Government at the moment when these are doing so much for Spain. This would suit neither his heart nor his loyalty, nor the interest of his crown."

In a note written the same day to Talleyrand,[2] Bonaparte spoke in a still stronger tone of the " misér-

[1] Correspondance, vii. 225; Projets de Notes, 27 Thermidor, An ix. (15 Aug. 1801).

[2] Correspondance, vii. 226; Talleyrand to Saint Cyr, 16 Frimaire, An x. (6 Dec. 1801); Lucien Bonaparte, Jung, ii. 468.

able" who was thus crossing his path, and he ordered that Lucien should let the King and Queen know "that I am long-suffering, but that already I am warmly affected by this tone of contempt and deconsideration which is taken at Madrid; and that if they continue to put the republic under the necessity either of enduring the shame of the outrages publicly inflicted on it, or of avenging them by arms, they may see things they do not expect."

Nevertheless Godoy held his ground, well aware that the existence of Spain was at stake, but confident that concession would merely tempt encroachment. History might render what judgment it would of Godoy's character or policy, — with this moral or political question the United States had nothing to do; but Bonaparte's hatred of Godoy and determination to crush him were among the reasons why Louisiana fell at a sudden and unexpected moment into the hands of Jefferson, and no picture of American history could be complete which did not show in the background the figures of Bonaparte and Godoy, locked in struggle over Don Carlos IV.

CHAPTER XV.

FORTUNATELY for the Prince of Peace, the world contained at that moment one man for whom Bonaparte entertained more hatred and contempt, and whom he was in still more haste to crush. The policy which Talleyrand had planned, and into which he had drawn the First Consul, could not be laid aside in order to punish Spain. On the contrary, every day rendered peace with England more necessary, and such a peace was inconsistent with a Spanish war. That Bonaparte felt no strong sympathy with Talleyrand's policy of peace in Europe and peaceful development abroad, is more than probable ; but he was not yet so confident of his strength as to rely wholly on himself, — he had gone too far in the path of pacification to quit it suddenly for one of European conquest and dynastic power. He left Godoy and Spain untouched, in order to rebuild the empire of France in her colonies. Six weeks after he had threatened war on Charles IV., his agent at London, Oct. 1, 1801, signed with Lord Hawkesbury preliminary articles of peace which put an end to hostilities on the ocean. No sooner did Bonaparte receive the news [1] than he summoned his

---

[1] Correspondance, vii. 279 ; Bonaparte to Berthier, 16 Vendémiaire, An x. (Oct. 8, 1801).

brother-in-law Leclerc to Paris. Leclerc was a general of high reputation, who had married the beautiful Pauline Bonaparte and was then perhaps the most promising member of the family next to Napoleon himself. To him, October 23, Napoleon entrusted the command of an immense expedition already ordered to collect at Brest, to destroy the power of Toussaint Louverture and re-establish slavery in the Island of St. Domingo.[1]

The story of Toussaint Louverture has been told almost as often as that of Napoleon, but not in connection with the history of the United States, although Toussaint exercised on their history an influence as decisive as that of any European ruler. His fate placed him at a point where Bonaparte needed absolute control. St. Domingo was the only centre from which the measures needed for rebuilding the French colonial system could radiate. Before Bonaparte could reach Louisiana he was obliged to crush the power of Toussaint.

The magnificent Island of St. Domingo was chiefly Spanish. Only its western end belonged by language as well as by history to France ; but this small part of the island, in the old days of Bourbon royalty, had been the most valuable of French possessions. Neither Martinique nor Guadeloupe compared with it. In 1789, before the French Revolution began, nearly two thirds of the commercial interests of France

[1] Correspondance, vii. 298. Bonaparte to Berthier, 1 Brumaire, An x. (23 Oct. 1801).

centred in St. Domingo;[1] its combined exports and imports were valued at more than one hundred and forty million dollars; its sugar, coffee, indigo, and cotton supplied the home market, and employed in prosperous years more than seven hundred ocean-going vessels, with seamen to the number, it was said, of eighty thousand. Paris swarmed with creole families who drew their incomes from the island, among whom were many whose political influence was great; while, in the island itself, society enjoyed semi-Parisian ease and elegance, the natural product of an exaggerated slave-system combined with the manners, ideas, and amusements of a French proprietary caste.

In 1789 the colony contained about six hundred thousand inhabitants, five sixths of whom were full-blooded negroes held in rigid slavery. Of the eighty or hundred thousand free citizens, about half were mulattoes, or had some infusion of negro blood which disqualified them from holding political power. All social or political privileges were held by forty or fifty thousand French creoles, represented by the few hundred planters and officials who formed the aristocracy of the island. Between the creoles and the mulattoes, or mixed-breeds, existed the jealousy sure to result from narrow distinctions of blood marking broad differences in privilege. These were not the only jealousies which raged in the colony; for the creoles were uneasy under the despotism of the colonial system, and claimed political rights which the

[1] Pamphile de Lacroix, Mémoires, ii. 277.

home government denied.   Like all colonists of that
day, in the quiet of their plantations they talked of
independence, and thought with envy of their neighbors in South Carolina, who could buy and sell where
they pleased.

When in 1789 France burst into a flame of universal
liberty, the creoles of St. Domingo shared the enthusiasm so far as they hoped to gain by it a relaxation of
the despotic colonial system; but they were alarmed
at finding that the mulattoes, who claimed to own a
third of the land and a fourth of the personalty in
the colony, offered to make the Republic a free gift
of one fifth of their possessions on condition of being
no longer subjected to the creole tyranny of caste.
The white and mulatto populations were thus brought
into collision.   The National Assembly of France
supported the mulattoes.   The creoles replied that
they preferred death to sharing power with what
they considered a bastard and despicable race.   They
turned royalists.   Both parties took up arms, and in
their struggle with each other they at length dropped
a match into the immense powder-magazine upon
which they both lived.   One August night in the
year 1791 the whole plain of the north was swept
with fire and drenched with blood.   Five hundred
thousand negro slaves in the depths of barbarism re-
volted, and the horrors of the massacre made Europe
and America shudder.

For several years afterward the colony was torn by
convulsions; and to add another element of confu-

sion, the Spaniards and English came in, hoping to
effect its conquest. Feb. 4, 1794, the National Assembly of France took the only sensible measure in
its power by proclaiming the abolition of slavery; but
for the moment this step only embroiled matters the
more. Among its immediate results was one of great
importance, though little noticed at the time. A
negro chief, who since the outbreak had become head
of a royalist band in Spanish pay, returned, in April,
1794, within French jurisdiction and took service under the Republic. This was Toussaint Louverture,
whose father, the son of a negro chief on the slave-
coast of Africa, had been brought to St. Domingo as
a slave. Toussaint was born in 1746. When he deserted the Spanish service, and with some four thousand men made the sudden attack which resulted in
clearing the French colony of Spanish troops, he was
already forty-eight years old.

Although Toussaint was received at once into the
French service, not until more than a year later, July
23, 1795, did the National Convention recognize his
merits by giving him the commission of brigadier-
general. Within less than two years, in May, 1797,
he was made General-in-Chief, with military command over the whole colony. The services he rendered to France were great, and were highly rewarded.
His character was an enigma. Hated by the mulattoes with such vindictiveness as mutual antipathies
and crimes could cause, he was liked by the whites
rather because he protected and flattered them at the

expense of the mulattoes than because they felt any
love for him or his race. In return they flattered
and betrayed him. Their praise or blame was equally
worthless; yet to this rule there were exceptions.
One of the best among the French officers in St.
Domingo, Colonel Vincent, was deep in Toussaint's
confidence, and injured his own career by obstinate
attempts to intervene between Bonaparte and Bonaparte's victim. Vincent described Toussaint, in colors
apparently unexaggerated, as the most active and in-
defatigable man that could be imagined, — one who
was present everywhere, but especially where his
presence was most needed; while his great sobriety,
his peculiar faculty of never resting, of tiring out a
half-dozen horses and as many secretaries every day;
and, more than all, his art of amusing and deceiving
all the world, — an art pushed to the limits of im-
posture, — made him so superior to his surroundings
that respect and submission to him were carried to
fanaticism.[1]

Gentle and well-meaning in his ordinary relations,
vehement in his passions, and splendid in his ambition, Toussaint was a wise, though a severe, ruler so
long as he was undisturbed; but where his own safety
or power was in question he could be as ferocious as
Dessalines and as treacherous as Bonaparte. In more
respects than one his character had a curious resemblance to that of Napoleon, — the same abnormal
energy of body and mind; the same morbid lust for

[1] Vie de Toussaint, par Saint-Remy, p. 322.

power, and indifference to means ; the same craft and vehemence of temper; the same fatalism, love of display, reckless personal courage, and, what was much more remarkable, the same occasional acts of moral cowardice. One might suppose that Toussaint had inherited from his Dahomey grandfather the qualities of primitive society; but if this was the case, the conditions of life in Corsica must have borne some strong resemblance to barbarism, because the rule of inheritance which applied to Toussaint should hold good for Bonaparte. The problem was the more interesting because the parallelism roused Napoleon's anger, and precipitated a conflict which had vast influence on human affairs. Both Bonaparte and Louverture were the products of a revolution which gave its highest rewards to qualities of energy and audacity. So nearly identical were the steps in their career, that after the 18th Brumaire Toussaint seemed naturally to ape every action which Bonaparte wished to make heroic in the world's eyes. There was reason to fear that Toussaint would end in making Bonaparte ridiculous; for his conduct was, as it seemed to the First Consul, a sort of negro travesty on the consular *régime*.

When the difficulties between France and America became serious, after Talleyrand's demand for money and sweeping attacks upon American commerce, Congress passed an Act of June 13, 1798, suspending commercial relations with France and her dependencies. At that time Toussaint, although in title only General-in-Chief, was in reality absolute ruler of St.

Domingo. He recognized a general allegiance to the French Republic, and allowed the Directory to keep a civil agent — the Citizen Roume — as a check on his power; but in fact Roume was helpless in his hands. Toussaint's only rival was Rigaud, a mulatto, who commanded the southern part of the colony, where Jacmel and other ports were situated. Rigaud was a perpetual danger to Louverture, whose safety depended on tolerating no rival. The Act of Congress threatened to create distress among the blacks and endanger the quiet of the colony; while Rigaud and the French authority would be strengthened by whatever weakened Louverture. Spurred both by fear and ambition, Toussaint took the character of an independent ruler. The United States government, counting on such a result, had instructed its consul to invite an advance; and, acting on the consul's suggestion, Toussaint sent to the United States an agent with a letter to the President [1] containing the emphatic assurance that if commercial intercourse were renewed between the United States and St. Domingo it should be protected by every means in his power. The trade was profitable, the political advantages of neutralizing Toussaint were great; and accordingly the President obtained from Congress a new Act, approved Feb. 9, 1799, which was intended to meet the case. He also sent a very able man — Edward Stevens — to St. Domingo, with the title of Consul-

[1] Toussaint to President Adams, 16 Brumaire, An vii. (Nov. 6, 1798); MSS. State Department Archives.

General, and with diplomatic powers. At the same
time the British Ministry despatched General Maitland to the same place, with orders to stop at Philadelphia and arrange a general policy in regard to
Toussaint. This was rapidly done. Maitland hurried
to the island, which he reached May 15, 1799, within
a month after the arrival of Stevens. Negotiations
followed, which resulted, June 13, in a secret treaty [1]
between Toussaint and Maitland, by which Toussaint
abandoned all privateering and shipping, receiving in
return free access to those supplies from the United
States which were needed to content his people, fill
his treasury, and equip his troops.

To this treaty Stevens was not openly a party ; but
in Toussaint's eyes he was the real negotiator, and
his influence had more to do with the result than all
the ships and soldiers at Maitland's disposal. Under
this informal tripartite agreement, Toussaint threw
himself into the arms of the United States, and took
an enormous stride toward the goal of his ambition, —
a crown.

Louverture had waited only to complete this arrangement before attacking Rigaud. Then the fruits
of his foreign policy ripened. Supplies of every kind
flowed from the United States into St. Domingo ; but
supplies were not enough. Toussaint began the siege
of Jacmel, — a siege famous in Haytian history. His
position was hazardous. A difficult war in a remote
province, for which he could not bring the necessary

[1] Treaty of June 13, 1799; MSS. State Department Archives.

supplies and materials by land; a suspicious or hos
tile French agent and government; a population
easily affected by rumors and intrigues; finally, the
seizure by English cruisers of a flotilla which, after
his promise to abandon all shipping, was bringing
his munitions of war along the coast for the siege, —
made Toussaint tremble for the result of his civil
war. He wrote once more to the President,[1] requesting him to send some frigates to enforce the treaty by
putting an end to all trade with the island except such
as the treaty permitted. Stevens again came to his
assistance. The United States frigate, " General
Greene," was sent to cruise off Jacmel in February
and March, 1800, and was followed by other vessels
of war. Rigaud's garrison was starved out; Jacmel
was abandoned; and Rigaud himself, July 29, 1800,
consented to quit the country.

Toussaint's gratitude was great, and his confidence
in Stevens unbounded. Even before the fall of Jacmel, Stevens was able to inform Secretary Pickering
that Toussaint was taking his measures slowly but
certainly to break connection with France.[2] "If he
is not disturbed, he will preserve appearances a little
longer; but as soon as France interferes with this
colony, he will throw off the mask and declare it
independent." Hardly was Rigaud crushed, when the

[1] Toussaint to President Adams, Aug. 14, 1799; MSS. State
Department Archives.

[2] Stevens to Pickering, Feb. 13, 1800; MSS. State Department
Archives.

first overt act of independence followed. Toussaint imprisoned Roume, and on an invitation from the municipalities assumed the civil as well as military authority, under the title of governor. In announcing to his Government that this step was to be taken, Stevens added : [1] " From that moment the colony may be considered as forever separated from France. Policy perhaps may induce him to make no open declaration of independence before he is compelled." A few days afterward Toussaint took the Napoleonic measure of seizing by force the Spanish part of the island, which had been ceded to France by the treaty of Bâle five years before, but had not yet been actually transferred. In thus making war on the ally of France, Toussaint had no other motive, as Stevens explained,[2] than to prevent the French government from getting a footing there. Bonaparte had given a new Constitution to France after the 18th Brumaire. Toussaint, after the deposition of Roume, which was his *coup d'état* and 18th Brumaire, gave a new Constitution to St. Domingo in the month of May, 1801, by which he not only assumed all political power for life, but also ascribed to himself the right of naming his own successor. Bonaparte had not yet dared to go so far, although he waited only another year, and meanwhile chafed under the idea of being imitated by one whom he called a " gilded African."

[1] Stevens to Pickering, April 19, 1800; MSS. State Department Archives.
[2] Ibid.

Perhaps audacity was Louverture's best policy; yet no wise man would intentionally aggravate his own dangers by unnecessary rashness, such as he showed in Bonaparte's face. He was like a rat defying a ferret; his safety lay not in his own strength, but in the nature of his hole. Power turned his head, and his regular army of twenty thousand disciplined and well-equipped men was his ruin. All his acts, and much of his open conversation, during the years 1800 and 1801, showed defiance to the First Consul. He prided himself upon being "First of the Blacks" and "Bonaparte of the Antilles." Warning and remonstrance from the Minister of Marine in France excited only his violent anger.[1] He insisted upon dealing directly with sovereigns, and not with their ministers, and was deeply irritated with Bonaparte for answering his letters through the Minister of Marine. Throwing one of these despatches aside unopened, he was heard to mutter before all his company the words, "*Ministre! . . . valet! . . .*"[2] He was right in the instinct of self-assertion, for his single hope lay in Bonaparte's consent to his independent power; but the attack on Spanish St. Domingo, and the proclamation of his new Constitution, were unnecessary acts of defiance.

When Jefferson became President of the United States and the Senate confirmed the treaty of Mor-

[1] Stevens to Pickering, May 24, 1800; MSS. State Department Archives.

[2] Pamphile de Lacroix, Mémoires, ii. 52.

fontaine, had Louverture not lost his balance he
would have seen that Bonaparte and Talleyrand had
out-manœuvred him, and that even if Jefferson were
not as French in policy as his predecessor had been
hostile to France, yet henceforth the United States
must disregard sympathies, treat St. Domingo as a
French colony, and leave the negro chief to his fate.
England alone, after the month of February, 1801,
stood between Toussaint and Bonaparte. Edward
Stevens, who felt the storm that was in the air,
pleaded ill-health and resigned his post of consul-
general. Jefferson sent Tobias Lear to Cap Français
in Stevens's place, and Lear's first interview showed
that Toussaint was beginning to feel Talleyrand's
restraints. The freedom he had enjoyed was disap-
pearing, and he chafed at the unaccustomed limitations. He complained bitterly that Lear had brought
him no personal letter from the President; and Lear
in vain explained the custom of the Government,
which warranted no such practice in the case of
consuls. "It is because of my color!" cried Toussaint.[1] Justice to President Jefferson and a keener
sense of the diplomatic situation would have shown
him that such a letter could not be written by the
President consistently with his new relations of
friendship toward France; and in fact almost the
first act of Pichon, on taking charge of the French
Legation in Washington after the treaty, was to re-

[1] Lear to Madison, July, 1801 ; MSS. State Department
Archives.

monstrate against any recognition of Toussaint, and
to cause Lear's want of diplomatic character which
offended Louverture.[1]

Rarely has diplomacy been used with more skill
and energy than by Bonaparte, who knew where
force and craft should converge. That in this skill
mendacity played a chief part, need hardly be repeated. Toussaint was flattered, cajoled, and held
in a mist of ignorance, while one by one the necessary preparations were made to prevent his escape;
and then, with scarcely a word of warning, at the
First Consul's order the mist rolled away, and the
unhappy negro found himself face to face with destruction. The same ships that brought news of the
preliminary treaty signed at London brought also
the rumor of a great expedition fitting at Brest and
the gossip of creole society in Paris, which made
no longer a secret that Bonaparte meant to crush
Toussaint and restore slavery at St. Domingo. Nowhere in the world had Toussaint a friend or a hope
except in himself. Two continents looked on with
folded arms, more and more interested in the result,
as Bonaparte's ripening schemes began to show their
character. As yet President Jefferson had no ink-
ling of their meaning. The British government was
somewhat better informed, and perhaps Godoy knew
more than all the rest; but none of them grasped the
whole truth, or felt their own dependence on Tous-

[1] Pichon to Decrès, 18 Fructidor, An ix. (Sept. 5, 1801); Archives de la Marine, MSS.

saint's courage. If he and his blacks should succumb
easily to their fate, the wave of French empire would
roll on to Louisiana and sweep far up the Mississippi;
if St. Domingo should resist, and succeed in resistance, the recoil would spend its force on Europe,
while America would be left to pursue her democratic
destiny in peace.

Bonaparte hurried his preparations. The month of
October, 1801, saw vast activity in French and Spanish ports, for a Spanish squadron accompanied the
French fleet. Not a chance was to be left for Toussaint's resistance or escape. To quiet English un-
easiness, Bonaparte dictated to Talleyrand a despatch
explaining to the British government the nature of
the expedition.[1] " In the course which I have taken
of annihilating the black government at St. Domingo,"
he said, " I have been less guided by considerations
of commerce and finance than by the necessity of sti-
fling in every part of the world every kind of germ of
disquiet and trouble ; but it could not escape me that
St. Domingo, even after being reconquered by the
whites, would be for many years a weak point which
would need the support of peace and of the mother
country ; . . . that one of the principal benefits of
peace, at the actual moment, for England was its conclusion at a time when the French government had not
yet recognized the organization of St. Domingo, and
in consequence the power of the blacks ; and if it had

[1] Correspondance, vii. 319 ; Bonaparte to Talleyrand, 22 Brumaire, An x. (Nov. 13, 1801).

done so, the sceptre of the new world would sooner
or later have fallen into the hands of the blacks."

No such explanations were given to the United
States, perhaps because no American minister asked
for them. Livingston landed at Lorient November
12, the day before Bonaparte wrote these words;
Leclerc's expedition sailed from Brest November 22;
and Livingston was presented to the First Consul
in the diplomatic audience of December 6. Caring
nothing for Toussaint and much for France, Livingston did not come prepared to find that his own
interests were the same with those of Toussaint, but
already by December 30 he wrote to Rufus King:
"I know that the armament, destined in the first
instance for Hispaniola, is to proceed to Louisiana
provided Toussaint makes no opposition."

While the First Consul claimed credit with England for intending to annihilate the black government
and restore slavery at St. Domingo, he proclaimed to
Toussaint and the negroes intentions of a different
kind. He wrote at last a letter to Toussaint, and
drew up a proclamation to the inhabitants of the
island, which Leclerc was to publish. "If you are
told," said this famous proclamation,[1] "that these
forces are destined to ravish your liberty, answer:
The Republic has given us liberty, the Republic will
not suffer it to be taken from us!" The letter to
Toussaint was even more curious, when considered

[1] Correspondance, vii. 315; Proclamation, 17 Brumaire, An x.
(Nov. 8, 1801).

as a supplement to that which had been written to
the British government only five days before. " We
have conceived esteem for you," wrote Bonaparte to
the man he meant to destroy,[1] " and we take pleasure
in recognizing and proclaiming the great services you
have rendered to the French people. If their flag
floats over St. Domingo, it is to you and to the brave
blacks that they owe it." Then, after mildly disap-
proving certain of Toussaint's acts, and hinting at
the fatal consequences of disobedience, the letter
continued : " Assist the Captain-General [Leclerc]
with your counsels, your influence, and your talents.
What can you desire ? — the liberty of the blacks ?
You know that in all the countries where we have
been, we have given it to the peoples who had it not."
In order to quiet all alarms of the negroes on the
subject of their freedom, a pledge still more absolute
was given in what Americans might call the Annual
Message sent to the French Legislature a week afterward. " At St. Domingo and at Guadeloupe there
are no more slaves. All is free there ; all will there
remain free." [2]

A few days afterward Leclerc's expedition sailed ;
and the immense fleet, with an army of ten thousand
men and all their equipments, arrived in sight of St.
Domingo at the close of January, 1802. Toussaint

[1] Correspondance, vii. 322 ; Bonaparte to Toussaint, 27 Brumaire, An x. (Nov. 18, 1801).

[2] Ibid., 327 ; Exposé de la situation de la République, 1 Frimaire, An x. (Nov. 22, 1801).

was believed to have watched them from a look-out
in the mountains while they lay for a day making
their preparations for combined action. Then Leclerc
sailed for Cap Français, where Christophe commanded.
After a vain attempt to obtain possession of the town
as a friend, he was obliged to attack. February 5
Christophe set the place in flames, and the war of
races broke out.

The story of this war, interesting though it was,
cannot be told here. Toussaint's resistance broke the
force of Bonaparte's attack. Although it lasted less
than three- months, it swept away one French army,
and ruined the industry of the colony to an extent
that required years of repair. Had Toussaint not
been betrayed by his own generals, and had he been
less attached than he was to civilization and despotic
theories of military rule, he would have achieved a
personal triumph greater than was won by any other
man of his time. His own choice was to accept the
war of races, to avoid open battle where his troops
were unequal to their opponents, and to harass instead of fighting in line. He would have made a war
of guerillas, stirred up the terror and fanaticism of
the negro laborers, put arms into their hands, and relied on their courage rather than on that of his army.
He let himself be overruled. "Old Toussaint," said
Christophe afterward, "never ceased saying this, but
no one would believe him. We had arms; pride in
using them destroyed us."[1] Christophe, for good

[1] Pamphile de Lacroix, Mémoires, ii. 228.

reasons, told but half the story. Toussaint was not
ruined by a few lost battles, but by the treachery
of Christophe himself and of the other negro generals. Jealous of Toussaint's domination, and perhaps afraid of being sent to execution like Moyse —
the best general officer in their service — for want
of loyalty to his chief, Christophe, after one cam-
paign, April 26, 1802, surrendered his posts and
forces to Leclerc without the knowledge and against
the orders of Toussaint. Then Louverture himself committed the fatal mistake of his life, which
he of all men seemed least likely to commit, — he
trusted the word of Bonaparte. May 1, 1802, he put
himself in Leclerc's hands in reliance on Leclerc's
honor.

Surprising as such weakness was in one who had
the sensitiveness of a wild animal to danger, — Leclerc himself seemed to be as much surprised that
the word of honor of a French soldier should be
believed as any bystander at seeing the negro believe it, — the act had a parallel in the weakness
which led Bonaparte, twelve years afterward, to
mount the deck of the "Bellerophon," and without even the guaranty of a pledge surrender himself to England. The same vacillations and fears,
the same instinct of the desperate political gambler,
the same cowering in the face of fate, closed the
active lives of both these extraordinary men. Such
beings should have known how to die when their
lives were ended. Toussaint should have fought on,

even though only to perish under the last cactus
on his mountains, rather than trust himself in the
hands of Bonaparte.

The First Consul's orders to Leclerc were positive, precise, and repeated.[1] " Follow exactly your
instructions," said he, " and the moment you have
rid yourself of Toussaint, Christophe, Dessalines,
and the principal brigands, and the masses of the
blacks shall be disarmed, send over to the continent all the blacks and mulattoes who have played a
rôle in the civil troubles. . . . Rid us of these gilded
Africans, and we shall have nothing more to wish." [2]
With the connivance and at the recommendation of
Christophe, by a stratagem such as Bonaparte used
afterward in the case of the Duc d'Enghien and of
Don Carlos IV., Toussaint was suddenly arrested,
June 10, 1802, and hurried on ship-board. Some
weeks later he was landed at Brest; then he disappeared. Except a few men who were in the secret,
no one ever again saw him. Plunged into a damp
dungeon in the fortress of Joux, high in the Jura
Mountains on the Swiss frontier, the cold and solitude of a single winter closed this tropical existence.
April 7, 1803, he died forgotten, and his work died
with him. Not by Toussaint, and still less by Christophe or Dessalines, was the liberty of the blacks

[1] Correspondance, vii. 413 ; Bonaparte to Leclerc, 25 Ventôse,
An x. (March 16, 1802).

[2] Ibid., 503, 504 ; Bonaparte to Leclerc, 12 Messidor, An x.
(July 1, 1802).

finally established in Hayti, and the entrance of
the Mississippi barred to Bonaparte.

The news of Leclerc's success reached Paris early
in June,[1] and set Bonaparte again in motion. Imag-
ining that the blacks were at his mercy, orders were
at once issued to provide for restoring them to slavery. The truth relating to this part of the subject, habitually falsified or concealed by Bonaparte
and his admirers,[2] remained hidden among the manu-
script records of the Empire; but the order to restore slavery at Guadeloupe was given, June 14, by
the Minister of the Marine to General Richepanse,
who commanded there, and on the same day a similar instruction was sent to General Leclerc at St.
Domingo, in each case leaving the general to act
according to his discretion in the time and manner
of proceeding.

"As regards the return of the blacks to the old
régime," wrote the Minister to General Leclerc,[3] "the
bloody struggle out of which you have just come victo-
rious with glory commands us to use the utmost caution.
Perhaps we should only entangle ourselves in it anew if
we wished precipitately to break that idol of liberty in
whose name so much blood has flowed till now. For
some time yet vigilance, order, a discipline at once rural
and military, must take the place of the positive and pro-

[1] Moniteur, 24 Prairial, An x. (June 13, 1802).
[2] Correspondance, xxx. 535 ; Notes sur St. Domingue.
[3] Decrès to Leclerc, 25 Prairial, An x. (June 14, 1802) ; Archives de la Marine, MSS. Cf. Revue Historique, "Napoléon
Premier et Saint Domingue," Janvier-Février, 1884.

nounced slavery of the colored people of your colony.
Especially the master's good usage must reattach them to
his rule.   When they shall have felt by comparison the
difference between a usurping and tyrannical yoke and
that of the legitimate proprietor interested in their preservation, then the moment will have arrived for making
them return to their original condition, from which it has
been so disastrous to have drawn them."

CHAPTER XVI.

SIMULTANEOUSLY with the order to restore slavery at Guadeloupe and St. Domingo, Bonaparte directed his Minister of Marine to prepare plans and estimates for the expedition which was to occupy Louisiana. "My intention is to take possession of Louisiana with the shortest delay, and that this expedition be made in the utmost secrecy, under the appearance of being directed on St. Domingo." [1] The First Consul had allowed Godoy to postpone for a year the delivery of Louisiana, but he would wait no longer. His Minister at Madrid, General Gouvion St.-Cyr, obtained at length a promise that the order for the delivery of Louisiana should be given by Charles IV. to the First Consul on two conditions : first, that Austria, England, and the dethroned Grand Duke of Tuscany should be made to recognize the new King of Etruria ; second, that France should pledge herself "not to alienate the property and usufruct of Louisiana, and to restore it to Spain in case the King of Tuscany should lose the whole or the greater part of his estates."

[1] Correspondance, vii. 485; Bonaparte to Decrès, 15 Prairial, An x. (June 4, 1802).

To these demands Talleyrand immediately replied
in a letter of instructions to Gouvion St.-Cyr, which
was destined to a painful celebrity.[1]   After soothing
and reassuring Spain on the subject of the King of
Etruria, this letter came at last to the required pledge
in regard to Louisiana : —

" Spain wishes that France should engage herself not
to sell or alienate in any manner the property or enjoyment of Louisiana.   Her wish in this respect perfectly
conforms with the intentions of the French government,
which parted with it in 1762 only in favor of Spain, and
has wished to recover it only because France holds to
a possession which once made part of French territory.
You can declare in the name of the First Consul that
France will never alienate it."

St.-Cyr accordingly gave a formal written pledge
in the name of the First Consul that France would
never alienate Louisiana.[2]

Even yet the formal act of delivery was delayed.
Bonaparte gave orders [3] that the expedition should
be ready to sail in the last week of September; but
the time passed, and delays were multiplied.   For
once the First Consul failed to act with energy.   His
resources were drained to St. Domingo as fast as

[1] Talleyrand to Gouvion St.-Cyr, 30 Prairial, An x. (June 19,
1802); Archives des Aff. Étr., MSS.

[2] St.-Cyr to Don Pedro Cevallos, 23 Messidor, An x. (July
12, 1802).   Yrujo to Madison, Sept. 4, 1803.   State Papers, ii.
569.

[3] Correspondance, viii. 5; Bonaparte to Decrès, 6 Fructidor,
An x. (Aug. 24, 1802).

he could collect them,[1] and the demands of the colonies on his means of transportation exceeded his supply of transports. The expedition to Louisiana was postponed, but, as he hoped, only to give it more scope.

From the time of Berthier's treaty of retrocession, Bonaparte had tried to induce the King of Spain to part with the Floridas ; but Charles IV. refused to talk of another bargain. In vain Bonaparte wrote to the young King of Etruria, offering to give him Parma, Piacenza, and Guastalla, if Don Carlos would add Florida to Louisiana.[2] When at length the King signed at Barcelona, October 15, the order which delivered Louisiana to France, Bonaparte pressed more earnestly than ever for the Floridas. Talleyrand made a report on the subject, dissuading him from acquiring more than West Florida.[3]

" West Florida," he wrote, " suffices for the desired enlargement of Louisiana ; it completes the retrocession of the French colony, such as it was given to Spain ; it carries the eastern boundary back to the river Appalachicola ; it gives us the port of Pensacola, and a population which forms more than half that of the two Floridas. By leaving East Florida to Spain we much diminish the difficulties of our relative position in regard to the United

---

[1] Correspondance, viii. 112; Bonaparte to Leclerc, 6 Frimaire, An xi. (Nov. 27, 1802).

[2] Ibid., 12; Bonaparte to the King of Tuscany, 11 Fructidor, An x. (Aug. 29, 1802).

[3] Rapport au Premier Consul; Frimaire, An xi. (November, 1802) ; Archives des Aff. Étr., MSS.

States, — difficulties little felt to-day, but which some day may become of the gravest importance."

Bonaparte did not follow this advice. On the death of the Duke of Parma he wrote with his own hand to the King of Spain, offering the old family estate of Parma as a gift for the King of Tuscany, in return for which France was to receive the Floridas.[1] The Queen, as before, favored the exchange, and all her influence was exerted to effect it; but Godoy was obstinate in evading or declining the offer, and after months of diplomatic effort Bonaparte received at last, toward the end of January, 1803, a despatch from General Beurnonville, his new representative at Madrid, announcing that the Prince of Peace, with the aid of the British Minister John Hookham Frere, had succeeded in defeating the scheme.[2]

" The Prince told me that the British Minister had declared to him, in the name of his Government, that his Britannic Majesty, being informed of the projects of exchange which existed between France and Spain, could never consent that the two Floridas should become an acquisition of the Republic; that the United States of America were in this respect of one mind with the Court of London; and that Russia equally objected to France disposing of the estates of Parma in favor of Spain, since the Emperor Alexander intended to have them granted as

[1] Correspondance, viii. 111; Bonaparte to the King of Spain, 6 Frimaire, An xi. (Nov. 27. 1802).

[2] Beurnonville to Talleyrand, 27 Nivôse, An xi. (Jan. 17, 1803); Archives des Aff. Étr., MSS.

indemnity to the King of Sardinia. In imparting to me this proceeding of the British Minister, the Prince had a satisfied air, which showed how much he wished that the exchange, almost agreed upon and so warmly desired by the Queen, may not take place."

Europe would have acted more wisely in its own interest by offering Bonaparte every inducement to waste his strength on America. Had England, Spain, and Russia united to give him Florida on his own terms, they would have done only what was best for themselves. A slight impulse given to the First Consul would have plunged him into difficulties with the United States from which neither France nor the United States could have easily escaped. Both Godoy and the Emperor Alexander would have done well to let French blood flow without restraint in St. Domingo and on the Mississippi, rather than drown with it the plains of Castile and Smolensk.

Although the retrocession of Louisiana to France had been settled in principle by Berthier's treaty of Oct. 1, 1800, six months before Jefferson came into office, the secret was so well kept that Jefferson hardly suspected it. He began his administration by anticipating a long period of intimate relations with Spain and France. In sending instructions to Claiborne as governor of the Mississippi Territory, — a post of importance, because of its relations with the Spanish authority at New Orleans, — President Jefferson wrote privately,[1] —

[1] Jefferson to W. C. C. Claiborne, July 13, 1801; Jefferson MSS.

"With respect to Spain, our disposition is sincerely amicable, and even affectionate. We consider her possession of the adjacent country as most favorable to our interests, and should see with an extreme pain any other nation substituted for them."

Disposed to be affectionate toward Spain, he assumed that he should stand in cordial relations with Spain's ally, the First Consul. Convinced that the quarrels of America with France had been artificially created by the monarchical Federalists, he believed that a policy of open confidence would prevent such dangers in the future. The First Consul would naturally cultivate his friendship, for every Federalist newspaper had for years proclaimed Jefferson as the head of French influence in America, and every Republican newspaper had branded his predecessors as tools of Great Britain. In spite of the 18th Brumaire, Jefferson had not entirely lost faith in Bonaparte, and knew almost nothing of his character or schemes. At the moment when national interest depended on prompt and exact information, the President withdrew half his ministers from Europe, and paid little attention to the agents he retained. He took diplomatic matters into his own hands, and meant to conduct them at Washington with diplomatists under his personal influence,— a practice well suited to a power superior in will and force to that with which it dealt, but one which might work badly in dealing with Bonaparte. When Chancellor Livingston, the new minister to Paris, sailed for France, Jefferson wrote him a private letter [1] in regard to the appointment of a new French minister at Washington. Two names had been suggested, — La Forest and Otto. Neither of these was quite satisfactory; some man would be preferred whose sympathies should be so entire as to make reticences and restraints unnecessary. The idea that Jefferson could put himself in Bonaparte's hands without reticence or restraint belonged to old theories of opposition, — a few months dispelled it; and when he had been a year in office, he wrote again to Livingston, withdrawing the objection to La Forest and Otto. "When I wrote that letter," said he,[2] "I did not harbor a doubt that the disposition on that side the water was as cordial as I knew ours to be." He had discovered his mistake, — "the dispositions now understood to exist there impose of themselves limits to the openness of our communications."

Even before Livingston sailed, the rumors of the retrocession of Louisiana had taken such definite shape [3] that, in June, 1801, Secretary Madison instructed the ministers at London, Paris, and Madrid on the subject. These instructions were remarkable for their mildness.[4] No protest was officially ordered against a scheme so hostile to the interests of the Union. On the contrary, Livingston was told, in Sep-

[1] Jefferson to R. R. Livingston, Aug. 28, 1801; Jefferson MSS.; State Department Archives.

[2] Jefferson to R. R Livingston, March 16, 1802; Jefferson MSS.

[3] Rufus King to Madison, June 1, 1801; State Papers, ii. 509.

[4] Madison to Pinckney, June 9, 1801; Madison to Livingston, Sept. 28, 1801; State Papers, ii. 510.

tember, 1801, that if he could obtain West Florida
from France, or by means of French influence, "such
a proof on the part of France of good-will toward
the United States would contribute to reconcile the
latter" to seeing Bonaparte at New Orleans. Even
after Rufus King, the United States minister at London, sent home a copy of Lucien Bonaparte's treaty
of Madrid, in which the whole story was told,[1] this
revelation, probably managed by Godoy in order to
put the United States and England on their guard,
produced no immediate effect. Jefferson yielded with
reluctance to the conviction that he must quarrel with
Bonaparte. Had not Godoy's delays and Toussaint's
resistance intervened, ten thousand French soldiers,
trained in the school of Hoche and Moreau, and
commanded by a future marshal of France, might
have occupied New Orleans and St. Louis before
Jefferson could have collected a brigade of militia
at Nashville.

By the spring of 1802 Jefferson became alive to the
danger. He then saw what was meant by the French
expedition against Toussaint. Leclerc had scarcely
succeeded, Feb. 5, 1802, in taking possession of the
little that Christophe left at Cap Français, when his
difficulties of supply began. St. Domingo drew its
supplies chiefly from the United States. Toussaint's
dependence on the American continent had been so
complete as to form one of the chief complaints
of French merchants. General Leclerc disliked the

---

[1] Rufus King to Madison, Nov. 20, 1801; State Papers, ii. 511.

United States, — not without reason, since the Government of that country, as was notorious, had done its utmost to punish France, and had succeeded beyond expectation. Leclerc was a soldier, — severe, impatient, quick to take offence, and also quick to forget it. He knew that he could expect no sympathy from Americans, and he found that all the supplies in St. Domingo were American property. Of course the owners asked extortionate prices; and had Leclerc paid them, he would within six weeks have seen his harbors glutted with goods from Baltimore and New York. Instead of doing this, he seized them, and insulted the American shipmasters and merchants. By the month of March the newspapers of the United States were filled with stories of Leclerc's arbitrary and violent conduct. He was reported as saying that the Americans were no better than Arabs; and one of his general officers was said to have told Lear, the American consul-general, that they were the scum of nations. Cargoes were taken without payment, American shipmasters were seized and imprisoned for offences unknown to the law; while Lear was notified that no consul could be received in St. Domingo as a colony of France, and that he must quit the island within a fortnight. No protest availed against such summary discipline. Lear obeyed; and returning to Madison at Washington, told him of American property confiscated and American citizens in prison.

Madison sent for Pichon, then in charge of the

French legation at Washington pending the appointment of a minister. Pichon was a relic of the French
republic; he had been long in the United States, and
felt little apparent sympathy with the consular *régime*
or its plans. At Madison's request, Pichon undertook
to interfere, and wrote to Leclerc letter upon letter of
remonstrance.[1]   America, he said, could either feed
or famish the French army: "Experience proves it;
our colonies were brought into revolt only by our
unlucky misunderstanding with her; through her
alone can we raise them up again." Leclerc resented
the tone of these letters, and wrote to Bonaparte
that Pichon was a scoundrel and a wretch, with
whom he would hold no further relations;[2] but before Leclerc's letter could have arrived, the First
Consul had already ordered[3] Talleyrand to rebuke the
chargé at Washington for his American officiousness.
Pichon's diplomatic career was closed; he retired
into private life as soon as the new minister arrived,
but meanwhile his remonstrances were not without effect upon Leclerc, whose anger rarely became
vindictive.

The conduct of Leclerc in expelling Lear and im-
prisoning American shipmasters because munitions of

[1] Pichon to Leclerc, 29 Ventôse–11 Messidor, An x. (March
20–June 30, 1802); Archives de la Marine, MSS.

[2] Leclerc to Bonaparte, 17 Prairial, An x. (June 6, 1802); Archives Nationales, MSS.

[3] Correspondance, vii. 508; Bonaparte to Talleyrand, 15 Messidor, An x. (July 4, 1802).

war were found among the cargoes lying in the ports
of Toussaint, first opened President Jefferson's eyes
to the situation into which he was drifting; but other
evidences were not wanting that Bonaparte was no
friend of the United States. Talleyrand's conduct
was almost as exasperating as when he provoked
reprisals four years before. Chancellor Livingston
reached France about Nov. 10, 1801, just in time to
see Leclerc's expedition sail. He was met by private
assurances that Louisiana and the Floridas had been
bought by France, and he went to Talleyrand with
inquiries.[1] The imperturbable Talleyrand looked
him in the face and denied the fact. "It had been
a subject of conversation," he said, "but nothing concluded." At that moment Rufus King was sending
from London the text of Lucien Bonaparte's treaty,
dated eight months before, which fixed the details of
the retrocession. President Jefferson received at the
same instant Talleyrand's explicit denial and the
explicit proof that Talleyrand was trying to deceive
him. Jefferson soon satisfied himself that Talleyrand's conduct rested on a system; and he became
angrier with every act of the French foreign minister.
Livingston, naturally somewhat suspicious and fret-
ful, soon became restive under the treatment he received; for his notes and remonstrances were left
equally without answer or attention, whether they re-
lated to Louisiana or to the debts due by the Govern-

[1] Livingston to Madison, Dec. 10, 1801; Livingston to King,
Dec. 30; King to Madison, Nov. 20; State Papers, ii. 511, 512.

ment of France to American citizens. As Livingston
grew hot, and Leclerc's temper burst into violence,
Madison became irritable, and by the month of May
had reached the point of saying that if such conduct should continue, "the worst events are to be
apprehended."[1]

The President himself then intervened. A French
gentleman, Dupont de Nemours, happened to be in
the United States on the point of returning to France.
Dupont's name was then as well and honorably
known in France as that of his descendants was to
become in the annals of the United States. To him
Jefferson turned as a medium of unofficial communication with the First Consul. He enclosed to Dupont
a letter addressed to Livingston on the Louisiana
affair, which he requested Dupont to read, and, after
reading, to seal.

"I wish you to be possessed of the subject," he wrote,[2]
"because you may be able to impress on the Government
of France the inevitable consequences of their taking possession of Louisiana; and though, as I here mention,
the cession of New Orleans and the Floridas to us would
be a palliation, yet I believe it would be no more, and
that this measure will cost France, and perhaps not very
long hence, a war which will annihilate her on the ocean,
and place that element under the despotism of two
nations, — which I am not reconciled to the more because my own would be one of them."

[1] Madison to Livingston, May 1, 1802; State Papers, ii. 516.
[2] Jefferson to Dupont de Nemours, April 25, 1802; Works,
iv. 435.

This idea was still more strongly expressed in the enclosure to Livingston, which Dupont was to read, in order that he might communicate its sense to Bonaparte : [1] —

" The day that France takes possession of New Orleans fixes the sentence which is to restrain her forever within her low-water mark. It seals the union of two nations, who in conjunction can maintain exclusive possession of the ocean. From that moment we must marry ourselves to the British fleet and nation. . . . Will not the amalgamation of a young and thriving nation continue to that enemy the health and force which are at present so evidently on the decline ? And will a few years' possession of New Orleans add equally to the strength of France ? "

Dupont was to impress on the First Consul the idea that if he should occupy Louisiana, the United States would wait " a few years," until the next war between France and England, but would then make common cause with England. Even a present cession of New Orleans and the Floridas to the United States, though it would remove the necessity of an immediate advance to England, would not prevent the risk of a quarrel with France, so long as France should hold the west bank of the Mississippi. To obviate such a quarrel was the object of Dupont's unofficial mission. " If you can be the means of informing the wisdom of Bonaparte of all its consequences, you have deserved well of both countries."

[1] Jefferson to Livingston, April 18, 1802; Works, iv. 431.

As though to alarm Bonaparte were not task enough for any one man, Jefferson suggested that it would be well to hoodwink Talleyrand.

" There is another service you can render. I am told that Talleyrand is personally hostile to us. This, I suppose, has been occasioned by the X. Y. Z. history ; but he should consider that that was the artifice of a party willing to sacrifice him to the consolidation of their power. This nation has done him justice by dismissing them."

To do Talleyrand justice was impossible; but his reflections on the letter which Dupont was tacitly authorized to show him could hardly have been just to Jefferson. With the X. Y. Z. history, as Jefferson called it, fresh in Talleyrand's mind, — an instance of his venality so notorious that it had cost him his office, and so outrageous that even his associates of the 18th Brumaire had not at first ventured to re-appoint him, — hostility to the United States had become with him a personal as well as a political passion. Accustomed to the penetrating candor of his own untroubled avowals, he read these words of Jefferson, announcing that an American President had been dismissed from office in order to do him justice : —

" This nation has done him justice by dismissing them ; those in power are precisely those who disbelieved that story, and saw in it nothing but an attempt to deceive our country. We entertain toward him personally the most friendly dispositions. As to the government of France, we know too little of the state of things there to understand what it is, and have no inclination to meddle in their settlement. Whatever government they establish, we wish to be well with it."

Talleyrand must have known enough of the American character to feel that a Republican President could not seriously mean to represent his own election as an act of national justice to a venal French politician; in his eyes, the letter could have seemed to show only simple-mindedness. One point needed no analysis of character. Jefferson said that he did not know what sort of government the 18th Brumaire created, or care to meddle in its affairs; he wished to be well with it, and in any case should not go to war until England did so. Dupont remonstrated against the nature of the message. "A young soldier," he wrote back,[1] "whose ministers can keep their places only by perpetually flattering his military pride, will be much more offended than touched by this reasoning; and if this be all that is advanced, we may regard the negotiation as a failure." To make its chances worse, it crossed the ocean at the same time with the news that Toussaint had submitted, and that no obstacle to the immediate occupation of Louisiana remained. Dupont talked in vain. Bonaparte answered only by pressing Spain for the Floridas, and demanding possession of New Orleans.

[1] Dupont to Jefferson, April 30, 1802; Jefferson MSS.

Thus far American diplomacy was not successful; Jefferson's efforts were no more effective than Madison's more cautious suggestions. As the summer began, the President watched anxiously the course of events at St. Domingo, and found consolation there for the baseness of Callender and the assaults on Paine at home. "Though I take for granted," he wrote to Governor McKean,[1] "that the colonization of Louisiana is a settled point, yet I suspect they must be much stronger in St. Domingo before they can spare troops to go there. What has been called a surrender of Toussaint to Leclerc, I suspect was in reality a surrender of Leclerc to Toussaint."

The seizure of Toussaint and his disappearance from the island, which occurred as Jefferson wrote this letter, overthrew its hopeful theories; but before long, reports began to arrive in the United States that Leclerc had met with a new disaster, so terrible as to surpass the horrors even of St. Domingo history. The first French army, of seventeen thousand men, had been consumed in the task of subjecting the negroes. A second army was next swept away by yellow fever. In the middle of September, 1802, Leclerc wrote to the First Consul that of twenty-eight thousand three hundred men sent to St. Domingo, four thousand remained fit for service.[2] "Add to

[1] Jefferson to Governor McKean, June 14, 1802; Jefferson MSS.

[2] Leclerc to Bonaparte, 29 Fructidor, An x. (Sept. 16, 1802); Archives Nationales, MSS.

our losses that of five thousand sailors, and the occupation of St. Domingo has cost us till now twenty-four thousand men, and we are not yet definitely masters of it." He was depending on Toussaint's generals and army for his support against an insurrection of the laborers, who were maddened by the rumor that slavery had been restored at Guadeloupe, and was soon to be re-established at St. Domingo. Nothing could be more discouraging than 'Leclerc's letters : [1] —

"I have no false measure to reproach myself with, Citizen Consul ; and if my position, from being a very good one, has become very bad, it is necessary to blame here only the malady which has destroyed my army, the premature re-establishment of slavery at Guadeloupe, and the newspapers and letters from France, which speak only of slavery. Here is my opinion on this country. We must destroy all the negroes in the mountains, men and women, keeping only infants less than twelve years old ; we must also destroy half those of the plain, and leave in the colony not a single man of color who has worn an epaulette. Without this the colony will never be quiet ; and at the beginning of every year, especially after murderous seasons like this, you will have a civil war, which will shake your hold on the country. In order to be master of St. Domingo, you must send me twelve thousand men without losing a single day."

Besides these twelve thousand men and twelve hundred thousand dollars in specie, Leclerc required

[1] Leclerc to Bonaparte, 15 Vendémiaire, An xi. (Oct. 7, 1802); Archives Nationales, MSS.

five thousand more men in the following summer. "If you cannot send the troops I demand, and for the season I point out, St. Domingo will be forever lost to France."

Long afterward, at St. Helena, Napoleon wrote comments [1] on the causes of his disaster at St. Domingo, severely blaming his brother-in-law Leclerc for failing to carry out his orders to arrest and send to Europe all the black generals, as he sent Toussaint. Napoleon's rule in politics, and one which cost him dear, was to disregard masses and reckon only on leaders. Toussaint came within a step of achieving the greatest triumph of his age. Had he been true to himself and his color, and had he hidden himself for a few months in the mountains, he need not have struck a blow in order to drive Bonaparte's generals back to Europe; the yellow fever and the blind despair of the negro laborers would have done the work alone. Bonaparte's theory in regard to the negro chiefs was an illusion. Christophe, Dessalines, Maurepas, and all Toussaint's chief officers served Leclerc faithfully till they saw his case to be hopeless. "Dessalines is at this moment the butcher of the blacks," wrote Leclerc Sept. 16, 1802, in the midst of insurrections; "Christophe has so maltreated them as to be execrated by them." The negro chiefs were traitors to both sides; and if not arrested by Leclerc, they deserved to be shot by their own people. While they helped to exterminate the

[1] Correspondance, xxx. 534.

black laboring class, Leclerc sent home reports that
might have frozen the blood of any man less callous
than Bonaparte:[1] —

" The decrees of General Richepanse [at Guadeloupe]
circulate here, and do much harm. The one which re-
stores slavery, in consequence of being published three
months too soon, will cost many men to the army and
colony of St. Domingo. . . . I get news of a bloody
combat sustained by General Boyer at the Gros Morne.
The rebels were exterminated; fifty prisoners were hung.
These men die with incredible fanaticism, — they laugh
at death; it is the same with the women. The rebels
of Moustique have attacked and carried Jean Rabel; it
should have been retaken by this time. This fury is the
work of General Richepanse's proclamation and of the
inconsiderate talk of the colonists."

As the insurrection spread, and the fever reduced
Leclerc's European force, the black generals and
troops began to desert. Shooting was useless; drown-
ing had no effect. No form of terror touched them.
" Few colonial troops remain with me," wrote Leclerc in almost his last letter. " A battalion of the
Eleventh Colonial, which had been joined with the
Legion of the Cape, having furnished a number of
deserters, 176 men of this battalion were embarked
at Jacmel for Port Republican. Of this number 173
strangled themselves on the way, the Chef de Batail-
lon at their head. There you see the men we have

[1] Leclerc to Decrès, 21 Thermidor, An x. (Aug. 9, 1802);
Archives de la Marine, MSS.

to fight!"[1]   At length the report came that Leclerc himself had succumbed.   Worn by anxieties, exertions, and incessant fever, he followed his army to the grave.

News of Leclerc's death, Nov. 1, 1802, and of the hopelessness of Bonaparte's schemes against St. Domingo, reached the Government at Washington nearly at the same time with other news which overshadowed this.   The people of the United States expected day by day to hear of some sudden attack, from which as yet only the dexterity of Godoy and the disasters of Leclerc had saved them.   Although they could see only indistinctly the meaning of what had taken place, they knew where to look for the coming stroke, and in such a state of mind might easily exaggerate its importance.   A few days before Congress met, the Western post brought a despatch from Governor Claiborne at Natchez announcing that the Spanish Intendant, Don Juan Ventura Morales, had forbidden the Americans to deposit their merchandise at New Orleans, as they had a right to do under the treaty of 1795.[2]

No one doubted that although the attack might come from a Spanish Intendant, the real party with whom America had to deal was not Spain, but France. The secret papers of the French government show

[1] Leclerc to Bonaparte, 15 Vendémiaire, An xi. (Oct. 7, 1802); Archives Nationales, MSS.

[2] Despatch of W. C. C. Claiborne, Oct. 29, 1802; State Papers, ii. 470.

what was said, but hardly believed at the time, that the First Consul was not directly responsible for the act; but they also prove that the act was a consequence of the retrocession. The colonial system of Spain was clumsy and disconnected. Viceroys, governors, commandants, intendants, acted in Mexico, Cuba, New Orleans, Peru, everywhere without relation to each other. At New Orleans the Governor, Don Juan de Salcedo, was powerless to control the Intendant, Don Juan Ventura Morales, and no authority nearer than Madrid could decide between them. The *entrepôt*, or right of deposit, not only prevented the Spanish Intendant from imposing duties on American produce, but also covered a large amount of smuggling which further diminished the revenue. The Intendant, who had charge of the revenues, and was partly responsible for the large deficit which every year drained the resources of Spain to Louisiana, was forced to hear the complaints of the Treasury at Madrid, continually asking him to find a remedy, and at last, in one of its despatches, letting slip the remark that " after all, the right of deposit was only for three years." The treaty of 1795 had in fact stipulated that the King of Spain would " permit the citizens of the United States, for the space of three years from this time, to deposit their merchandise and effects in the port of New Orleans, and to export them from thence, without paying any other duty than a fair price for the hire of the stores ; and his Majesty promises either to continue this permis-

sion if he finds during that time that it is not preju-
dicial to the interests of Spain, or if he should not
agree to continue it there, he will assign to them
on another part of the banks of the Mississippi an
equivalent establishment."

According to the explanation given by Morales to
Laussat,[1] the new French prefect whom Bonaparte
sent to receive possession of Louisiana, the Spaniard
acted on his own responsibility, in what he believed
to be the interests of the colony, and within the stipu-
lations of the treaty. Thinking that the retrocession
offered a chance, which might never recur, for re-
opening a question which had been wrongly decided,
Morales, defying the opposition and even the threats
of Governor Salcedo, proclaimed the right of deposit
to be at an end. He reasoned that Spain as a
result of peace with England had shut her colonial
ports to strangers, and this measure, so far as it included Louisiana, was illusory so long as the right
of deposit should exist. The right had been granted
for three years from 1795; and if the practice had
been permitted to continue after these three years
expired, it might have been owing, not to the treaty,
but to the general privileges granted to neutrals during the war; and as for the Americans, it was their
own fault not to have looked more carefully to their
rights at the close of the three years, when they
should have secured the continuation or the prom-

[1] Laussat to Decrès, 29 Germinal, An xi. (April 19, 1803);
Archives de la Marine, MSS.

ised substitute. As Spain was about to lose Louisiana
in any case, Morales remarked that she need not
trouble herself about the quarrel he was making
with the United States; while the French republic
took Louisiana as it actually stood under the treaties, and ought therefore to be glad of whatever improved the actual situation, or opened the path to
negotiations more advantageous. This view of the
matter, as Morales presented it, was the more interesting because it was in the spirit of Talleyrand's
plans, and reversed Godoy's policy.

The rumor that Spain had closed the Mississippi
roused varied sensations as it spread eastward. Tennessee and Kentucky became eager for war. They
knew that Morales's act was a foretaste of what they
were to expect from France; and they might well ask
themselves how many lives it would cost to dislodge
a French army once fortified on the lower Mississippi.
The whole power of the United States could not at
that day, even if backed by the navy of England,
have driven ten thousand French troops out of Louisiana. On the contrary, a vigorous French officer,
with a small trained force and his Indian allies, could
make Claiborne uneasy for the safety of his villages
at Natchez and Vicksburg. No one could foresee
what might be the effect of one or two disastrous
campaigns on the devotion of the Western people to
the Government at Washington. The existence of
the Union and the sacrifice of many thousand lives
seemed, in the opinion of competent judges, likely to

be risked by allowing Bonaparte to make his position at New Orleans impregnable.

The New England Federalists were satisfied that President Jefferson must either adopt their own policy and make war on France, or risk a dissolution of the Union. They had hardly dared hope that democracy would so soon meet what might prove to be its crisis. They too cried for war, and cared little whether their outcry produced or prevented hostilities, for the horns of Jefferson's dilemma were equally fatal to him. All eyes were bent on the President, and watched eagerly for some sign of his intentions.

CHAPTER XVII.

AFTER the letters sent to Europe by Dupont de Nemours in May, neither the President nor the Secretary of State again stirred before the meeting of Congress in December. The diplomacy of 1800 was slow. Nearly six months were required to decide upon a policy, write to Europe, receive a reply, and decide again upon an answer. An entire year was needed for taking a new line of action, and ascertaining its chances of success. In October, Madison wrote to Livingston that the President still waited to learn the impression produced at Paris by Dupont.[1] Livingston, on his side, had been active and unsuccessful. The President again wrote to him, by the October packet, a letter which would have perplexed any European diplomatist.[2]

" We shall so take our distance between the two rival nations," said Jefferson, " as, remaining disengaged till necessity compels us, we may haul finally to the enemy of that which shall make it necessary. We see all the disadvantageous consequences of taking a side, and shall be forced into it only by a more disagreeable alternative ;

[1] Madison to Livingston, Oct. 15, 1802; State Papers, ii. 525.
[2] Jefferson to Livingston, Oct. 10, 1802; Works, iv. 447.

in which event we must countervail the disadvantages by measures which will give us splendor and power, but not as much happiness as our present system. We wish, therefore, to remain well with France; but we see that no consequences, however ruinous to them, can secure us with certainty against the extravagance of her present rulers. . . . No matter at present existing between them and us is important enough to risk a breach of peace, — peace being indeed the most important of all things for us, except the preserving an erect and independent attitude."

" Peace is our passion!" This phrase of President Jefferson, taken from a letter written a few months later,[1] expressed his true policy. In spite of his frequent menaces, he told Livingston in October, 1802, that the French occupation of Louisiana was not "important enough to risk a breach of peace." Within a week after this letter was written, New Orleans was closed to American commerce, and a breach of peace seemed unavoidable. Down to that time the Executive had done nothing to check Napoleon. The President had instructed his agents at Paris and Madrid to obtain, if they could, the cession of New Orleans and West Florida, and had threatened an alliance with England in case this request were refused; but England was at peace with France, and Bonaparte was not likely to provoke another war until he should be able to defend Louisiana. So far as any diplomatic action by the United States government was

---

[1] Jefferson to Sir John Sinclair, June 30, 1803; Works, iv. 490.

concerned, Madison and Jefferson might equally well
have written nothing; and when news arrived that
the Mississippi was closed, alarming as the situation became, no new action was at first suggested.
The President was contented to accept the assistance of the Spanish and French representatives at
Washington.

In Jefferson's domestic as well as in his political
household Don Carlos Martinez de Yrujo, — created
in 1802 Marquis of Casa Yrujo, — the minister of
Spain, was thoroughly at home, for he had a double
title to confidence, and even to affection. His first
claim was due to his marriage with a daughter of
Governor McKean of Pennsylvania, whose importance
in the Republican party was great. His second claim
was political. Some years earlier he had so exasperated Timothy Pickering, then Secretary of State, as
to provoke a demand for his recall. One of President
Jefferson's first diplomatic acts was to ask from the
Spanish government that Yrujo should be allowed to
remain at Washington; and Godoy, who knew even
better than Jefferson the character and merits of
Yrujo, readily granted the favor.

Thus Yrujo was doubly and trebly attached to the
Administration. Proud as a typical Spaniard should
be, and mingling an infusion of vanity with his pride;
irascible, headstrong, indiscreet as was possible for
a diplomatist, and afraid of no prince or president;
young, able, quick, and aggressive; devoted to his
King and country; a flighty and dangerous friend,

but a most troublesome enemy ; always in difficulties, but in spite of fantastic outbursts always respecta- ble, — Yrujo needed only the contrast of characters such as those of Pickering or Madison to make him the most entertaining figure in Washington politics. He had become an American in language, family, and political training.   He loved the rough-and-tumble of democratic habits, and remembered his diplomatic dignity only when he could use it as a weapon against a secretary of state.   If he thought the Government to need assistance or warning, he wrote communica- tions to the newspapers in a style which long expe- rience had made familiar to the public and irritating to the Government whose acts he criticised.   For natural reasons the American Executive, which never hesitated to use the press without limit for its own purposes, held it indecorous that a foreign minister should attempt to affect public opinion.   The example of Genet was regarded as a proof even more than a warning that such action was highly improper ; but from Yrujo's point of view, as from Genet's, the ques- tion of decorum was ridiculous in a country which prided itself on the absence of etiquette, and the only question he cared to consider was whether the press answered his purpose.   His success could be best measured by the exasperation it caused to the tempers of Pickering and Madison.

Yrujo felt no love for Bonaparte, and no wish to serve his ends.   At this moment of anxiety, stepping forward to assist the President, he asserted that there

was no cause for alarm;[1] that the act of Morales
was not authorized by the King of Spain, but rose
from some excess of zeal or mistaken interpretation
of the treaty on the part of the Intendant; and that
a packet-boat should be instantly sent to New Orleans
to inquire the reasons of the measure. His letter to
the Intendant was in reality extremely sharp, — " a
veritable diatribe," according to Laussat, the new
French prefect, to whom Morales showed it. Yrujo
pointed out the fatal consequences of Morales's conduct, and the ground it gave to United States citizens
for claiming indemnity for their commercial losses.[2]
At the same time Madison instructed Charles Pinckney at Madrid to inform the Spanish government that
the President expected it to lose not a moment in
countermanding the order of Morales, and in repairing
every damage that might result from it.[3]

There the matter rested until December 6, when
Congress met. Even at so exciting a moment, senators were slow in arriving at Washington, and a week
passed before a quorum was formed. Not till December 15 could the Annual Message be read. No message could be more pacific in tone. The President discussed everything except the danger which engrossed
men's minds. He talked of peace and friendship,

[1] Yrujo to Madison, Nov. 27, 1802; MSS. State Department
Archives.

[2] Yrujo to Morales, Nov. 26, 1802; Gayarré, History of Louisiana, iii. 576.

[3] Madison to Pinckney, Nov. 27, 1802; State Papers, ii. 527.

of law, order, and religion, of differential duties, distressed seamen, the blockade of Tripoli, Georgia lands, Indian treaties, the increase in revenue, "the emancipation of our posterity from that mortal canker" a national debt, "by avoiding false objects of expense;" he said that no change in the military establishment was deemed necessary, but that the militia might be improved; he regretted that the behavior of the Barbary Powers rendered a small squadron still necessary to patrol the Mediterranean, but at the same time he strongly urged Congress to take measures for laying up the whole navy, by constructing a large dry-dock on the Eastern Branch, where the seven frigates might be stowed away side by side under cover, and kept from decay or expense. All these subjects he touched in a spirit of peace and good-will toward mankind; but when he came to the question of Louisiana, about which he had written so many alarming letters to Europe, he spoke in a tone of apparent indifference. "The cession of the Spanish province of Louisiana to France," he said, "which took place in the course of the late war, will, if carried into effect, make a change in the aspect of our foreign relations which will doubtless have a just weight in any deliberations of the Legislature connected with that subject." No allusion was made to the closure of the Mississippi.

Nothing could more disconcert the war party than this manner of ignoring their existence. Jefferson afterward explained that his hope was to gain time;

but he could not more effectually have belittled his
Federalist enemies than by thus telling them that a
French army at New Orleans would "make a change
in the aspect of our foreign relations." This manner of treating Congress was the more dexterous,
because if the President did not at once invite the
Legislature to realize the alarming state of foreign
affairs, he abstained only in order to carry out
other tactics. Two days after the Message was read,
December 17, John Randolph, the Administration
leader in the House, moved for the papers relating to the violated right of deposit. Great curiosity
was felt to know what course the President meant
to take.

" However timid Mr. Jefferson may be," wrote Pichon
to Talleyrand,[1] " and whatever price he may put on his
pacific policy, one cannot foresee precisely what his
answer will be. . . . I find in general a bad temper as
regards us ; and I cannot help seeing that there is a tendency toward adopting an irrevocably hostile system.
This circumstance will be decisive for Mr. Jefferson. If
he acts feebly, he is lost among his partisans ; it will
be then the time for Mr. Burr to show himself with
advantage."

Thornton watched with equal anxiety the movement which promised to throw the United States
into the arms of England. He expected as little as
Pichon that the President would act with energy, but

[1] Pichon to Talleyrand, 2 Nivôse, An xi. (Dec. 22, 1802);
Archives des Aff. Étr., MSS.

he hoped that the situation would force him into taking a side.[1]

" From the language of his ministers, and from the insinuations of some members of the Federal party, it will not be, I doubt, such a measure of vigor as would place the country on a commanding ground in the negotiation with Spain, or eventually with France ; and the latter persons have some of them designated it to me as likely to be a very foolish thing."

Five days passed before Jefferson answered the call of the House; and when he did so, he sent papers which might have been prepared in five minutes, for most of them had been long printed in the newspapers.[2]   In communicating these documents, the President added that he had not lost a moment in causing every step to be taken which the occasion claimed from him ; but he did not say what these steps were.   A week later he sent another document, which he requested the House to return without publication ; [3] it was a letter which Governor Claiborne had received from Governor Salcedo, denying responsibility for the Intendant's act, and asserting that it was not authorized by the Spanish government.   The House shut its doors and debated a week.   Then it reopened its doors, and announced to the world that by a party

[1] Thornton to Lord Hawkesbury, Jan. 3, 1803; MSS. British Archives.

[2] Message of Dec. 22, 1802; State Papers, ii. 469.

[3] Message of Dec. 30, 1802; State Papers, ii. 471.

vote of fifty to twenty-five, the following resolution
had been adopted : [1] —

" Adhering to that humane and wise policy which
ought ever to characterize a free people, and by which
the United States have always professed to be governed ;
willing at the same time to ascribe this breach of compact to the unauthorized misconduct of certain individuals rather than to a want of good faith on the part of his
Catholic Majesty ; and relying with perfect confidence on
the vigilance and wisdom of the Executive, — they will
wait the issue of such measures as that department of the
Government shall have pursued for asserting the rights
and vindicating the injuries of the United States."

Strenuously as the President exerted himself to
stifle the warlike feeling in Congress, his influence
did not extend far enough to check the same feeling
elsewhere. Successful in Washington, he found himself exposed to an alarming pressure from the West.
One State legislature after another adopted resolutions which shook the ground under his feet. Eighteen months had passed since the seriousness of
Napoleon's schemes became known to him, but as
yet he had done nothing that could be construed as
an attempt to represent the demands of the western
country ; all his ingenuity had, in fact, been exerted
to evade these demands. The West wanted troops
at Natchez, to seize New Orleans at the first sign
of a French occupation ; but the use of force at that

[1] Resolutions of Jan. 7, 1803; Annals of Congress, 1802–1803,
p. 339.

stage was not in Jefferson's thoughts. To quiet
Kentucky and Tennessee without satisfying them was
a delicate matter; but, delicate as it was, Jefferson
succeeded in doing it. He explained his plan in
a letter to Monroe, written at the moment when
everything depended on Monroe's aid:[1] —

"The agitation of the public mind on occasion of the
late suspension of our right of deposit at New Orleans
is extreme. In the western country it is natural, and
grounded on honest motives; in the seaports it proceeds
from a desire for war, which increases the mercantile lot-
tery; in the Federalists generally, and especially those
of Congress, the object is to force us into war if possible, in order to derange our finances; or if this cannot be
done, to attach the western country to them as their best
friends, and thus get again into power. Remonstrances,
memorials,.etc., are now circulating through the whole
of the western country, and signed by the body of the
people. The measures we have been pursuing, being invisible, do not satisfy their minds. Something sensible,
therefore, has become necessary."

This sensible, or rather this tangible, measure was
the appointment of a minister extraordinary to aid
Livingston in buying New Orleans and the Floridas.
The idea was adopted after the secret debate in the
House. As Madison wrote soon afterward to Livingston,[2] "such has been the impulse given to the
public mind" by these debates and by the press,
"that every branch of the government has felt the

[1] Jefferson to Monroe, Jan. 13, 1803; Works, iv. 453.
[2] Madison to Livingston, Jan. 18, 1803; State Papers, ii. 529.

obligation of taking the measures most likely not only to re-establish our present rights, but to promote arrangements by which they may be enlarged and more effectually secured." According to this view, the impulse of Congress and the Press alone made the Executive feel its obligation. For more than a year the Executive had known the danger and had done nothing; being obliged to do something, its first object was to avoid doing too much.

Accordingly, General Smith of Maryland, Jan. 11, 1803, carried the House again into secret session, and moved to appropriate two million dollars " to defray any expenses which may be incurred in relation to the intercourse between the United States and foreign nations." The next day a committee reported, through Joseph Nicholson, in favor of appropriating the money, with a view to purchasing West Florida and New Orleans.[1] The Report argued that there was no alternative between purchase and war. Meanwhile, January 11, the President sent to the Senate the name of James Monroe as minister extraordinary to France and Spain to help Livingston and Pinckney in " enlarging and more effectually securing our rights and interests in the river Mississippi and in the territories eastward thereof."

The nomination was approved by the Senate January 13; and without losing a moment, Jefferson

[1] Report of Jan. 12, 1803; Annals of Congress, 1802–1803, pp. 371–374.

wrote to Monroe, explaining the reasons which made
his course necessary : [1] —

"The measure has already silenced the Federalists
here.   Congress will no longer be agitated by them ; and
the country will become calm as fast as the information
extends over it.   All eyes, all hopes, are now fixed on
you ; and were you to decline, the chagrin would be
universal, and would shake under your feet the high
ground on which you stand with the public.   Indeed, I
know nothing which would produce such a shock ; for on
the event of this mission depend the future destinies of
this Republic.   If we cannot, by a purchase of the country, insure to ourselves a course of perpetual peace and
friendship with all nations, then, as war cannot be distant, it behooves us immediately to be preparing for that
course, without however hastening it ; and it may be
necessary, on your failure on the Continent, to cross the
Channel.   We shall get entangled in European politics ;
and, figuring more, be much less happy and prosperous."

With infinite pertinacity Jefferson clung to his own
course.   He deserved success, although he hardly
expected to win it by means of Monroe, whom he
urged to go abroad, as his letter implied, not so much
to purchase New Orleans, as to restore political quiet
at home.   For the purchase of New Orleans, Livingston was fully competent ; but the opposition at home,
as Jefferson candidly wrote to him,[2] were pressing
their inflammatory resolutions in the House so hard
that "as a remedy to all this we determined to name

[1] Jefferson to Monroe, Jan. 13, 1803; Works, iv. 453.
[2] Jefferson to Livingston, Feb. 3, 1803; Works, iv. 460.

a minister extraordinary to go immediately to Paris
and Madrid to settle this matter.   This measure
being a visible one, and the person named peculiarly
popular with the western country, crushed at once
and put an end to all further attempts on the Legislature.   From that moment all has been quiet."
The quiet was broken again, soon after this letter was
written, by a sharp attack in the Senate.   Ross of
Pennsylvania, White of Delaware, and Gouverneur
Morris of New York, assailed the Administration for
the feebleness of its measures.   In private, Jefferson
did not deny that his measures were pacific, and
that he had no great confidence in Monroe's success ; he counted rather on Bonaparte's taking possession of New Orleans and remaining some years on
the Mississippi.[1]

" I did not expect he would yield until a war took
place between France and England ; and my hope was to
palliate and endure, if Messrs. Ross, Morris, etc., did not
force a premature rupture, until that event.   I believed
the event not very distant, but acknowledge it came on
sooner than I expected."

" To palliate and endure " was therefore the object
of Jefferson's diplomacy for the moment.   Whether
the Western States could be persuaded to endure or
to palliate the presence of a French army at New
Orleans was doubtful; but Jefferson's success in
controlling them proved his personal authority and
political skill.   Meanwhile the interest and activity of

[1] Jefferson to Dr. Priestley, Jan. 29, 1804; Works, iv. 524.

the little diplomatic world at Washington increased.
Monroe accepted his appointment and came for his
instructions. Every one was alive with expectation.
As public opinion grew more outspoken, the President was obliged to raise his tone. He talked with
a degree of freedom which seemed more inconsistent
than it really was with his radical policy of peace.
With Thornton he was somewhat cautious.[1] Immediately after Monroe's nomination, Thornton asked
the President whether he intended to let the new
envoy pass to England and converse with British
ministers about the free navigation of the Mississippi,
— a right to which Great Britain, as well as the
United States, was entitled by treaty.

" The inquiry was somewhat premature, and I made it
with some apology. Mr. Jefferson replied, however, un-
affectedly, that at so early a stage of the business he had
scarcely thought himself what it might be proper to do;
that I might be assured the right would never be abandoned by this country; that he wished earnestly for a
tranquil and pacific recognition and confirmation of it;
that on the whole he thought it very probable that Mr.
Monroe might cross the Channel. He reiterated to me
with additional force the resolution of the country never
to abandon the claim of the free navigation, — which indeed cannot be without dissevering the Western States
from the Union, — declaring that should they be obliged
at last to resort to force, *they would throw away the
scabbard.*"

[1] Thornton to Lord Hawkesbury, Jan. 31, 1803; MSS. British Archives.

Thornton added that the President still hoped the French would not for some time take possession of Louisiana, and rested his hope on the demand which the Island of St. Domingo would create for every soldier that could be spared; but he also talked of building gunboats for the navigation of the Mississippi.

"In the mean time," continued Thornton, "the country seems in general well satisfied with the resolution taken by the House and the measure adopted by himself; and, what is more important, authentic information is received that the people of Kentucky will wait with patience the result of the steps which the executive government may think it right to take, without recurring, as was apprehended would be the case to force, for the assertion of their claims. The President regards this circumstance (with great justice, it appears to me) as the surest pledge of the continuance of his authority, and as the death-blow of the Federal party."

Upon Pichon the Government concentrated its threats, and Pichon sent to Talleyrand cry after cry of distress: —

"It is impossible to be more bitter than this Government is at the present posture of affairs and at the humiliating attitude in which our silence about Louisiana places them. . . . Mr. Jefferson will be forced to yield to necessity his pretensions and scruples against a British alliance. I noticed at his table that he redoubled his civilities and attentions to the British *chargé*. I should also say that he treats me with much consideration and politeness, in spite of the actual state of affairs."

No sooner had Monroe been confirmed by the Senate, than Secretary Madison sent for Pichon and asked him to do what he could for the success of Monroe's mission.[1] At ample length he explained that the undivided possession of New Orleans and West Florida was a necessity for the American settlements on the upper Mississippi and Mobile rivers, and that Monroe was instructed to obtain the whole territory east of the Mississippi, including New Orleans, at a price not exceeding two or three million dollars. This part of the Secretary's argument was simple; but not content with this, "he entered into details to prove that New Orleans had no sort of interest for us, that its situation was acknowledged to be bad, the choice of it was due to accident, and we might very soon build a city on the opposite bank." He argued further that the true policy of France required her to make the river her boundary against the United States; for "the United States had no interest in seeing circumstances rise which should eventually lead their population to extend itself on the right bank. In point of fact, was it not evident that since these emigrations tended to weaken the State and to slacken the concentration of its forces, sound policy ought not to encourage them? In spite of affinities in manners and language, no colony beyond the river could exist under the same government, but would infallibly give birth to a separate State having

[1] Pichon to Talleyrand, 4 Pluviôse, An xi. (Jan. 24, 1803); Archives des Aff. Étr., MSS.

in its bosom germs of collision with the East, the easier to develop in proportion to the very affinities between the two empires." The Secretary ended by hinting that should the First Consul not be persuaded by these suggestions, " it might happen that the conduct of France would decide political combinations which, getting the upper hand of all these considerations, would tend to produce results no doubt disagreeable to the United States, but certainly still more so to France and her allies."

Pichon was a sore trial to the moderate amount of patience which Bonaparte possessed. Instead of hinting to Madison that these arguments would have more weight if the President proposed to support them by acts such as a military First Consul was accustomed to respect, Pichon wrote melancholy accounts of his situation to Talleyrand. The Americans, he said, were throwing themselves into the arms of England; they thought they held the balance of power between France and Great Britain, and meant to make the nation which should force them into war regret the inconsiderate act; the States of New York, Virginia, Maryland, and Pennsylvania, either through their legislatures or their governors, had energetically announced their readiness to risk everything to maintain the dignity and rights of the nation; Madison refused to do business, on the ground that Talleyrand's want of attention to Livingston required reprisals; the Secretary of the Treasury talked of war; a public dinner had been given to Monroe, at which

General Smith offered the toast, "Peace, if peace is honorable; war, if war is necessary!" the President was open in denouncing Bonaparte's ambition; Monroe who had talked long with Pichon, used lan·guage even more startling than that of the President or the Cabinet : —

"He did not conceal from me that if his negotiation failed, the Administration had made up its mind to act with the utmost vigor, and to receive the overtures which England was incessantly making. He repeated to me several times that I could only imperfectly imagine the extent of those overtures, and that if the tie were once made between the two States, they would not stop half way."[1]

If Monroe made such an assertion as Pichon reported, he carried his diplomacy beyond the line of truthfulness; for although Thornton, without instructions, had offered one or two suggestions of concert, England had made no overture. Monroe's own instructions rested on the opposite principle, — that England was to receive, not to make, overtures. Jefferson wished only to create the impression that disaster impended over France if she persevered in closing the Mississippi. He spoke clearly to this effect in a letter written to Dupont at the time he was alarming Pichon : —

"Our circumstances are so imperious as to admit of no delay as to our course, and the use of the Mississippi

[1] Pichon to Talleyrand, 29 Pluviôse, An xi. (Feb. 17, 1803); Archives des Aff. Étr., MSS.

so indispensable that we cannot hesitate one moment to hazard our existence for its maintenance. If we fail in this effort to put it beyond the reach of accident, we see the destinies we have to run, and prepare at once for them." [1]

Alarmed by such language, Pichon volunteered to imitate Yrujo and write a letter to the future French prefect whose arrival at New Orleans was expected, urging him to raise the interdict on American commerce.[2] Madison was pleased with the offer, and in return communicated to Pichon a despatch just received from Livingston, which announced that Talleyrand had consented to speak, so far as to promise that France would strictly observe in Louisiana the treaties which existed between America and Spain. " I quickly saw, by the rapidity with which this news circulated in the two houses of Congress, the salutary effect it produced. On all sides I was talked with, and the Administration is sincerely satisfied by it." Small as the favor was, the Administration had reason to be grateful, as it served for the moment to pacify Kentucky and Tennessee.

The months of January and February passed. Not until spring came, and the Seventh Congress was about to expire, did Monroe receive his instructions and prepare to sail. The nature of these in-

[1] Jefferson to Dupont, Feb. 1, 1803 ; Works, iv. 456.
[2] Pichon to Talleyrand, 24 Pluviôse, An xi. (Feb. 12, 1803) ; Archives des Aff. Étr., MSS.

structions was so remarkable as to deserve a moment
of study.[1]

They were framed to provide for three contingen-
cies. Should the French government be willing to
sell New Orleans and the Floridas, the President
would bid high rather than lose the opportunity.
Should France refuse to cede any territory whatever, even the site for a town, the two commissioners were to content themselves with securing the right
of deposit, with such improvements as they could obtain. Should Bonaparte deny the right of deposit
also, the commissioners were to be guided by instructions specially adapted to the case. For New Orleans
and West Florida Monroe and Livingston were to
offer any sum within ten million dollars, commercial privileges for ten years in the ceded ports, in-
corporation of the inhabitants on an equal footing
with citizens without unnecessary delay, and, if absolutely necessary, a guaranty of the west bank of
the Mississippi.

These were the main ideas of Monroe's instructions. In brief, they offered to admit the French to
Louisiana without condition. Bonaparte could have
regarded nothing in these instructions as hostile to
his own plans, and could have satisfied every demand
by giving the United States, in the terms of the Spanish treaty, a place of deposit anywhere on the banks
of the Mississippi, or by merely allowing American

[1] Instructions to Livingston and Monroe, March 2, 1803 ;
State Papers, ii. 540.

vessels to pass up and down the river.[1] In private, Jefferson professed preference for Natchez over New Orleans as the seat of American trade.[2] He made no secret of his intention to put off the day of forcible resistance until the national debt should be reduced and the Mississippi Valley filled with fighting men.

The tenor of these expressions seemed inconsistent with that of his letters by Dupont. After telling Bonaparte that[3] "the cession of New Orleans and the Floridas to us would be a palliation," but no more, to the presence of France on the west bank, which would "cost France, and perhaps not very long hence, a war which will annihilate her on the ocean," then within a year to guarantee France forever in possession of the west bank,—had an air of vacillation. After telling Dupont again in February that if the United States failed to put the use of the Mississippi beyond the reach of accident, they should see the destinies they had to run, and at once prepare for them; then within a month to admit Bonaparte to possession of all Spanish rights at New Orleans, without guaranty of any kind for putting the use of the river beyond accident, — looked like fear. The instructions contained one positive expression:

[1] Madison to Monroe, April 20, 1803; Madison's Writings, ii. 181.

[2] Jefferson to Hugh Williamson, April 30, 1803; Works, iv. 483.

[3] Jefferson to Dupont, April 25, 1802; Works, iv. 435.

"The United States cannot remain satisfied, nor the Western people be kept patient, under the restrictions which the existing treaty with Spain authorizes." This sentence introduced only a moderate request: "Should it be impossible to procure a complete jurisdiction over any convenient spot whatever, it will only remain to explain and improve the present right of deposit by adding thereto the express privilege of holding real estate for commercial purposes, of providing hospitals, of having consuls residing there," and other commercial agents. Even this moderate condition was not an ultimatum. Madison required only that the Spanish treaty of 1795 should be respected, and this had already been promised by Talleyrand.

In truth the inconsistency was more apparent than real. Jefferson explained to the French government that the war he had in his mind was a contingent result. While assuring Dupont that if he failed to put the use of the Mississippi beyond the reach of accident he should prepare for war, he added in italics an explanation:[1] —

"Not but that we shall still endeavor to go on in peace and friendship with our neighbors as long as we can, *if our rights of navigation and deposit are respected;* but as we foresee that the caprices of the local officers and the abuse of those rights by our boatmen and navigators, which neither government can prevent, will keep up a state of irritation which cannot long be kept inac-

[1] Jefferson to Dupont, Feb. 1, 1803; Works, iv. 456.

tive, we should be criminally improvident not to take at once eventual measures for strengthening ourselves for the contest."

The essence and genius of Jefferson's statesmanship lay in peace. Through difficulties, trials, and temptations of every kind he held fast to this idea, which was the clew to whatever seemed inconsistent, feeble, or deceptive in his administration. Yielding often, with the suppleness of his nature, to the violence of party, he allowed himself to use language which at first sight seemed inconsistent, and even untruthful; but such concessions were momentary: the unswerving intent could always be detected under every superficial disguise; the consistency of the career became more remarkable on account of the seeming inconsistencies of the moment. He was pliant and yielding in manner, but steady as the magnet itself in aim. His manœuvres between the angry West and the arbitrary First Consul of France offered an example of his political method. He meant that there should be no war. While waiting to hear the result of Monroe's mission he wrote to an English correspondent a letter [1] which expressed his true feelings with apparent candor: —

"We see . . . with great concern the position in which Great Britain is placed, and should be sincerely afflicted were any disaster to deprive mankind of the benefit of such a bulwark against the torrent which has

[1] Jefferson to Sir John Sinclair, 30 June, 1803; Works, iv. 490.

for some time been bearing down all before it. But her power and prowess by sea seem to render everything safe in the end. Peace is our passion, and wrongs might drive us from it. We prefer trying *every* other just principle, right and safety, before we would recur to war."

END OF VOL. I.